Child Protection, Domestic Violence and Parental Substance Misuse

Quality Matters in Children's Services

Series Editor: Mike Stein

Consultant Editor: Caroline Thomas

The provision of high quality children's services matters to those who use and provide children's services. This important series is the result of an extensive government-funded research initiative into the *Quality Protects* programme which aimed to improve outcomes for vulnerable children, as well as transform the management and delivery of children's services. Focussing on current challenges in making every child matter, the titles in this series are essential reading for all those working in the field.

also in the series

The Pursuit of Permanence
A Study of the English Child Care System
Ian Sinclair, Claire Baker, Jenny Lee and Ian Gibbs
ISBN 978 1 84310 595 4

of related interest

Making an Impact
Children and Domestic Violence – A Reader
2nd edition
Marianne Hester, Chris Pearson and Nicola Harwin
With Hilary Abrahams
ISBN 978 1 84310 157 4

Domestic Violence and Child Protection
Directions for Good Practice
Edited by Cathy Humphreys and Nicky Stanley
ISBN 978 1 84310 276 2

Supporting Women after Domestic Violence
Loss, Trauma and Recovery
Hilary Abrahams
Foreword by Cathy Humphreys
ISBN 978 1 84310 431 5

Mothering Through Domestic Violence
Lorraine Radford and Marianne Hester
ISBN 978 1 84310 473 5

Talking About Domestic Abuse
A Photo Activity Workbook to Develop Communication
Between Mothers and Young People
Cathy Humphreys, Ravi K Thiara, Agnes Skamballis and Audrey Mullender
ISBN 978 1 84310 423 0

Quality Matters in Children's Services

Child Protection, Domestic Violence and **Parental Substance Misuse**

Family Experiences and Effective Practice

▶ Hedy Cleaver
▶ Don Nicholson
▶ Sukey Tarr
▶ Deborah Cleaver

Foreword by **Kevin Brennan MP**
Parliamentary Under Secretary of State for
Children, Young People and Families

JKP

Don Nicholson's death earlier this year was a great loss to the research world and he is sadly missed by all who knew him. He was a major contributor to this book, but sadly a terminal illness prevented him seeing its publication. His career in research started in 1996 having spent a lifetime providing services, both as a practitioner and manager, to children and adults. This experience gave Don both the authority and confidence to successfully negotiate with chief executives and senior managers as well as the insight and sensitivity to interview distressed and anxious children and adults. To the research team he also brought humour, tenacity and a clear-headed approach. This book reflects the dedication Don gave to all his work with vulnerable children and families.

First published in 2007
by Jessica Kingsley Publishers
116 Pentonville Road
London N1 9JB, UK
and
400 Market Street, Suite 400
Philadelphia, PA 19106, USA

www.jkp.com

Copyright © Hedy Cleaver, Don Nicholson,
Sukey Tarr and Deborah Cleaver 2007

Library of Congress Cataloging in Publication Data
A CIP catalog record for this book is available from the Library of Congress

British Library Cataloguing in Publication Data
A CIP catalogue record for this book is available from the British Library

ISBN 978 1 84310 582 4

Printed and bound in Great Britain by
Athenaeum Press, Gateshead, Tyne and Wear

6/8/10

Contents

FOREWORD 7

ACKNOWLEDGEMENTS 9

Chapter 1 Introduction 11

Chapter 2 The Response of Children's Social Care 27

Chapter 3 Collaborative Working 58

Chapter 4 Families' Experience of Referral and Assessment 83

Chapter 5 Families' Experience of Services 106

Chapter 6 Plans, Procedures and Joint Protocols 131

Chapter 7 Training 150

Chapter 8 Conclusions and Implications for Policy and Practice 169

APPENDIX I AIMS AND METHODS 187

APPENDIX II FAMILY STORIES 202

REFERENCES 224

SUBJECT INDEX 228

AUTHOR INDEX 232

List of Figures, Tables and Boxes

Table 2.1	Source of referral	28
Table 2.2	Reason for referral	31
Table 2.3	Association between parental awareness of the referral and the source of the referral	32
Table 2.4	Reasons for the initial assessment	36
Table 2.5	Proportion of cases where key agencies were involved during the initial assessment	52
Table 3.1	Questionnaire responses	59
Box 3.1	Organisations identified by managers	60
Table 3.2	Managers' assessment of the quality of inter-agency relationships	65
Table 3.3	Assessed quality of inter-agency working relationships	66
Box 3.2	Commonly identified factors which support good working relationships	68
Table 3.4	Levels of communication between organisations and families	70
Table 3.5	Impact of confidentiality issues on inter-agency working	76
Table 3.6	Do effective systems exist for resolving confidentiality issues?	79
Table 6.1	Research assessment of the ACPC Annual Report/Business Plan	133
Table 6.2	Research assessment of the Domestic Violence Forum Annual Report/Business Plan	135
Table 6.3	Research assessment of the Drug Action Team and Drug and Alcohol Action Team Plans	137
Table 6.4	Research assessment of the Crime and Disorder Reduction Strategy/Community Safety Plan	139
Table 6.5	Research assessment of the Children's Services Plan	141
Table 6.6	Research assessment of ACPC procedures	143
Table 7.1	The number of questionnaires broken down by authority and professional group	151
Table 7.2	Managers' levels of understanding of the impact of parental substance misuse and domestic violence on children's development	157
Table 7.3	Managers' understanding of child protection procedures	161
Table A.1	Distribution of cases from the participating authorities	194

Foreword

The Government is firmly committed to safeguarding and promoting the welfare of children, and in particular those who grow up in families where there is domestic abuse or parental substance misuse. This commitment is demonstrated by recent legislation and statutory guidance in relation to both children and adults. The Government's guidance on making arrangements to safeguard and promote the welfare of children under s11 of the Children Act 2004, and *Working Together to Safeguard Children* stress the importance of collaborative working to improve outcomes for children. Domestic violence and drug and alcohol misuse have also been at the forefront of government policy and guidance with the introduction of the Domestic Violence, Crime and Victims Act 2004; the Every Child Matters Programme; Young People and Drugs guidance; the Government's response to Hidden Harm – the Advisory Council on the Misuse of Drugs' report on the needs of children of problem drug users and the *Alcohol Harm Reduction Strategy for England* (2004).

To achieve better outcomes for these vulnerable children, policy makers and professionals need to understand not only how domestic violence and parental substance misuse affect children and young people, but also what makes a difference, which services are valued by families, and which factors support effective collaborative working between children's and adult services. I, therefore, welcome the publication of this research which was commissioned as part of the Government's Quality Protects research initiative. It seeks to address these challenging issues. The focus of the study is on how well children living in families where there is domestic violence and/or parental substance misuse are protected from emotional, physical, sexual abuse and neglect. It provides important findings on: the impact of domestic violence, parental alcohol and drug misuse on children; what factors enable different agencies to successfully work together; and what supports parents to engage with services.

I hope that this publication will be widely read and inform the development and training of staff in all relevant disciplines. Also that its important messages will find expression in more effective inter-agency working which aims to improve outcomes for our children and young people who are growing up in families where there is domestic abuse and parental substance misuse.

Kevin Brennan, MP
Parliamentary Under Secretary of State
for Children, Young People and Families, UK

Acknowledgements

The research on which this book is based was done in partnership with six local authorities and we acknowledge with sincere thanks the many people who gave generously of their time to help with the study. We are especially indebted to the parents who let us into their homes at adverse times and willingly answered our many questions as fully and as honestly as they could. Their openness in discussing subjects which were often painful and distressing provided valuable insights into their circumstances and experience of services. We hope that we have done justice to their accounts as they hold important messages for all those working with children and families.

Of equal importance were the observations of the service providers who were involved in this research. Despite the pressure that most were experiencing due to the considerable changes that were taking place, they took time to talk at length or complete questionnaires for us. We would like to thank them all.

This study was commissioned and funded by the Department of Health (and transferred to the Department for Education and Skills, now the Department for Children, Schools and Families) under the *Quality Protects* research initiative, which is being published in the Quality Matters in Children's Services series by Jessica Kingsley Publishers. We are particularly indebted to Caroline Thomas (Department for Children, Schools and Families) and Mike Stein (York University), co-ordinators of this initiative, for steering the research through from the proposal stage to completion. The study was undertaken with the help of an advisory group chaired by Caroline Thomas and Mike Stein. We would like to express our gratitude for their support and guidance. The members of this group were: Paul Boyce (Strategic Development Manager, Cumbria); Bas Chandry (Co-ordinator Substance Misusers Group, Sutton); Carolyn Davies (Department for Children, Schools and Families); Jenny Gray (Department for Children, Schools and Families); Anna Gupta (Royal Holloway University of London); Judith Longhill (Assistant Director Children and Families, Bury); Carole Malone (Domestic Violence Project, Hillingdon); Ellen Malos (Bristol Women's Study Group); Gaynor Mears (Domestic Violence Services, Cambs); Mike Stein (York University), Caroline Thomas (Department for Children, Schools and Families) and Richard Velleman (Bath University).

Chapter 1

Introduction

> Listen to what we have to say, understand the situation better. Give more information and make us feel involved in what they are doing. I felt intimidated, and so I suppose other people do. Give us support. They need to look after the children but we also need support and help. I felt I could have given them information. They don't seem to understand what is happening, what people go through or how difficult it is. They look at the children, I agree they have to do that, but they don't look at the others in the family. (Mother describing her experiences of children's social care and other agencies)

The experience of this mother reflects that of many families referred to children's social care because of concerns about the children's welfare and evidence of parental substance misuse or domestic violence. This book focuses on how child protection practices and procedures respond to children and families when there are these sorts of concerns, and explores parents' experience of the process.

Aims and methods

The study on which this book is based was commissioned under the Government's *Quality Protects* research initiative and examines how Objective 2 of the *Quality Protects* programme *Protection from Significant Harm* is working for children and young people referred to Children's Social Services. (Since the implementation of the Children Act (2004) Children's Social Services are referred to as Children's Social Care). The referrals discussed here are those where there are safeguarding concerns and evidence of domestic violence and/or parental substance misuse (Department of Health 1999).

It is an empirical study carried out over two years that specifically aimed to:

- explore how children's social care responds to families where problems require the intervention by both adult and children's services

- identify the factors that enable different agencies to work successfully together at the various stages of assessment, planning, service delivery and review

- explore children and parents' experiences of professional interventions – what factors do they find most supportive?

Six English local authorities participated in the study. The authorities were selected in partnership with the Social Services Inspectors in three of the former Social Services Inspectorate regions. Two criteria were used in making the selection – the type of authority, and how well developed were the working practices between their children's services and services working with domestic violence and substance misuse (see Appendix I for details on the aims and methods). The selection resulted in two London Boroughs, two Metropolitan Boroughs and two Shire Counties taking part in the study. Throughout the book these authorities are referred to as:

- London Borough 1 and London Borough 2.
- Metropolitan Borough 1 and Metropolitan Borough 2.
- Shire County 1 and Shire County 2.

The participating local authorities varied in the degree to which they had developed their working practices between children's and adult services. Two authorities had well-developed working practices, two were in the middle range, and two had less developed working practices.

Having selected the authorities there were three parts to the study. The first part explored the extent to which staff were aware of existing protocols, policies, and working practices in relation to cases that involve children where there is evidence of domestic violence, and/or parental substance misuse. Information was gathered using the following methods:

- a scrutiny of documentation such as Area Child Protection Committee (ACPC) procedures and other relevant local policy documents, and training plans

- a postal questionnaire to gather information on practitioners' awareness of these documents.

The second part identified the factors associated with different working practices through studying social work case files. The following criteria were used to select cases for the sample:

- referred because of concerns about the child's safety
- the case progressed to an initial assessment (or other form of assessment)

- the assessment (or referral) identified concerns of either domestic violence and/or parental substance misuse.

Cases were identified retrospectively from 1 December 2002. Identifying cases retrospectively ensured that the typology of working practices used to select the local authorities remained relevant and referrals and consequent intervention could be followed up for a period of at least 6 months. The sample included 357 cases, approximately half with evidence of domestic violence and half with evidence of parental substance misuse. In a fifth of cases, domestic violence and parental substance misuse coexisted.

The final part explored the experiences of families. This involved a qualitative case study of a small group of families identified from the case file study. The original plan was to include seven families from each of the participating authorities. However, gaining access to families proved particularly difficult, and only 17 families fully participated in the study. Sadly children's views could not be included because in only one case was it deemed suitable to interview the young person. Interviews were carried out with parents/carers with whom the child was living at the time of the referral and with relevant professionals, such as the child's social worker and the professional working with the parent.

A detailed description of the aims and methods can be found in Appendix I.

The legal context

In order to place the research findings in context, some of the key developments in law and policy as they relate to children living with domestic violence and/or parental substance misuse need to be revisited briefly, so that central debates can be understood and their impact on practice highlighted.

Safeguarding and promoting children's welfare

It is recognised that the majority of children benefit from growing up within their own families. However, there are occasions when parents are experiencing difficulties, such as substance misuse or domestic violence, that impact on their capacity to meet the developmental needs of their children (Cleaver, Unell and Aldgate 1999). In such cases services and support from outside the family are needed to safeguard and promote the welfare of the children. Recent government guidance provides the following definition of what is meant by safeguarding and promoting the welfare of children:

> The process of protecting children from abuse or neglect, preventing impairment of their health and development, and ensuring they are growing up in circumstances consistent with the provision of safe and effective care that enables

children to have optimum life chances and enter adulthood successfully. (HM Government 2006a, p.27)

The Children Act (1989) places a duty on every local authority to provide a range of appropriate services to ensure that children in need within their area are safeguarded and their welfare is promoted. Children are defined as 'in need' when they are unlikely to reach or maintain a satisfactory level of health or development, or their health and development will be significantly impaired without the provision of services (s17(10) of The Children Act (1989)). Some children are in need because they are suffering or likely to suffer significant harm – this is the threshold that justifies compulsory intervention in family life in the best interest of children. The Act places a duty on local authorities to make, or cause enquiries to be made, where there is reasonable cause to suspect that a child is suffering, or likely to suffer, significant harm (s47).

The Children Act (1989) also recognises that to promote the welfare of children, services may need to be provided to address the difficulties their parents are experiencing.

> Parents are individuals with needs of their own. Even though services may be offered primarily on behalf of their children, parents are entitled to help and consideration in their own right… Their parenting capacity may be limited temporarily or permanently by poverty, racism, poor housing or unemployment or by personal or marital problems, sensory or physical disability, mental illness or past life experiences. (Department of Health 1991, p.8)

In some cases to safeguard and promote the welfare of the children within their family, services may need to be provided by a number of agencies. The failure of agencies to work together in such cases is a common theme in the reports from inquiries into the serious injury or death of a child over the past 20 years, and re-iterated in the *Victoria Climbié Inquiry Report* (Cm 5730 2003).

> The support and protection of children cannot be achieved by a single agency… Every service has to play its part. All staff must have placed upon them the clear expectation that their primary responsibility is to the child and his or her family. (Cm 5730 2003, paragraphs 17.92 and 17.93)

The Children Act (2004) and the accompanying statutory guidance on making arrangements under s11 of the Act, and *Working Together to Safeguard Children* (HM Government 2006a), respond to the findings of the Victoria Climbié Inquiry by making clear that safeguarding and promoting the welfare of children are everyone's responsibility and central to all local authority functions.

> Safeguarding and promoting the welfare of children – and in particular protecting them from significant harm – depends on effective joint working between

agencies and professionals that have different roles and expertise. (HM Government 2006a, p.33, paragraph 1.14)

The guidance strengthens the responsibilities of local authorities to safeguard and promote the welfare of children in need in accordance with the *Framework for the Assessment of Children in Need and their Families* (Department of Health *et al.* 2000), *Safeguarding Children* (Chief Inspector of Social Services *et al.* 2002), *Safeguarding Children in Education* (Department for Education and Skills 2004a) and *Working Together to Safeguard Children* (HM Government 2006a).

The implementation of Local Safeguarding Children Boards (a requirement of the Children Act 2004) requires statutory agencies and other relevant local agencies and organisations to co-operate with the authority to achieve the following objective:

(a) to co-ordinate what is done by each person or body represented on the Board for the purposes of safeguarding and promoting the welfare of children in the area of the authority by which it is established; and

(b) to ensure the effectiveness of what is done by each such person or body for those purposes.

(Children Act 2004 s14(1))

A key function of the Local Safeguarding Children Board (LSCB) is to ensure the effective safeguarding of children by all local stakeholders and the promotion of their welfare, both in a multi-agency context and within individual agencies. The implementation of LSCBs should ensure better collaboration and co-ordination in cases which require services from both children's and adult services such as agencies working with parents experiencing domestic violence or substance misuse. Although not Board partners, section 5 of The Children Act (2004) enables the Board to include representatives from other relevant agencies and *Working Together to Safeguard Children* states that LSCBs should make appropriate arrangements at a strategic management level to involve among others, domestic violence forums, drug and alcohol misuse services and Drug Action Teams (HM Government, 2006a p.86, paragraph 3.63).

The government's response to the *Victoria Climbié Inquiry Report* has also raised the priority of safeguarding children within specific services. For example, the National Policing Plan for 2003–6 implements all the recommendations directed at the police. This includes, at a local level, arrangements to strengthen information sharing and partnership working with other agencies dealing with child protection, and to ensure policing plans include child protection strategies. The National Policing Plan also specifies the 'need to respond quickly and effectively to domestic violence incidents' as part of one of its four over-arching

member of the family, or when these adults are aware of potential danger but do not take reasonable steps to protect the child (Domestic Violence, Crime and Victims Act 2004, s4).

Parental substance misuse

> Whilst there has been huge concern about drug misuse in the UK for many years, the children of problem drug users have largely remained hidden from view. The harm done to them is also usually unseen: a virus in the blood, a bruise under the shirt, resentment and grief, a fragmented education. (Home Office 2003, p.90, paragraph 8.1)

When it comes to parental substance misuse there is less evidence of national prioritisation, although there has been some progress. In 1997 SCODA (Standing Committee on Drug Abuse) produced *Drug Using Parents: Policy Guidelines for Inter-agency Working*. These were the first national guidelines specifically covering drug using parents and their children. In 1998 the Government launched its 10-year strategy *Tackling Drugs to Build a Better Britain* (Drugs Strategy Directorate) which had four key aims: to help young people resist drug misuse; to protect our communities from drug related anti-social and criminal behaviour; to enable people with drug problems to overcome them; and to stifle the availability of illegal drugs on the street. However, it has little to say concerning children of parents with a drug or alcohol problem.

The Government's *Updated Drug Strategy for England* (Home Office *et al.*, 2002) is wide ranging but still devotes little attention to the children of problem drug users, although the then Home Secretary David Blunkett acknowledged the vulnerability of the children in his foreword: 'Very often jobs and homes are lost; friendships and family ties are broken. Where children are involved there is the danger of abandonment and neglect' (Home Office *et al.* 2002, p.3). The Strategy acknowledges that the children of problem drug users are at a higher risk of misusing drugs themselves. It also recognises that there are often shortcomings in the support women drug users receive from treatment services in terms of child care. However, apart from these references the lack of attention to the needs of children of problem drug users suggests that at a strategic level, neither the number of children involved nor the extent of their needs has yet been fully recognised. Nonetheless, the proposed investment in services, the production of new guidance and improved training and support for front line drugs workers should help all drug users including those with dependant children.

The needs of children of drug users were explored by the Advisory Council on the Misuse of Drugs in their inquiry *Hidden Harm – Responding to the Needs of Children of Problem Drug Users* (2003). The aims of the inquiry included examining the immediate and long-term consequences for children of problem drug users and identifying best policy and practice. The inquiry resulted in 48 recommendations and six key messages:

- We estimate there are between 250,000 and 350,000 children of problem drug users in the UK – about one for every problem drug user.

- Parental problem drug use can and does cause serious harm to children at every age from conception to adulthood.

- Reducing the harm to children from parental problem drug use should become a main objective of policy and practice.

- Effective treatment of the parent can have major benefits for the child.

- By working together, services can take many practical steps to protect and improve the health and well-being of affected children.

- The number of affected children is only likely to decrease when the number of problem drug users decreases.

(Home Office 2003, p.3)

In March 2005 the Government published its response to the inquiry which accepted 42 of the 48 recommendations across children's services, primary health care and maternity services, drug and alcohol treatment services and criminal justice agencies (Department for Education and Skills 2005).

The main focus of the *Hidden Harm* Inquiry was children of problem drug users. Less attention has been given to children of problem alcohol users, although alcohol is involved in one-third of child abuse cases and 40 per cent of domestic violence incidents (National Family and Parenting Institute and Alcohol Concern 2001). The Government's *Alcohol Harm Reduction Strategy* (Strategy Unit 2004) places alcohol firmly on the national agenda. The Strategy focuses on four key areas to reduce harm: better communication with the public; preventing and tackling harms to health; reducing alcohol-related crime and disorder; and working with the alcohol industry. However, although noting that there are between 780,000 and 1.3 million children who are affected by parental alcohol problems, children of problem alcohol users are not addressed in the report.

Models of Care for Alcohol Misusers (Department of Health and National Treatment Agency for Substance Misuse 2006) has been developed to achieve the second aim of the *Alcohol Harm Reduction Strategy* by providing best practice guidance for local health organisations and their partners in the commissioning and provision of interventions and treatment for adults affected by alcohol misuse. Although it specifically acknowledges the impact of parental alcohol misuse on children, recommendations relating to screening and early assessments do not include the children of alcohol misusing parents. It does, however, recommend that comprehensive and risk assessments should be targeted at, among others, users with complex needs including those who are pregnant or have children 'at risk'.

Despite the escalation of substance misuse (both alcohol and drugs) during the 1980s and 1990s, and the recent figures that indicate an increasing number of women users and a younger population of substance misusers as a whole, there is still little information available concerning the relationship between parental drug and alcohol misuse and harm to children.

However, the profile of parental substance misuse has been raised with the revised *Working Together to Safeguard Children*, making clear that adult mental health services, including those providing services for alcohol and substance misuse 'have a responsibility in safeguarding children when they become aware of, or identify, a child at risk of harm' (HM Government 2006a, p.59, paragraph 2.92). The importance of collaborative working between these services and children's services to safeguard and promote the welfare of children is reinforced by naming 'drug and alcohol misuse services' and 'drug action teams' as organisations which the Local Safeguarding Children Boards need to link to.

The research context

A major theme to emerge from the child protection studies summarised in *Child Protection: Messages from Research* (Department of Health 1995) was the high proportion of children referred to children's social care, who were exposed to domestic violence, parental drug and alcohol misuse within their families. This is reflected in social work caseloads which involve a high proportion of children living with domestic violence or parents with problem drug or alcohol use. For example, at the point of initial assessment, approximately 17 per cent of children were found to be living with a parent or carer with a known history of violence and 11.6 per cent with a parent or carer with a known history substance misuse (Cleaver and Walker with Meadows 2004a). The rate increases exponentially with increasing concerns about the ability of parents to safeguard and promote the welfare of their children. At the conference stage of the child protection process, there are issues relating to parental drug or alcohol misuse in between 25 per cent (Farmer and Owen 1995; Thoburn, Lewis and Shemmings 1995) and 60 per cent (Brisby, Baker and Hedderwick 1997) of cases, and domestic violence in 52 per cent of cases (Farmer and Owen 1995).

The impact of domestic violence and parental substance misuse on children's safety and welfare

There is a considerable body of research that shows children who grow up in families where there is domestic violence and parental drug or alcohol misuse are at increased risk of significant harm (see for example: Barnard 2007; Cawson 2002; Cleaver *et al.* 1999; Harbin and Murphy 2000; Humphreys and Stanley 2006; Kroll and Taylor 2003; Lindstein 1996; Mullender and Morley 1994; Tunnard 2002; Velleman and Orford 2001).

Children may be vulnerable to direct harm. For example, the unborn children of women exposed to domestic violence may be at risk of direct harm because women are more likely to suffer moderate to severe violence and homicide during pregnancy (Humphreys and Stanley 2006). Some 40–60 per cent of pregnant women exposed to domestic violence experience punches or kicks directed at their abdomen (Cleaver *et al.* 1999). Once children are born, domestic violence continues to place children and young people at risk of direct harm. Children are witnesses, to a greater or lesser extent, to every aspect of domestic violence against their mothers and may be physically injured during such incidents, either by accident or because they attempt to intervene (Humphreys and Stanley 2006). In at least 40 per cent of domestic violence cases there is also childhood physical and sexual abuse involving the same perpetrator, usually the father or father figure (Itzin 2006).

Parental substance misuse can also result in direct harm to the child. For example, maternal alcohol or drug misuse can impact on the unborn child resulting in premature birth, foetal alcohol syndrome which may damage the central nervous system and result in a range of anatomical abnormalities and behaviour problems (Abel 1997), or neonatal abstinence syndrome which can have severe short-term physical affects on the child (Klee 2002).

Alternatively children's vulnerability may stem from the impact of domestic violence and/or substance misuse on parenting capacity. Domestic violence and parental drug or alcohol misuse may result in parents having difficulty in organising their lives. For example, excessive alcohol intake or drug misuse may mean parents are less attentive to the baby or child's needs. The preoccupation with getting and using drugs means parents place their own needs above those of their children (Barnard 2007). Parents may not be able to concentrate long enough to complete feeding or bathing or to ensure the environment is safe for children (Barnard 2007; Cleaver *et al.* 1999). Children may also be at risk of physical harm from parents dropping cigarettes or falling asleep with electrical appliances on (Hart and Powell 2006).

Domestic violence or substance misuse can also affect parents' ability to control their emotions. Severe mood swings which may result from substance misuse or domestic violence can frighten children and leave them feeling uncertain, anxious and over-vigilant (Barnard 2007; Cleaver *et al.* 1999). This may have considerable consequences for child–parent attachment patterns and therefore for children's feelings of emotional safety, quite apart from the implications for their physical safety (Kroll and Taylor 2003).

A chaotic lifestyle is a frequent consequence of domestic violence and substance misuse. Parents may fail to shop, cook, wash, clean the home or generally look after their children. As a result children, many of whom are very young, have to assume responsibility for cooking and cleaning and the care of younger siblings (Bancroft *et al.* 2004).

Domestic violence or parental substance misuse may also affect the parent–child relationship. For example, parents may come to depend on their children for emotional support and for these children their childhood is foreshortened as roles are reversed and they assume the care of their parent (Bancroft *et al.* 2004). In addition, domestic violence or substance misuse may affect parents' ability to engage with their children. Children's needs for play, attention and fun are not met or only met intermittently (Humphreys and Stanley 2006).

The short and long-term impact on children will depend on a multitude of factors including their age, level of understanding, personality, circumstances, coping strategies and degree of support. Moreover, children's response can alter over time as circumstances change and children adopt different coping strategies (Cleaver *et al.* 1999; Humphreys and Stanley 2006).

The social consequences of domestic violence and parental substance misuse

Parents' capacity to meet the needs of their children is further hampered because of the social consequences of domestic violence and parental substance misuse. For example, living standards are likely to be reduced as family income for rent and essential household bills, such as for food, heating and clothing, is used to satisfy parental needs, or bills are simply overlooked or regarded as irrelevant (Velleman 1996). The exaggerated mood swings and irritability associated with problem drinking and drug misuse can affect the parents' ability to maintain regular working patterns, and jobs are lost. Living standards may also decline because violent and aggressive outbursts, associated with domestic violence and alcohol misuse, may lead to parents damaging and destroying property making the home an unsafe place for children. Finally, the effects of substance misuse or domestic violence on parents' consciousness and energy can result in the home being littered with food scraps and other debris, and used needles and syringes may be left accessible to children.

A further social consequence of domestic violence and substance misuse is the loss of friends and family. For example, friendships may be curtailed because parents in violent relationships wish to hide their experience, or keep silent through fear or a lack of opportunity to develop close relationships (Malos and Hague 1997). Alternatively parents may cut themselves off from family and friends because they are ashamed of their behaviour, or because their social activities have come to be based around the procurement and use of drugs. As a result friends and family drift away, relationships become increasingly strained and families are left isolated and without the support needed to ensure their children are safely parented (Barnard 2007; Cleaver *et al.* 1999; Harbin and Murphy 2000; Turning Point 2006).

Finally, domestic violence and parental substance misuse can have social consequences due to the way they affect can relationship between spouses or intimate partners. Relationships may become greatly strained and break down, because coping on a day-to-day basis with a substance misusing partner or with domestic violence is exhausting and dispiriting. Moreover, there is much evidence to show that problem drinking is associated with domestic violence (Coleman and Cassell 1995); some 80 per cent of cases of domestic violence are alcohol-related (Velleman 1993).

The impact of domestic violence and parental substance misuse on the child protection process

Not only do such parenting issues impact on children's health and development, they also influence the process of safeguarding and promoting the welfare of children. Research has shown that the process may be influenced in a number of ways. For example, fear that children may be removed makes parents and children reluctant to admit parental problem drinking or problems with drug use or domestic violence. The fear of sharing such information may also be the result of threats made by the male perpetrator either to the mother herself or the child. As a result parents may appear unco-operative and even hostile towards offers of support and services (Cleaver *et al.* 1999; Debbonaire 1999; Farmer and Owen 1995).

The process may also be affected because practitioners faced with erratic or possibly violent parents may visit families less frequently or avoid broaching sensitive issues. To confront families on issues which are likely to result in a violent response is frightening, and when practitioners feel unsupported or must visit alone there is a danger that concerns are not thoroughly investigated (James 1994; Littlechild and Bourke 2006).

A lack of knowledge, expertise and training may also influence the process. Practitioners may not recognise the symptoms of domestic violence or parental substance misuse, understand the consequences for the family, or how these issues impact on children and young people (Cleaver and Freeman 1995; Cleaver *et al.* 1998; Forrester and Harwin 2003; Turning Point 2006).

The importance of inter-agency working

A further factor that may influence the child safeguarding process in cases where there are concerns of domestic violence or parental substance misuse is the variety of agencies that may need to be involved in assessment, planning and service provision. Although inter-agency work within the child welfare field has all too often been unco-ordinated, haphazard and plagued with difficulties (Chief Inspector of Social Services *et al.* 2002) more recently agencies are working together better to identify and act on welfare concerns (Chief Inspector, Commission for Social Care Inspection 2005).

The importance of effective inter-agency working has been acknowledged in relation to safeguarding children (Department of Health and Department for Education and Skills 2004a), in relation to preventing domestic violence and its recurrence (Cm 5847) and in relation to working with parental substance misuse (Home Office 2003).

However, the splits between adult and children's services, the different legal frameworks and professional perspectives can mitigate against effective inter-agency working and the provision of services. Practitioners find it difficult to collaborate with others outside their own sphere because:

> ...practitioners are brought up or accultured in one agency. The practitioner in a particular agency will speak that particular language, will understand the roles and structure within that practice system and will automatically and unconsciously see the world through that single agency perspective. (Murphy and Oulds 2000, in Harbin and Murphy, p.116)

Agencies develop and deliver services according to a particular client group. For example, professionals tend to focus on the needs of their client, which may result in polarised views that block effective joint working. Similarly, different professional notions of confidentiality can further impede agencies effectively working together. Even when specific inter-agency initiatives are established, such as domestic violence forums, in general the focus has remained on women themselves and children's issues have not been addressed (Hague and Malos 1998).

To support greater communication, information sharing and joint working when there are concerns about children's welfare, the Government expects all local authority areas to implement the Common Assessment Framework (CAF) between 2006 and the end of 2008. The CAF provides a standard approach to assessing the needs of children and young people and deciding on how they should be met. A key aim is to improve joint working and communication between practitioners by helping to embed a common language of assessment (HM Government 2006b).

The emphasis on inter-agency co-operation is reinforced when there are concerns about children's safety and welfare. Section 27 of The Children Act (1989) places a specific duty on agencies to co-operate in the interests of children in need and Section 47 places a duty on agencies to help the local authority social services with their enquiries in cases where there is reasonable cause to suspect a child is suffering or likely to suffer significant harm. The Children Act (2004) strengthens the 1989 Act by placing a duty on statutory agencies to co-operate to improve children's well-being.

Moreover, an inter-agency approach to safeguarding and promoting the welfare of children is a fundamental tenant of the *Framework for the Assessment of Children in Need and their Families*. This is Government Guidance for those undertaking assessments of children in need and their families under The Children Act (1989) (Department of Health *et al.*, 2000).

> A key principle of the Assessment Framework is that children's needs and their families' circumstances will require inter-agency collaboration to ensure full understanding of what is happening and to ensure an effective service response. (Department of Health *et al.* 2000, p.63, paragraph 5.1)

The implementation of the Assessment Framework and the *Integrated Children's System*, which ensures these principles are applied to all children in need including those looked after, should support an inter-agency approach which will avoid duplicating or unnecessarily repeating assessments, and ensure the assessment benefits from the knowledge of experts from other organisations and disciplines (Department for Education and Skills 2006a). Of importance for the focus of this study is that it should improve the identification and assessment of children in need when there are issues of domestic violence and drug and alcohol misuse within families. However, little is known on the effectiveness of this initiative and existing child protection practices to meet children's needs in these circumstances.

The context of the research study

The findings from the study cannot be fully understood without an awareness of the issues and challenges facing local authorities at the time. The data were gathered between August 2002 and August 2004; a period of considerable change for children's social care. During the life of the research the joint chief inspectors report *Safeguarding Children* (2002), the *Victoria Climbié Inquiry Report* (Cm 5730 2003) and the Government's response *Keeping Children Safe* (Cm 5861

2003) were published. In addition, consultation on the Government's Green paper *Every Child Matters* (Cm 5860 2003) was underway. Finally, the *Integrated Children's System* (Department of Health 2002) and *Information Sharing and Assessment* (Cleaver *et al.* 2004b; Department for Education and Skills 2006b) were launched and being tested out. Much of this overhaul of legislation and guidance focuses on inter-agency working and the role and effectiveness of local Area Child Protection Committees (now Local Safeguarding Children Boards under the Children Act 2004).

In addition to this plethora of new guidance and legislation, children's social care was experiencing serious difficulties nationally in the recruitment and retention of social workers. These staff issues affected the ability of children's social care to effectively bring about the necessary changes in practice such as improved inter-agency working and service provision for children in need and their families. The employment of locum workers does not fully compensate for a shortfall in permanent staff and at the same time increases the challenge of implementing new government policy and working procedures (Cleaver *et al.* 2004a).

Summary points

- The findings from research have drawn attention to the vulnerability of children who experience domestic violence or parental substance misuse by illustrating how these issues impact negatively on all aspects of children's lives. Moreover, children's vulnerability is compounded because domestic violence and parental substance misuse can affect the process of identification and assessment.

- To ensure children are safe and their welfare is promoted, when they live in families where there is domestic violence or parental problem alcohol or drug use, may require the services from both agencies working with children and those working with adults. The importance of inter-agency working has been acknowledged in policy documents relating to safeguarding children and work with domestic violence and parental substance misuse.

- However, Government inquiries into serious injury or death of a child have, over the past 20 years, consistently highlighted the failure of agencies to work together. The Government has acknowledged the need to address the issues raised by these inquiries and has published a suite of legislation and guidance to support better inter-agency collaboration.

- This book focuses on children referred to children's social care when there are concerns of domestic violence and/or parental substance misuse and describes the extent to which children and adult services work together, identifies factors that support collaborative working, and explores what aspects of the services provided to families parents find most helpful.

Chapter 2

The Response of Children's Social Care

To understand the extent to which agencies work together when children living with domestic violence or parental substance misuse are referred to children's social care, 357 social work case files were examined. Cases were included in the sample when a child had been referred for services to safeguard or promote his or her welfare during 2002, and concerns about domestic violence and/or parental substance misuse were identified at the point of referral or during the initial assessment.

The chapter identifies the extent of inter-agency collaboration and working, through focusing on the:

- route to children's social care
- characteristics of the children
- response of children's social care
- degree of inter-agency collaboration during assessment, planning and service provision.

The route to children's social care

The evidence of how children and families were referred to children's social care and what subsequently happened is based on records held within the social work case file. However, this may not be a complete picture of the decisions made on particular cases because, although at the time of the research the Assessment Framework had been implemented, not all the participating local authorities were using the accompanying records consistently. Moreover, there was some you make your referral by telephone, confirm it in writing within 48 hours' (HM Government 2006d, p.13, paragraph 11.5).

Non-professionals such as parents and children, wider family and neighbours were most likely to use the telephone when contacting children's social care (80%).

Re-referrals

Information was available on 338 cases. In practically half the cases (48.5%) the current referral was a re-referral. A rather higher proportion than the national average; Government statistics for the year ending 31 March 2003 (the year the data was collected) showed 22 per cent of referrals were repeat referrals (Department for Education and Skills 2004b). 'A re-referral is a referral about the same child/young person within a 12-month period from when the child's case was last closed' (Department of Health 2000a, p.2).

A greater proportion of referrals from non-professionals sources were re-referrals than those from professional sources. Re-referrals accounted for 61.4 per cent of all referrals from non-professionals sources, compared with 45.1 per cent of those from professional sources.

The reasons driving this bias are complex. Part of the trend may result from social work practitioners acting more readily on referrals made by professionals than those coming from non-professionals. 'When families are unknown to welfare agencies and/or there is little evidence of severe abuse, professional judgement on what to do can be unduly influenced by the status of the referrer' (Cleaver, Wattam and Cawson 1998, p.5). In addition, the greater re-referral rate may partly result from previous requests for help, made by family, friends and neighbours, not having been effectively dealt with and additional help is needed.

Alternatively, a factor leading to the bias may be that families, who felt they had previously benefited from services, sought further help.

Reason the child was referred

Information was available on 349 cases. Social workers frequently recorded more than one reason why the child and family were referred to children's social care. In over three-quarters of cases (77.4%) the recorded reason for referral included child protection concerns, in 60 per cent of cases domestic violence, and in half the cases (52%) parental substance misuse. In a fifth of cases (20.3%) both parental substance misuse and domestic violence were noted (see Table 2.2).

Table 2.2 Reason for referral

	Number	Percentage
Child protection concerns	271	77
History of domestic violence	206	59
Parental substance misuse	182	52
Parental mental illness	42	12
Parental learning or physical disability	6	4
Other parenting issues	65	19
Disabled child	5	1
Child beyond control	13	4
Financial concerns	13	4
Housing	42	12
Other	51	15

Because individual cases may have more than one reason for referral the percentages refer to all referrals and do not add up to 100 per cent.

Parental awareness of the referral

Information was available on 250 cases. Parents were aware of the referral in over half the cases (57.2%). In the remaining 107 cases they did not know a referral to children's social care had been made. An exploration of the data shows no correlation between the reason for referral and parental awareness of the referral. However, there was a strong association between the agency making the referral and whether parents knew a referral had been made. Health practitioners and the police were most likely to inform parents before making a referral to children's social care while other social services' departments (includes drug and alcohol teams and other adult services), schools and voluntary agencies were less likely to talk to parents before making the referral (see Table 2.3).

the total population served by all six authorities; 92.5 per cent were classified as White British, Irish or other White, although there was considerable variation between the six participating authorities.

In the study sample the children from other ethnic backgrounds were made up of six children who were classified as Caribbean or African; eight as Indian or Pakistani, and 16 as mixed heritage. Although, in most instances this distribution reflected the total population served by all six authorities, the proportion of children from Asian backgrounds was slightly lower than expected, accounting for 2.9 per cent of the group compared with 3.7 per cent of the total population served by the six authorities.

To try and understand why children from the Asian community may be under represented, the research team met with a member of the Drug and Alcohol Team in one local authority who had specific responsibility for working with the local Asian community. His experiences suggest that the incidence of drug misuse and domestic violence are similar in Asian communities as in the overall population, reflecting findings of previous research (see for example, Butt and Box 1998; Dutt and Phillips 2000). His reflections suggest the reasons for the lower take-up of services are complex and influenced by a number of factors, including:

- Services not generally geared to Asian communities; not ethnically sensitive, and lack an understanding of the needs of the Asian community.

- Racism within the caring institutions, or at least a perception of racist attitudes.

- Possible racism from the Asian community towards non-Asian workers, not wishing to be helped by non-Asians.

- Ignorance, perhaps due to language difficulties, as well as a lack of awareness of the agencies that can offer help.

- Embarrassment at seeking help for problems within a very tight knit community; a general acceptance that problems should be held within the community – 'keep it under the carpet'.

These findings suggest that children's social care cannot solve the problem of low take-up of services alone. They will need to work more closely with the community in order to break down racism (perceived or otherwise), build up trust, and develop services that safeguard and promote the welfare of children that are perceived as consistent with the culture of the community.

Principal carer for the child

Information was available on 349 cases. In the majority of cases (89.6%) the mother had been noted as the child's principal carer, the father in only 25 cases (10.1%) and another member of the family in one case.

The response of children's social care

The scrutiny of social work case files suggest that in carrying out their duties, children's social care did not always follow Government Guidance as laid out in *Framework for the Assessment of Children in Need and their Families* (Department of Health *et al.* 2000) and *Working Together to Safeguard Children* (Department of Health *et al.* 1999). For example, all cases resulting in an initial child protection conference should be preceded by an:

- initial assessment (which may be very brief depending on the child's circumstances)
- a strategy discussion to decide whether to initiate s47 enquiries
- s47 enquiries (the purpose of which is to decide whether the authority should take any action to safeguard or promote the child's welfare)
- a core assessment (which is the means by which an s47 enquiry is carried out).

Initial assessments

> An initial assessment is defined as a brief assessment of each child referred to social services with a request for services to be provided. (Department of Health *et al.* 2000, p.32, paragraph 3.9)

In 267 cases (74.8%) an initial assessment was found on the case file.

Completing initial assessments within the required time

Information was available on 214 cases. Government Guidance acknowledges how critical time is in a child's life. Timescales were introduced to ensure assessments do not continue unchecked over prolonged periods without any analysis or action being made. 'A decision to gather more information constitutes an initial assessment... This should be undertaken within a maximum of seven working days but could be very brief depending on the child's circumstances' (Department of Health *et al.* 2000, p.32, paragraph 3.9). The case files show that in less than half the cases (46%) the initial assessment had been completed within the required seven working days. This is a lower proportion than had been found in previous research (where two-thirds were completed on time – Cleaver *et al.* 2004a) or Government national statistics for that year (which showed 57 per cent of initial assessments were completed within 7 working days – Department for Education and Skills 2004b). The reason why a greater proportion of initial assessments in the present study were not completed on time may be the result of a number of factors. For example, despite the complexity of the case, social workers may be reluctant to embark on a core assessment, a task which they perceive to be onerous and time consuming, and resort to extending the initial assessment beyond its remit and time frame. Alternatively it may reflect organisational difficulties, problems with staffing, or poor supervision.

Reasons for the initial assessment

Information was available on 267 cases. The reasons for the initial assessment (see Table 2.4) reflect the concerns that triggered the referral, and indeed the criteria used to select the cases for study. In three-quarters of cases (75.3%) safeguarding concerns about the children was recorded as the reason for the assessment and in practically two-thirds of cases either concern over domestic violence and/or parental substance misuse were noted (61.7% and 60.7% respectively). The rate of recording most other concerns also reflects the recorded reasons for referral.

However, at the initial assessment stage environmental factors were more frequently recognised than at the point of referral. For example, housing was a factor noted on 12 per cent of referrals, but a feature in a quarter of initial assessments, financial difficulties were noted in only 3.7 per cent of referrals, but featured in 12 per cent of initial assessments (see Table 2.4).

Table 2.4 Reasons for the initial assessment

	Number	Percentage
Child protection concerns	201	75.3
History of domestic violence	165	61.7
Parental substance misuse	162	60.7
Parental mental illness	57	21.3
Parental learning or physical disability	6	2.2
Other parenting issues	61	22.8
Disabled child	4	1.5
Child beyond control	17	6.4
Financial concerns	32	12.0
Housing	66	24.7
Other	51	19.1

Because individual cases may have more than one reason for the initial assessment the percentages refer to all initial assessments and do not add up to 100 per cent.

Seeing the child

Information was available on 267 cases. When carrying out an initial assessment, social workers should see the child according to an agreed plan, which may include seeing the child alone or with his or her carers. The reason for seeing children is to gather information for the assessment through observing their behaviour and communicating with them. It is also to ensure that the child's views are ascertained and understood (HM Government 2006d).

The initial assessment records showed that in three-quarters of cases (74.2%) the social worker had seen the child when undertaking the initial assessment. In the 69 cases where the child was not seen, 10 involved unborn children. The remaining 59 cases were made up of: 16 children below the age of 5 years, 23 children aged 5 to 9 years, 15 children aged 10 to 14 years, and 5 young people aged 15 years or more. The case file provided no information to explain why these children had not been seen in the course of carrying out the initial assessment.

The reason for the assessment was not significantly associated with whether the child was seen. When the reason for the initial assessment included concerns about domestic violence, in 77.6 per cent of cases the social worker saw the child, and in cases where the reason for the assessment included concerns over parental substance misuse in 72.2 per cent of cases the social worker saw the child as part of the initial assessment.

Findings from the initial assessment

The findings from the initial assessment determines 'whether the child is in need, the nature of any services required, and whether a further, more detailed core assessment should be undertaken' (Department of Health *et al.* 2000, p.31, paragraph 3.9). In carrying out an initial assessment the social worker needs to focus on safeguarding and promoting the welfare of the child through gaining an understanding of the child's developmental needs, the capacity of parents to meet the child's needs, and the impact of wider family and environmental factors. Of particular relevance in these cases was for social workers to identify and understand the difficulties parents were experiencing themselves and how these impacted on their ability to carry out their parental tasks and duties.

EVIDENCE OF DOMESTIC VIOLENCE AND PARENTAL SUBSTANCE MISUSE

The findings of the initial assessment reflect the focus of the study. Half the children were living with parents who were experiencing domestic violence, a third with parents who had a drug problem and just over a third with parents who were misusing alcohol. However, these issues did not exist in isolation; there was neighbourhood and social networks in which they live. (Department of Health *et al.* 2000, p.22, paragraph 2.13)

In carrying out an initial assessment social workers should explore the impact of the wider family and environment on the child and his or her parents. This includes assessing four dimensions: family history and functioning; social resources; housing; employment and income. In all but 12 cases, social workers recorded information relating to these issues. An examination of these data shows that the majority (80.6%) of children and their parents were experiencing problems in relation to family history and functioning. Moreover, between 40 per cent and 50 per cent of children and their parents were experiencing problems in relation to the other 4 dimensions: wider family, social resources, housing, and employment and income.

Once again a research rating of 'severe difficulties' was calculated (difficulties identified by the social worker in two or more of the four dimensions covered in the *family and environmental domain*). Using this criterion resulted in two-thirds of cases (66.3%) being classified as having severe difficulties in relation to the domain of family and environmental factors, again a much greater proportion than the 37 per cent found in previous research which looked at a consecutive sample of cases (Cleaver *et al.* 2004a).Most children and families were negatively affected by at least one aspect of their family and environmental factors. In only 32 cases (12.5%) had social workers not recorded a problem in any of the dimensions.

The findings from the initial assessment highlight the vulnerability of children living with domestic violence and/or parental drug or alcohol misuse. Practically a third of the children had severe unmet developmental needs, half had parents who were experiencing severe difficulties in meeting their children's needs, and two-thirds were severely affected by factors within their wider family and environment.

Multiple-problem cases

Cases were classified as *multiple-problem* when children had severe unmet developmental needs *and* there were severe difficulties in relation to parenting capacity *and* there were severe difficulties in relation to family and environmental factors. These criteria applied to over a fifth of children (22.3%) a much greater proportion than the 7 per cent identified in previous research that took a consecutive sample of initial assessments (Cleaver *et al.* 2004a).

However, it should not be assumed that domestic violence, parental alcohol misuse and parental drug misuse have a similar impact. Separating the issues shows how differently parental alcohol misuse, drug misuse and domestic violence affect children and families.

THE IMPACT OF DOMESTIC VIOLENCE AND PARENTAL SUBSTANCE MISUSE ON CHILDREN'S DEVELOPMENTAL NEEDS

Over a third (39.1%) of the children, living in families where there was evidence of domestic violence *and* parental substance misuse (drug and/or alcohol) were identified as having severe developmental needs. Separating out the issues showed considerable similarities. A third (34.5%) of children exposed only to domestic violence had severe unmet developmental needs; 29.5% of those exposed only to parental drug misuse did so, and 38.2% of children where there was evidence of only parental alcohol misuse.

THE IMPACT OF DOMESTIC VIOLENCE AND PARENTAL SUBSTANCE MISUSE ON PARENTING CAPACITY

Parenting capacity was severely affected in 71 per cent of cases where there was evidence of domestic violence *and* parental substance misuse (drug and/or alcohol). Looking at each issue suggests that domestic violence has less of an adverse affect on parenting capacity than parental substance misuse. In 37.9 per cent of cases where there was evidence only of domestic violence, severe parenting issues were identified compared with 50 per cent of cases where there was only evidence of parental alcohol misuse and 53.8 per cent of cases where there was only evidence of parental drug misuse.

THE IMPACT OF DOMESTIC VIOLENCE AND PARENTAL SUBSTANCE MISUSE ON FAMILY AND ENVIRONMENTAL FACTORS

Evidence of domestic violence *and* parental substance misuse (drug and/or alcohol) was associated with severe difficulties in relation to family and environmental factors in 82.9 per cent of cases. An exploration of the three issues shows that the association is most strongly found for parental drug misuse where 79.6 per cent of cases were classified as having severe problems in relation to family and environmental factors. In contrast, in cases where domestic violence was not associated with parental substance misuse 55.9 per cent of cases were classified as having severe problems, and when only parental alcohol misuse was identified 57.1 per cent were classed as experiencing severe problems.

This exploration of the data suggests that the co-morbidity of domestic violence and parental substance misuse has a much greater negative impact on children's welfare and safety. Separating out the issues shows that although domestic violence and parental substance misuse result in a similar rate of

15.3% of cases) than when there was evidence of domestic violence (provided in 23.2% of cases).

The interviews with families (see Chapter 4) suggest that deciding not to provide families with a copy of the assessment did not mean that the outcome of the initial assessment was not discussed. This was reinforced by the notation found in two-thirds (67.2%) of case records, that the outcome of the initial assessment had been communicated to families.

Strategy discussion

When there is reasonable cause to suspect the child is suffering or is likely to suffer significant harm, the initial assessment should be brief and children's social care should convene quickly a strategy discussion (Department of Health *et al.* 2001). To hold a strategy discussion does not require a face-to-face meeting, but 'a meeting is likely to be the most effective way of discussing the child's welfare and planning future action' (Department of Health *et al.* 2001, p.23, paragraph 3.24).

The strategy discussion should be used to:

- share available information
- agree the conduct and timing of any criminal investigation
- decide whether a core assessment under s47 of The Children Act (1989) (s47 enquiries) should be initiated, or continued if it has already begun
- plan how the s47 enquiry should be undertaken (if one is to be initiated), including the need for medical treatment, and who will carry out what actions, by when and for what purpose
- agree what action is required immediately to safeguard and promote the welfare of the child, and/or provide interim services and support. If the child is in hospital, decisions should also be made about how to secure the safe discharge of the child
- determine what information from the strategy discussion will be shared with the family, unless such information sharing may place a child at increased risk of significant harm or jeopardise police investigations into any alleged offence(s)
- determine if legal action is required.

(HM Government 2006a, p.116, paragraph 5.55)

A strategy discussion was held in 65 cases. In 49 cases the strategy discussion followed on from an initial assessment. However, no initial assessment predated the strategy discussion in the other 16 cases, suggesting that Government Guidance was not always followed (HM Government 2006a, p.115).

The results of the strategy discussion

In the majority of cases the decision following the strategy discussion was to initiate s47 enquiries; the result in 55 cases (84.6%). The remaining cases were dealt with in a variety of ways. In three cases the discussion led to a criminal investigation being conducted, in four cases a core assessment was initiated, and in one the child and family were referred to another agency. In two cases the results of the strategy discussion had not been recorded on the case file.

Enquiries under s47 of The Children Act (1989)

> The core assessment is the means by which a s47 enquiry is carried out... In these circumstances, the objective of the LA's involvement is to determine whether action is required to safeguard and promote the welfare of the child or children who are the subjects of the enquiries. (HM Government, 2006, p.118, paragraph 5.60)

A record of s47 enquiries was found on the case file in 73 cases. The scrutiny of social work case files suggests that systematic recording of strategy discussions and subsequent s47 enquiries was not always routine practice. For example, in 55 cases the recorded decision of the strategy discussion was to conduct an enquiry under s47, but in six cases there was no evidence on the case file of s47 enquiries having been conducted. In a further 24 cases, where there was a record of s47 enquiries on the case file, there was no record of a strategy discussion having taken place.

A scrutiny of the characteristics of the cases suggests some are more associated with enquiries being conducted under s47, than others.

Age of child

Although a greater proportion of referrals of middle year children and early teens were involved in s47 enquiries (25% and 21.9% respectively) younger children did not lag far behind; 17.6% of referrals involving children under the age of 5 years resulted in enquiries under s47. However, young people aged 15 years and more, were less often (13.3%) involved in s47 enquires.

Gender of child

A similar proportion of boys and girls, referred to children's social care because there were concerns about domestic violence or parental substance misuse, were involved in enquiries under s47 (20.8% and 18.5% respectively).

Evidence of parental substance misuse or domestic violence

Cases where there was evidence of domestic violence were slightly more likely to result in s47 enquiries being conducted than referrals where there was evidence of parental substance misuse. A fifth (19.4%) of referrals involving domestic violence concerns led to enquiries under s47 compared with 14.8% of those where there were concerns of parental substance misuse.

The identity of the local authority

The rate of s47 enquiries being conducted varied with the identity of the local authority. Rates clustered for four participating authorities with an average of 18.1 per cent of referrals going on to enquiries under s47 with a range of 10 per cent. However, the rate in the two participating London Boroughs was rather different; in London Borough 2 no referrals led to enquiries being made under s47, whereas in the other 43.3 per cent of referrals resulted in enquiries under s47. No significance can be placed on this finding because it reflects differences in identifying the sample rather than differences in social work practice. In London Borough 2, a member of the research team scrutinised all referrals to identify relevant cases, while in the other social workers took responsibility for the task. On discovering that their IT system could not provide the relevant information at the point of referral the sample was gathered in a variety of ways including identifying cases from the child protection register where information about domestic violence and parental substance misuse was recorded.

Core assessments

A core assessment was carried out in 95 cases; a quarter (26.6%) of all the referrals included in the study.

> A core assessment is deemed to have commenced at the point the initial assessment ended, or a strategy discussion decided to initiate enquires under s.47, or new information obtained on an open case indicates a core assessment should be undertaken. (Department of Health *et al.* 2000, p.32, paragraph 3.11)

The information held on the social work case files suggests social work practice was not always consistent with government guidance. For example, core assessments were not always preceded by an initial assessment; in 43 cases there was no evidence of an initial assessment. Moreover, a core assessment record was not found in every case where there was evidence of enquiries conducted under s47; in 33 cases where s47 enquiries had been recorded there was no evidence of a core assessment having been undertaken.

A scrutiny of the findings for individual authorities shows a wide scattering in the rate of core assessments being undertaken with an average of 28.3 per cent.

For example, a core assessment was undertaken in every case where enquiries under s47 had been initiated in Shire County 1, in two-thirds of cases in London Borough 1, and in over half (57%) in Metropolitan Borough 1. However, in two authorities (Shire County 2 and Metropolitan Borough 2) very few core assessments ($n = 3$ and $n = 2$ respectively) were undertaken at all and this was reflected in that only some 16 per cent of cases where enquiries under s47 were recorded, had a core assessment been carried out. This variation may reflect the fact that authorities were at different stages in their implementation of the Assessment Framework.

In cases where a core assessment was undertaken the characteristics of the cases showed both similarities and differences to cases where enquiries under s47 had been recorded.

Age of the child

The skew towards middle year children and early teens found in relation to s47 enquiries was not evident in core assessments. Although a third (32.3%) of middle year children referred to children's social care because of concerns of parental substance misuse and/or domestic violence underwent a core assessment, this applied to a similar proportion (30.1%) of children under 5 years. In contrast only 18.7 per cent of children aged 10 to 14 years and few (6.7%) young people aged 15 years or more were involved in a core assessment.

Gender of the child

A greater proportion of boys referred to children's social care were involved in a core assessment than girls (29.8% compared with 19.1%).

Evidence of parental substance misuse or domestic violence

As was found for s47 enquiries, referrals relating to domestic violence were more likely to result in a core assessment than those where there were concerns of parental substance misuse, although the difference was not great. A quarter (25%) of all referrals where concerns included domestic violence went on to a core assessment compared with less than a fifth (18.7%) of those where parental substance misuse was a cause for concern.

The use of scales and questionnaires

The publication of the Assessment Framework was accompanied by a set of questionnaires and scales to help social workers carry out their assessments in complex cases. The set includes the following:

- Strengths and Difficulties Questionnaire
- The Parenting Daily Hassle Scale
- Home Conditions Scale
- Adult Wellbeing Scale
- The Adolescent Wellbeing Scale
- The Recent Life Events Questionnaire
- The Family Activities Scale
- The Alcohol Scale.

The use of the scales and questionnaires can provide the evidence base for judgements and recommendations regarding the child and inform the child's plan (Department of Health, Cox and Bentovim 2000).

The case files showed that practitioners rarely used the scales and questionnaires; in only seven cases (7.4%) had one or more of the scales and questionnaires been used to inform the assessment. The most frequently used test was *The Parenting Daily Hassle Scale* (six cases) followed by the *Home Conditions Scale* and the *Strengths and Difficulties Questionnaire* (both used in four cases). Of interest, considering the focus of the study was the finding that *The Alcohol Scale* had been used in only three cases. Although the rate for using the scales and questionnaires is rather higher than that found in previous research, it remains low (Cleaver *et al.* 2004a).

In eight cases the social work case file showed that a specialist assessment had been commissioned.

Child in Need Plan

The core assessment should result in a Child in Need Plan.

> The analysis, judgement and decisions made will form the basis of a plan of work with a child in need and his or her family. The complexity or severity of the child's needs will determine the scope and detail of the plan. (Department of Health *et al.* 2000, p.60, paragraph 4.33)

In 62 cases (65.3%) the core assessment resulted in a plan. Although every core assessment should result in a plan, nonetheless this is practically twice the rate found in earlier research (Cleaver *et al.* 2004a).

In 33 cases the core assessment did not result in a plan. It could be argued that a plan had not been recorded following the core assessment because the case had been taken to an initial child protection conference where a separate plan would be drawn up. However, the holding of an initial child protection conference was not related to whether the core assessment resulted in a plan:

- In 27 of the 33 cases (81.8%) where no plan was found as a result of the core assessment an initial child protection conference had been held.

- In 52 of the 62 cases (83.9%) where a plan was recorded as a result of the core assessment an initial child protection conference had been held.

Less than a third of plans (20.6%) had a recorded date for it to be reviewed.

Time taken to carry out a core assessment

Social workers had recorded both the start and end date of the core assessment in 38 cases (40%). In less than a third of these cases (31.6%) the core assessment had been completed within the required 35 working days (Department of Health *et al.* 2000). This is lower than the 73.5 per cent found to have been completed on time in the author's early study (Cleaver *et al.* 2004a).

Initial Child Protection Conference

The purpose of the initial child protection conference is to:

- bring together and analyse, in an inter-agency setting, the information that has been obtained about the child's developmental needs, and the parents' or carers' capacity to respond to these needs to ensure the child's safety and promote the child's health and development within the context of their wider family and environment

- consider the evidence presented to the conference, make judgements about the likelihood of a child suffering significant harm in future, and decide whether the child is at continuing risk of significant harm

- decide what future action is required to safeguard and promote the welfare of the child, how that action will be taken forward, and with what intended outcomes.

(HM Government 2006a, p.123, paragraph 5.80)

One hundred and twenty one referrals (33.9%) resulted in an initial child protection conference.

Government Guidance is clear that an initial assessment, strategy discussion and enquiries under s47 should have taken place prior to the initial child protection conference (HM Government 2006a). The scrutiny of social work case files suggests that this guidance was not routinely followed. In cases where an initial child protection conference had been held there was a record of an initial assessment in two-thirds of cases (62.8%), a record of a strategy discussion in less than half the cases (43.8%), a record of s47 enquiries in half the cases (52.8%) and evidence that a core assessment had been started in two-thirds of cases (65.3%).

Table 2.5 Proportion of cases where key agencies were involved during the initial assessment

Agency	DV only (n = 77)	PSM only (n = 72)	DV and PSM (n = 72)
Health	62.3%	58.3%	72.2%
Education	51.9%	56.9%	52.8%
Police	46.8%	22.2%	38.9%
Other agencies/ voluntary	20.8%	23.6%	25.0%
Housing	1.3%	6.9%	8.3%
DAT	1.3%	11.1%	20.8%
Domestic violence agency	3.9%	–	4.2%

DAT = Drug and Alcohol Team; DV = domestic violence; PSM = parental substance misuse.

For example, health and education were just as likely to be involved in cases where there was evidence of domestic violence or/and parental substance misuse. In contrast, the police and agencies providing services to help those involved in domestic violence were more likely to be involved in cases were there was evidence of domestic violence. Likewise, agencies providing services to parents who have drug or alcohol problems (DAT) and housing were more likely to be involved in cases where there was evidence of parental substance misuse.

However, most striking was that irrespective of the family circumstances, the relatively few cases where services for domestic violence, substance misuse or housing were involved or consulted during the initial assessment.

Agencies involved in the provision of services following an initial assessment

Children's social care provided services to the child and family in over half the cases (55.8%). In addition, 30 cases (12.4%) were referred to an agency providing services to families experiencing domestic violence, 41 cases (17.1%) were referred to a drug and alcohol team or other agency working with substance misuse, 13 (5.4%) were referred to probation services and 106 (43.3%) to another agency. In a quarter of cases, no agency continued to be involved with the family, as the result of the initial assessment was to take no further action.

Referring to a domestic violence service or to substance misuse service was related to whether these issues featured in the reason for the assessment.

- A referral was made to an agency providing services for substance misuse in over a quarter (27.8%) of cases where there was evidence of parental substance misuse.

- A referral was made to an agency providing services for families experiencing domestic violence in a fifth (20.1%) of cases where there was evidence of domestic violence.

The findings suggest that following an initial assessment that identified either domestic violence and/or parental substance misuse, referring cases to agencies providing services to address these issues is not routine. However, not all cases where there is evidence of domestic violence may warrant a referral to services for domestic violence, for example, when the violent partner has left the home. In cases where there are fears that the separated violent partner will continue with the assaults the police may provide a protective service. Although this could not be identified from the social work case record, it did emerge from interviews with some police officers and families.

Communicating the outcome of the initial assessment to the relevant agencies

Social workers had noted on the initial assessment record that the outcome of the initial assessment was communicated to other agencies in three-quarters of cases (75.2%).

Agencies involved in strategy discussions

> Whenever there is reasonable cause to suspect that a child is suffering, or is likely to suffer, significant harm, there should be a strategy discussion involving LA children's social care and the police, and other bodies as appropriate (e.g. children's centre/school and health), in particular any referring agency. (HM Government 2006a, p.116, paragraph 5.54)

As would be expected the police were most frequently involved in strategy discussions; they were involved in 81.5 per cent of cases. Health took part in practically two-thirds (63%) of strategy discussions, education in nearly a fifth (18.5%), and other social services departments in 17 per cent. However, specialist agencies providing services to families experiencing domestic violence or substance misuse were not involved routinely; taking part in nine (13.8%) and four (6.2%) strategy discussions respectively.

Agencies involved in s47 enquiries

The involvement of other agencies in s47 inquiries closely mirrors the findings for involvement in the strategy discussion. Once again, in the majority of cases the police and health services took part (86.3% and 65.4% respectively). The involvement of agencies providing services for families experiencing domestic violence or substance misuse continued to be uncommon. The drugs and alcohol team were involved in six cases (8.2%) and domestic violence agencies in five cases (6.8%) where s47 inquiries took place.

Agencies involved in the Initial Child Protection Conference

A third (n = 121) of referrals resulted in an initial child protection conference. A similar pattern of agency involvement found for s47 enquiries was evident at the initial child protection conference. Police and health services were involved in most initial child protection conferences (found in 95% and 85% respectively) whereas the involvement of services for domestic violence or substance misuse was not common. For example, agencies providing services for domestic violence took part in 5 per cent of initial child protection conferences, and, although the participation of DAT improved, nonetheless, they were involved in less than a fifth (18.2%) of conferences.

This continuing low level of involvement is perhaps more striking in the light of the initial child protection conference identifying domestic violence as an issue in 72.7 per cent of cases and parental substance misuse in 60.3 per cent of cases.

Agencies involved in the core assessments plans

> In order to ensure optimal outcomes for children, whilst at the same time avoiding duplication of services or children receiving no service at all, it is important for all disciplines and agencies to work in a co-ordinated way to an agreed plan. (Department of Health 2000b, p.63, paragraph 5.2)

An exploration of the agencies involved in the 62 plans following a core assessment shows that health services were involved in over two-thirds (69.4%) of plans, and education in a fifth (20.9%) of plans.

In a quarter of cases (24.2%) the drug and alcohol team was involved in the plan. However, the relative absence of agencies providing services for families experiencing domestic violence was once again evident; in only 8 per cent of cases was such an agency involved in the child's plan.

Discussing the plan following a core assessment with the relevant agencies

Social workers should note on the core assessment record whether the plan has been discussed with the agencies who were party to the plan. In practically two-thirds of cases the social worker had noted that the plan had been discussed with the relevant agencies (62.9%). It cannot be assumed that in the remaining third of cases the relevant agencies were not aware of the plan; it may simply reflect a failure of the social worker to note this on the core assessment record.

Summary points

- The sample included 357 referrals to children's social care where there were concerns over the welfare or safety of the child and concerns about domestic violence and/or parental substance misuse.

- Professionals made three-quarters of the referrals to children's social care; 'non-professionals' referred to the child, parent, relative or neighbour. The police and health services were the main source of referrals.

- Parents were aware of the referral in over half the cases. Police and health services were more likely to inform parents prior to making the referral than other agencies.

- The sample included a greater proportion of younger children. Boys and girls were similarly represented.

- The sampling criteria meant that referrals led to some form of action being taken. In three-quarters of cases the referral led to an initial assessment, in 18.2 per cent of cases a strategy discussion was convened, in a fifth of cases s47 enquiries were conducted, and in just over a quarter of cases a core assessment was carried out.

- Less than half the initial assessments were concluded within the required time; a lower proportion than the figure of two-thirds found in a consecutive sample of initial assessments (Cleaver *et al.* 2004a).

- The initial assessment showed that issues of domestic violence and parental substance misuse rarely existed in isolation. A quarter of children were living in families where there was evidence of both domestic violence and parental substance misuse, a further quarter where parents had poor mental health, and in 10 per cent of cases a parent had physical or learning disabilities.

- Children living in families where there is evidence of domestic violence and/or parental substance misuse are particularly vulnerable. The social workers' initial assessment shows that three-quarters of children had needs in at least one area of their development, 85 per cent were living with parents who were not able to undertake all key parenting tasks, and the wider family and environment was having a negative impact on most children (87.5%). Indeed, a fifth of cases were classified by the research team as *multiple-problem* (that is children experiencing severe difficulties in relation to all three domains: developmental needs *and* parenting capacity *and* family and environmental factors).

- The coexistence of domestic violence *and* parental drug or alcohol misuse was found to have a more serious impact on all aspects of children's lives. A separate focus on domestic violence, alcohol misuse and drug misuse showed they had similar negative effects on children's development, but parental substance misuse (drugs or alcohol) had a more negative impact on parenting capacity than did domestic violence, while parental drug misuse was more strongly linked with negative family and environmental factors than the other two issues.

- Practitioners working in agencies providing services for domestic violence or substance misuse were rarely consulted or involved in the initial assessment. Domestic violence agencies were consulted or involved in only 2.6 per cent of cases and substance misuse agencies in 10.6 per cent of cases.

- As a result of the initial assessment some form of action was taken to support the child and his or her family in three-quarters of cases. This action included children's social care providing services and/or a referral for services to another agency. Following an initial assessment referrals to agencies providing services for domestic violence or parental substance misuse, however, were not routine. For example, a referral to a domestic violence service provider was made in only a fifth of cases where there was evidence of domestic violence and to an agency working with drugs and alcohol in a quarter of cases where there was evidence of parental substance misuse.

- Over a third of the cases where the outcome of the initial assessment was no further action involved children identified as having no severe needs in any of the three domains. The converse, however, was that 38 children where the decision was no further action did have severe needs in at least one domain, two of which had been classified as *multiple-problem* (having severe difficulties in all three domains).

- A strategy discussion was held in just under a fifth of cases. Agencies providing services for domestic violence or substance misuse were not routinely involved (taking part in 13.8% and 6.2% respectively).

- Only a fifth of referrals resulted in s47 enquiries being conducted. When enquiries were undertaken agencies providing services for domestic violence or substance misuse were rarely involved (found in 6.8% and 8.2% of cases respectively).

- A third of cases resulted in an initial child protection conference. Involvement of domestic violence or substance misuse services was again not common (taking part in 5% and 18.2% respectively) even though domestic violence was identified as an issue in 72.7 per cent of cases and parental substance misuse in 60.3 per cent of cases.

- A core assessment was carried out in just over a quarter of cases. Practitioners rarely used scales or questionnaires to inform the assessment and plan. Two thirds of the core assessments resulted in a plan. The involvement of drug and alcohol teams increased somewhat at the planning stage being involved in a quarter of plans following a core assessment. However, this level of involvement did not apply to services for domestic violence who were involved in only 8 per cent ($n = 5$) of plans.

Chapter 3

Collaborative Working

> Good information sharing is the key to successful collaborative working and
> early intervention to help children and young people at risk of poor outcomes.
> (Cm, 5860 2003, Department for Education and Skills 2006b)

In cases of parental substance misuse and domestic violence a number of different
service providers should share information and work together in order to address
the needs of all members of the family. To be effective, practitioners need to be
aware of the range of relevant organisations and agencies within their local
authority. A thorough knowledge of these will provide the bedrock for information sharing and inter-agency collaboration. Multi-agency working to address
the needs of vulnerable children is supported by a number of recent Government
initiatives and guidance (see for example, Cm 5860 2003; Department of Health
et al. 1999; HM Government 2006a; HM Government 2006d).

This chapter is based on findings from the questionnaires completed by
managers from a range of different relevant agencies and examines:

- managers' awareness of the agencies and organisations that provide
  relevant services and those they would contact in cases involving
  substance misuse and domestic violence

- the quality of inter-agency relationships

- factors which support multi-agency working and communication

- factors which hinder multi-agency working and communication.

The link person in each participating local authority agreed to pass on the questionnaire to senior and first line managers within children's social care and a
senior manager in the following services: police, health (including hospital
managers, health visitor managers and GPs) substance misuse, housing, domestic
violence, and education. The breakdowns by authority and service are shown in
Table 3.1.

Table 3.1 Questionnaire responses

Authority		Service	(n = 78)
Metropolitan Borough 1	10	Police	5
Metropolitan Borough 2	12	Health	22
Shire County 1	16	Substance misuse	17
Shire County 2	19	Housing	3
London Borough 1	13	Children's social care	17
London Borough 2	8	Domestic violence	13
		Education	1

Managers' awareness of the agencies and organisations

Managers identified a wide range of organisations that provide services or which they would contact in cases of parental substance misuse or domestic violence. These included all the major statutory agencies and a number of voluntary agencies. The voluntary agencies were often local groups and have been categorised as either support organisations, housing organisations, substance misuse organisations or domestic violence organisations. Box 3.1 lists the agencies in the order in which they were most frequently mentioned.

The number of agencies and organisations mentioned

Knowledge of organisations varied from four managers mentioning just one agency that they would involve, to one manager mentioning 16 agencies. The average number of agencies mentioned by managers was 6.4. There was a suggestion in the data that the length of time that managers had been in post correlated with the number of agencies mentioned (longer serving managers mentioning more agencies) but this was not shown to be statistically significant.

Children's social care managers within the same local authority did not always have a similar awareness of the specialist services available for domestic violence and substance misuse within their authority. For example, in one authority three of the children's social care senior managers identified only two organisations working with substance misusers, while a fourth senior manager identified six such organisations.

Managers need a comprehensive knowledge of the local services that support children and families experiencing domestic violence or substance misuse; it is the responsibility of service managers to ensure that this information is effectively updated and distributed to all relevant staff. It is also a management responsibility to ensure that practitioners use the information for the benefit of service users.

The *Information Sharing and Assessment* (ISA) work should help make information about local services more readily available to practitioners and service users. The Government produced a set of minimum requirements for local authorities, one of which was that by March 2004 they should 'have a service directory providing comprehensive information on local providers, eligibility criteria, geographical location and referral procedures' (Cm 5860 2003, p.102).

An evaluation of progress found that 85.7 per cent of authorities had met this requirement or were close to meeting it as of April 2004 (Cleaver *et al.* 2004c). If these service directories are kept up to date with contact names and numbers they will be a useful tool to help practitioners identify relevant local services.

Box 3.1 Organisations identified by managers

Most frequently mentioned	Children's social care
	Substance misuse organisations – statutory and voluntary
	Domestic violence organsiations – statutory and voluntary
	Police
	Health
	Support organisations – statutory and voluntary
	Housing violence organsiations – statutory and voluntary
	Education
	Probation
Least frequently mentioned	CAMHS
	Solicitors

Involving children's social care

Nearly all (89%) managers from organisations other than children's social care (*n* = 61) mentioned that they would involve children's social care when concerned about a child living with parental substance misuse or domestic violence.

This finding suggests managers from a variety of organisations (health, police, education, housing, domestic violence services and substance misuse services) see children's social care as a key agency to safeguarding and promoting the welfare of children living in these circumstances.

It is of concern that not every manager mentioned children's social care as an agency that they would contact when working with such cases, and suggests that in a few cases the needs of adults may be placed before those of the children. The seven managers who failed to mention children's social care did not come from any specific local authority or service.

Involving substance misuse services

The majority (79%) of managers not working in substance misuse or domestic violence services ($n = 48$) said that in cases where vulnerable children were living with a substance misusing parent, they would involve either a statutory or voluntary substance misuse service. Those who did not mention involving a substance misuse service were split across professions. However, seven of the ten managers were based in one local authority (Shire County 2).

The overall number of substance misuse services identified by the managers in different authorities showed considerable variation. In four authorities (Metropolitan Borough 1, Shire County 1, Metropolitan Borough 2 and London Borough 2) managers as a group identified between five and seven different substance misuse services in their authority; in the remaining two authorities the managers identified only two organisations providing services for substance users. This difference may reflect a lack of substance misuse services in these authorities. However, brief enquiries suggest that service provision does not differ markedly from their matched authorities, where managers had identified a greater number of service providers. Moreover, there were a number of agencies offering substance misuse services, known to the research team that had not been identified by the managers completing the questionnaires.

Involving domestic violence services

Three-quarters (75%) of managers not working in substance misuse or domestic violence organisations ($n = 48$) said that in cases where vulnerable children were living with domestic violence, they would involve either a statutory or voluntary domestic violence service. Those not mentioning a domestic violence service were spread across the different organisations. However, 7 of the 12 managers who did not mention involving services for domestic violence were from the same authority as the managers who had failed to identify any substance misuse service.

Unlike the findings for substance misuse services there was greater consistency between managers' awareness of local domestic violence service providers. As a group, managers in each local authority mentioned between five and seven different agencies providing services for families experiencing domestic violence.

Why managers in one local authority were less aware of local services for substance misuse and domestic violence

The local authority where managers identified few or no services for substance misuse or domestic violence is a large rural authority and both the population and available services are widely distributed. As a result managers may be less aware of particular services. For example, even if managers in one part of the authority were aware of services available in another part of the authority they may not refer cases to them because they are simply too far away from the family in question. The problem of distance was highlighted by one of the social workers interviewed in this authority:

> Services provided on the basis of the initial assessment: Outreach support from the family centre – this is based in XXX so mum could not benefit from visiting the centre as it is a round trip of about 80 miles. (Social worker – Shire County 2)

However, comparing this shire county (Shire County 2) with the other participating shire county (Shire County 1) suggests a more complex picture. Although the first is one of the largest shire county in England, both local authorities are characterised by a combination of large rural and urban areas. The issues that particularly differentiated the two authorities were staffing levels and management.

While staff recruitment and retention is a problem common to all participating authorities, it appeared to be most acute in children's social care within this particular shire county, as noted in a recent inspection:

> The long-standing staff shortages in the intake, area teams and administrative staff had been compounded by increased work loads. This had led to managers prioritising work with the result that eligibility criteria and thresholds for intervention had been superseded by other locally determined factors. The effect of these circumstances was that consistency of service delivery to children and their families was not possible. (Social Services Inspection [SSI] report 2003 – Shire County 2)

The reference in the above quotation, to thresholds for intervention being superseded by 'locally determined factors', may be the result of poor central management. A comparison with Shire County 1 shows that the management structure in this authority lacked central control, and the impression was that at team level there was non-compliance with centrally decided policy and practice guidelines.

A lack of robust central management is likely to be a factor in the relatively low level of awareness of the available service provision for substance misuse and domestic abuse. The management issue cannot however, be separated out from the staffing difficulties. Sixteen management posts in children's services were covered by acting up arrangements.

Involving the police

Seventy-one per cent of the 73 managers other than the police mentioned that they would involve the police in cases where children for whom they had concerns were living with domestic violence or a substance misusing parent. A willingness to involve the police was not associated with a particular local authority. However, it was linked with the identity of the service. For example, 91 per cent of the 22 health managers, 76 per cent of the 17 children's social care managers and 69 per cent of the 13 domestic violence managers mentioned involving the police, compared with only 35 per cent of the 17 substance misuse managers. It is perhaps surprising that 24 per cent of children's social care managers reported that they would not routinely involve the police in domestic violence cases.

Managers' willingness to involve the police may be associated with their client group. Domestic violence services work mainly with the victims of 'crime', the abused women and children. Outside help from statutory agencies may be welcomed by the family. However, the reverse is true for drug and alcohol services. Their client group are the 'offenders'. Families fear that revealing their situation to statutory agencies, particularly the police, may result in punitive rather that supportive actions. This notion is reflected by some service providers who find other professionals often hold prejudicial views about their clients.

Involving health

The health service was seen as an important organisation to involve when there were concerns about children living with domestic violence or parental substance misuse. Nearly two-thirds (63%) of the 56 managers outside the health service noted that they would involve one or more parts of the health service. There was a wide range of health services mentioned including health visitors, PCTs, GPs, midwives and school nurses.

Involving support organisations

Half (49%) of the 79 managers, not working in support organisations, reported that they would involve a voluntary or statutory support organisation. These included family centres, NSPCC, Surestart, counselling services and Homestart.

Involving housing

Practically half (48%) of the 77 managers, excluding housing managers, mentioned involving statutory or voluntary housing organisations when there were concerns about children living with domestic violence or parental substance misuse. The reports of parents (see Chapter 4) suggest that housing is a major problem for many families, and a delay in getting housing issues resolved can hamper the timing of other service provision.

> Lack of service from Housing has stopped things changing… Get Housing to pull their finger out. I will get the drug support once the housing is sorted. (Parent)

The managers' reports suggest contacting and working with housing organisations is not a high priority when vulnerable children live with domestic violence or parental substance misuse. This contrasts with the perceptions of families; the interviews found that practically a quarter of parents interviewed for the study reported that their housing circumstances were unacceptable.

Others

Education, probation, Child and Adolescent Mental Health Services (CAMHS) and solicitors seem to be rarely involved and were only mentioned by a few managers. Of some concern is the apparent failure of many managers to routinely involve the education services when children live with domestic violence or parental substance misuse; schools play a crucial role in promoting the welfare of children and providing information to assess their developmental needs.

The quality of inter-agency relationships

> Respecting and having a positive view of the role and the workers of the other agency is a fundamental component of an effective collaborative relationship. (Darlington *et al.* 2005, p.1087)

Managers were asked to define the quality of the working relationship between their own organisation and the organisations they had identified as providing services in cases where children live with domestic violence or parental substance misuse. They categorised the relationships as either: generally very good, generally fairly good, or generally poor. The responses are shown in Table 3.2.

Table 3.2 Managers' assessment of the quality of inter-agency relationships

Quality of relationship	Responses (n = 377)
Generally very good	51% (192)
Generally fairly good	41% (156)
Generally poor	8% (29)

The data show that where inter-agency relationships exist they appear to be good, with only a small percentage of relationships (8%) being classed as poor.

This positive finding may reflect a propensity for managers to mention only organisations with which their service had good working relationships. However, reflecting on the managers' reports of the agencies they would involve when children live with domestic violence or parental substance misuse, shows that most would contact children's social care, police, health, substance misuse services and domestic violence services. This indicates that agencies were involved because of their role in promoting the welfare of the child and family rather than because of the quality of the working relationship. All six authorities had a range of very good, fairly good and poor relationships and no one authority appeared to have worse inter-agency working relationships than any other.

Table 3.3 breaks down the quality of inter-agency working relationships by the organisation with which the relationship is held.

Relationships between agencies were rated as poor in 29 cases. Poor inter-agency working relationships were reported most frequently by managers working in agencies whose clients are children, and about two-thirds of these poor working relationships are with organisations whose clients are adults. For example, children's social care managers accounted for 12 reports of poor working relationships and health managers for a further 12 reports. In most cases the poor working relationship was with either: housing, substance misuse services, hospitals or GPs.

Housing

Relationships with housing appear to be worse than relationships with the other main organisations. This could be a factor that contributes to the finding that less than half the managers identified housing as an agency which provides a service or which they would contact in cases of parental substance misuse or domestic violence. If housing is to be more frequently involved in these cases the barriers to good working relationships need to be addressed.

Table 3.3 Assessed quality of inter-agency working relationships

Organisation	Very good	Fairly good	Poor	(n = 333)
Police	66%	34%	–	47
Domestic violence services	60%	38%	2%	53
Health (combined)	48%	48%	4%	46
Health – Health visitors	81%	19%	–	16
Health – Hospitals/PCTs	27%	64%	9%	11
Health – GPs	20%	70%	10%	10
Children's social care	47%	44%	9%	57
Substance misuse services	40%	47%	13%	62
Housing	23%	48%	29%	31

Substance misuse services

Managers from children's social care and health services accounted for the eight relationships with substance misuse services that had been classed as poor. Their comments suggest the different client group on which their service is focused and a policy of being non-judgemental and inclusive (Barnard 2007) creates a barrier to good working relationships. Substance misuse services focus primarily on the needs of adults and do not necessarily acknowledge or take into account the ways the parent with the drug problem affects the children. In contrast, children's social care and many health providers, such as health visitors and school nurses, focus primarily on children.

> [It is] Occasionally difficult to make substance misuse see the needs of children, as the focus of their work is the adult. (Health manager PCT/HV – Metropolitan Borough 2)

This difference in focus will inevitably lead to situations where priorities conflict, as described below by a substance misuse manager.

> We are in the middle of a very disappointing case where children have been put into foster care as a result of police concerns and are now being put forward for adoption by social services. There has been poor communication with our service and actions which seem consistent with the view that any substance misuse parent provides grounds for adoption, even when, as in this case, the client is on a stable and carefully monitored methadone prescription. (Substance misuse manager – Metropolitan Borough 2)

In the above case children's social care may have had well-founded reasons for their actions, however, these were not shared with the substance misuse service. This example reflects either poor inter-agency communication or unresolved issues over information sharing and confidentiality.

A history of poor communication may lead to an erosion of the trust between organisations. Substance misuse services have a reputation for withholding information from other organisations, particularly children's social care, to protect their clients (Barnard 2007).

> Drug misuse worker not wanting to share information regarding a child's welfare if this will mean significant changes for the care of the child, e.g. permanent removal. (Senior children's social care manager – London Borough 1)

Potentially difficult inter-agency working relationships are further endangered by the perception that agencies not specifically focussed on drug and alcohol problems are prejudiced against parents with such problems.

> Understanding of the need to act according to child's needs rather than prejudice about drug use. (Substance misuse manager – Metropolitan Borough 2)

Discussions with children's social care managers and practitioners also highlighted how the different time scales for intervention may affect working relationships between adult and children's services. Services for adult drug users work to long time scales matching the provision of services to the pace of change their clients can realistically achieve. In contrast, services working with children, particularly where there are safeguarding concerns, must seek a far more immediate response.

Finally, the scrutiny of procedures and protocols (see Chapter 6) found that Area Child Protection Committee (ACPC) procedures did not adequately cover parental substance misuse and no supporting procedures were provided by individual agencies.

Domestic violence services

Relationships with domestic violence services were very rarely classed as poor. A poor working relationship was noted in only one instance; contrasting with the finding for substance misuse services. Reflecting on the issues identified as linked with poor relationships with services for substance users suggests these may not apply to services for domestic violence. For example, services for domestic violence generally focus on working with the mother and her children who are seen as victims of the domestic violence. The need to remove the children from the caring parent in order to keep them safe rarely happens because in most cases the primary objective is to remove the abusive parent and protect the victims from further assaults.

Timescales for services are less likely to conflict because both children's social care and domestic violence services focus on the needs of the victims – the abused parent and the children.

Finally, the scrutiny of procedures and protocols found ACPC procedures were more likely to include adequate information on domestic violence. In addition, many individual agencies provided guidance on how to deal with domestic violence.

Factors which support multi-agency working

Supporting good working relationships between agencies and organisations is the responsibility of senior, middle and line management. Without management commitment, good multi-agency working will not succeed.

Managers were asked to identify factors which support a good working relationship, factors which help communication between agencies, and factors which help to involve other organisations. Box 3.2 shows the most common responses.

Box 3.2 Commonly identified factors which support good working relationships

- Understanding and respecting the roles and responsibilities of other services.

- Good communication.

- Regular contact and meetings.

- Common priorities.

- Inter-agency training.

- Knowing what services are available and who to contact.

- Clear guidelines and procedures for working together.

- Low staff turnover.

These factors reflect those identified by Birchall and Hallett (1995) in their work on inter-agency co-ordination in child protection services and Kroll and Taylor (2003) in their exploration of parental substance misuse and child welfare, and are discussed in detail below.

Understanding and respecting the roles and responsibilities of other services

All evidence indicates that children are safeguarded best where there is clarity and understanding between different agencies about roles and responsibilities, underpinned by good working relationships at all levels. (Commission for Social Care Inspection 2005, p.33, paragraph 4.32)

A clear understanding of the roles and responsibilities of other services will help ensure that relevant agencies are involved in the assessment, planning and service provision in cases where children live with domestic violence or parental substance misuse. It will also enable practitioners to have greater confidence in each others' abilities, and lead to fewer misunderstandings, inappropriate referrals and misdirected services.

An awareness and appreciation of the role of others is essential for effective collaboration between organisations and their practitioner. (HM Government 2006a, p.39, paragraph 2.1)

Managers from all the services questioned thought that understanding the roles and responsibilities of other service providers was important in supporting good working relationships. Organisations with different perspectives need to respect, value and trust each others' assessments and decisions, and work together to safeguard and promote the welfare of children and their families.

Understanding each others perspectives. I think we sometimes seek to explain our own perspective too much rather than try to understand the others' perspective. We can end up mistrusting each other which is silly as we are seeking the same thing. We need to educate each other ourselves, about what each other's agency roles are and take responsibility for building relationships. (Senior children's social care manager – Shire County 1)

...not trying to convince other practitioners that your service is 'right'. Respecting the skills/knowledge and practice of other practitioners. (Substance misuse manager NHS Trust – Shire County 1)

Understanding what other organisations do and their cultures. The systems they operate. The language they use... Not thinking that you are the 'be all and end all' and castigating others in other agencies. (Domestic violence manager probation – London Borough 2)

Some managers did not feel that their agency was always respected.

Being treated as a professional all the time not just when social services want us to be! For example, social services want reports written etc. for core groups and case conferences but then will not send copies even though we attend meetings as we are not a professional body. (Impact Housing – Metropolitan Borough 1)

Good communication

> Communication is a key aspect which will set the foundation of a good relationship. (Domestic violence manager, Asian women's domestic violence project – Metropolitan Borough 1)

Managers were asked to describe communication generally between organisations working with families affected by substance misuse or domestic violence. The results are shown below in Table 3.4.

Table 3.4 Levels of communication between organisations and families

Communication	Cases involving substance misuse (n = 50)	Cases involving domestic violence (n = 47)
Excellent	8%	6%
Good	28%	34%
Variable	58%	51%
Poor	6%	9%

Very few managers classed communication as poor and the findings show a similar pattern in the quality of communication whether it involved children living with domestic violence or parental substance misuse. Nonetheless, the findings suggest there is little reason for complacency. In practically two-thirds of cases (64% in cases involving parental substance misuse, and 60 per cent of cases involving domestic violence) managers rated the quality of communication as either variable or poor.

Managers reported that the following factors need to be in place for effective communication:

- clear communication channels
- clear lines of responsibility
- workers with a knowledge of the legal framework who are open and share information
- workers with good inter-personnel skills
- common language
- ready access to email/telephones/fax machines

- keeping people informed, involving them in discussions and decision making and giving feedback, prompt correspondence and communication
- communicating concerns at an early stage.

This list identifies a range of issues that require a multi-pronged approach. For example, an audit would establish current practice and processes, the findings of which should be used to inform training plans, the development of procedures, guidelines and investment in electronic hardware.

Regular contact and meetings

Many practitioners felt that it was important to have regular contact in order to develop and maintain good working relationships.

> Networks are effective when the individuals concerned meet together and share information. (Senior children's social care manager – London Borough 1)

Supporting good inter-agency working relationships did not necessarily depend on face-to-face meetings. Working relationships could be sustained through a range of methods; what was essential was to keep relevant colleagues in other agencies up to date with what was happening in the cases they were involved with.

Common priorities

When children's social care are making enquiries under s47 of The Children Act (1989), because there are concerns about a child's safety, all agencies have a duty to assist them by providing relevant information or advice (Children Act 1989 s47 (9)). However, the findings from this study suggest collaboration may be hampered by the different working cultures that develop in organisations providing services to adults and those that develop in agencies working with children.

> …the child/adult divide has made the success of bringing in joint working much slower. (Senior children's social care manager – London Borough 2)

There were many comments from health and children's social care managers which highlighted the different priorities between adult and children's services and the way these impacted on good inter-agency working relationships.

> Not considering child protection concerns if adult service. (Health manager PCT – London Borough 2)

> …makes a difference if other organisation is child focused and can understand why focus is on the child. (Senior children's social care manager – London Borough 2)

> Acceptance that child's needs are paramount. (Senior children's social care manager – Metropolitan Borough 1)

> Practitioners who work with adults not recognising child protection issues. (Health manager PCT senior nurse – Shire County 2)

The Children Act (2004), the National Service Framework for Children, Young People and Maternity Services and *Working Together to Safeguard Children* (2006) have helped to raise awareness that the safeguarding and welfare of children is everyone's responsibility. However, when children are not the primary focus of an agency's work, child protection is not always a priority. The scrutiny of plans for domestic violence services, services for substance misuse, and the police (see Chapter 6) shows that the service plans did not always cover child protection, a finding also highlighted in the recent Joint Chief Inspectors' Report (Commission for Social Care Inspection 2005) in relation to the police.

> All but one of the 43 police forces have clear child protection procedures and guidance. However, child protection is not a priority in 41 per cent (18) of policing plans, mainly because there is a lack of focus on children's safeguards at a national level. Child protection is not a national priority area or currently monitored by means of a national performance indicator. (Commission for Social Care Inspection 2005, p.24, paragraph 4.17)

Inter-agency training

> Training delivered on an inter-agency basis is a highly effective way of promoting a common and shared understanding of the respective roles and responsibilities of different professionals, and contributes to effective working relationships. (HM Government 2006a, p.91, paragraph 4.2)

Managers acknowledged the importance of inter-agency training to promote an understanding of the roles and responsibilities of professionals working in different organisations, their different thresholds for services, and issues surrounding confidentiality and information sharing. More specifically, managers thought inter-agency training was needed to enable practitioners to gain a greater understanding of how children's safety and welfare is affected by domestic violence or parental substance misuse.

> Joint training is very important, understanding of others' remits, what are the boundaries, good understanding of issues around confidentiality and how to deal with confidentiality issues. (Substance misuse manager NHS trust – Shire County 1)

Managers from services for substance misuse reported that a lack of adequate training and poor understanding of the relevant procedures hampered communication and inter-agency working. The scrutiny of ACPC annual training plans supports this perception; in only three of the six participating authorities did the ACPC training plan include training on parental substance misuse. What training existed was often brief; no authority provided more than two days' training on the subject and in one authority training on substance misuse was not provided every year.

> Communication in hindered by *staff who are not trained or are unsure of procedures* (Substance misuse children's social care – London Borough 1)

> Communication is hindered by *knowledge/training re client group and the process of drug treatment services.* (Substance misuse manager – Metropolitan Borough 2)

A more detailed exploration of the importance of training can be found in Chapter 7.

Knowing what services are available and who to contact

Managers reported that it was important that practitioners had a comprehensive awareness of the local organisations that could provide services to children and families in cases of parental substance misuse or domestic violence.

> Being aware of who to contact – names and position. (Health manager PCT – Shire County 2)

As mentioned earlier in this chapter, it is a management responsibility to ensure practitioners are aware of local services and who to contact within the service. This task will be supported by the development of service directories as set out in *Every Child Matters* (Cm 5860 2003).

Clear guidelines and procedures for working together

In order to support inter-agency relationships there needs to be in place clear guidelines and procedures for practitioners to follow when concerned about the safety and welfare of children living with domestic violence or parental substance misuse. Workers need to be aware of their own agency's guidelines and procedures and have ready access to them. The scrutiny of agency's procedures (see Chapter 6) showed that the issue of domestic violence was more comprehensively covered than parental substance misuse. For example, ACPC procedures generally covered domestic violence and frequently included specific guidance for practitioners, and links to other relevant documentation. Moreover, agencies working with domestic violence also produced guidance targeted at practitioners in other organisations. Similar documentation was rare in relation to parental substance misuse.

> Clear policies and procedures. Clear implementation and training on these from managers down to frontline staff. (Senior children's social care manager – London Borough 1)

> Current levels of inter-agency liaison are informal, need greater levels of formal acknowledgement at managerial level. (Substance misuse manager – Shire County 1)

When there is a lack of robust, clear guidelines and procedures good multi-agency working relationships will depend on the personalities of the individuals involved, a situation that is far from satisfactory (Commission for Social Care Inspection 2005).

Low staff turnover

There is considerable evidence to show the difficulties children's social care departments experience in recruiting and retaining their staff. A high staff turnover was found to affect the capacity of practitioners to communicate and work effectively with colleagues in other agencies (Cleaver *et al.* 2004a). Newly recruited staff need time to familiarise themselves with local service provision, the agency's protocols, procedures and guidelines, and establish personal contacts.

Although there was no direct link between the length of time managers had been in their present position and the quality of relationships between their agencies and others working in this field, nonetheless stability of staff was a factor mentioned by some managers. Working with the same people over a number of years was thought to help in building up trust between professionals in different agencies and thus supporting positive relationships.

> In this authority there is not very much change of personnel…a stable group helps build good relationships. (Education social inclusion service manager – Metropolitan Borough 1)

> Close and good networking – this is a relatively small place, certainly in terms of population, and there is continuity of staff – same people working together for a long time. (Domestic violence manager probation – Shire County 2)

Factors which hinder multi-agency working and communication

Managers were asked to identify factors which hinder inter-agency working relationships. The following issues were reported:

- confidentiality
- lack of resources

- lack of trust
- preconceptions of parents.

The issues identified by the managers reflect those found in previous research that explored multi-agency collaboration (see for example, Birchall and Hallett 1995; Darlington, Feeney and Rixon 2005; Hudson 2000).

Confidentiality

Effective information sharing by professionals is central to safeguarding and promoting the welfare of children.

> Sharing information is vital for early intervention to ensure that children and young people with additional needs get the services they require. It is also essential to protect children and young people from suffering harm from abuse or neglect and to prevent them from offending. (HM Government 2006d, p.55, paragraph 1.2)

Practitioners need to be confident about the information held on children and families that can and cannot be shared, and when information must be shared regardless of whether consent has been obtained, or when to seek consent will place the child at risk of increased harm. Appendix 3 in *What to Do if You're Worried A Child Is Being Abused* (HM Government 2006d) and the cross-government guidance on information sharing in respect of children and young people (HM Government 2006c) provide guidance for managers and practitioners on the legal and ethical considerations when sharing information in order to safeguard and promote the welfare of children. Most agencies and organisations have developed protocols for information sharing between some agencies. *Every Child Matters* (Cm 5860 2003) expects all local authorities to:

> have protocols in place for information sharing covering health services, education services and social care; and in development for all other agencies providing services to children and young people, including the police and Youth Offending Teams. (Cm 5860 2003, p.102)

The scrutiny of documentation showed that although all six local authorities had in place ACPC protocols for information sharing and client confidentiality, the protocols did not routinely include services for domestic violence and parental substance misuse. Protocols for sharing information about children and families where there was concerns or evidence of domestic violence or parental substance misuse tended to be drawn up between two or three service providers, such as the police and children's social care or a substance misuse service and children's social care. Moreover, three of the six participating local authorities had no protocols for information sharing that included services for domestic violence or substance misuse services.

THE VIEWS AND EXPERIENCES OF MANAGERS IN SERVICES OTHER THAN DOMESTIC VIOLENCE AND SUBSTANCE MISUSE

The lack of information sharing protocols covering domestic violence and parental substance misuse is related to the experiences of managers working with cases of domestic violence or parental substance misuse. Three-quarters of managers from services other than substance misuse or domestic violence reported that confidentiality issues negatively impacted on information sharing and inter-agency working between their agency and others working with the family. Approximately a fifth of managers reported this occurred on a regular basis (see Table 3.5).

Table 3.5 Impact of confidentiality issues on inter-agency working

Frequency	Substance misuse cases (n = 46)	Domestic violence cases (n = 46)
Often	24%	20%
Occasionally	52%	57%
Rarely	24%	24%

Table 3.5 shows confidentiality issues negatively affected inter-agency working at a similar rate irrespective of whether cases involved children living with parental substance misuse or domestic violence.

Examples of when confidentially issues had hampered inter-agency working, provided by these managers (those not from substance misuse or domestic violence agencies) show confidentiality difficulties were not restricted to any particular agency and included GPs, substance misuse services, health service and children's social care.

> GPs not sharing information re domestic violence. (First line children's social care manager – Shire County 2)

> Worker from drug and alcohol team not sharing information about mother abusing substances while caring for child and putting child at risk. (First line children's social care manager – Shire County 2)

Particularly in relation to health practitioners where there is failure to share significant information as unwilling to disclose information because of patient confidentiality. (First line children's social care manager – London Borough 1)

Workers from the mental health team not passing on information in order to 'protect' their client. Seeing client in isolation and not considering the effect on the children. (Health manager PCT HV – Shire County 1)

Social Services are not always prepared to give relevant information. (Housing – London Borough 1)

Client/worker alliance has made worker less inclined to report issues that may be judged by social services to impact the welfare of the child. (First line children's social care – London Borough 2)

A factor mentioned by managers as hindering inter-agency communication was practitioners hiding behind their own agency's confidentiality procedures and using them as a reason for not sharing information.

Codes of conduct and individual practice guidelines/policies/procedures relating to sole agencies often hamper effectiveness of communication. (Health manager PCT, senior nurse – Metropolitan Borough 1)

Not having all the information because practitioners are being very protective about 'their' confidential information. (Health manager hospital – Shire County 2)

To aid a universal approach, training and clear information sharing protocols and guidelines are urgently needed so that practitioners within all relevant services know what information they can share and what information they can expect to receive from other agencies and organisations. *Every Child Matters* (Cm 5860 2003) and the cross-Government Guidance (HM Government 2006c) should ensure that protocols for information sharing across agencies providing services to children and young people are established. However, unless adult services are included in these protocols, information sharing to safeguard children and promote their welfare, between children's services and adult services, will continue to be problematic.

It would be very useful to develop formal procedures between agencies so that we all knew what we could get in the way of information – an agreement would be very helpful. (Housing – Shire County 2)

Social work department demanding information about patients that cannot be given over the phone, then threats being issued! (Health manager, hospital senior nurse – Shire County 2)

Some managers felt that communication and information sharing about children living with domestic violence or parental substance misuse only happened when there were serious child protection concerns. Some managers thought information should be shared at an earlier stage to prevent problems escalating.

> Confidentiality. Discussions only occur when there are serious child welfare concerns. (Domestic violence service manager – Metropolitan Borough 2)

> Children, whose parents were being seen because of domestic violence and drug misuse, have been killed. (Health manager PCT, nursing sister – Shire County 2)

Some managers felt that to safeguard and promote the welfare of children living with domestic violence or parental substance misuse, it should be obligatory for information to be shared between relevant agencies and organisations.

> It should be obligatory that when adults with children are being seen (because of domestic violence or substance misuse) the information is shared. (Health manager PCT, senior nurse – Shire County 2)

THE VIEWS AND EXPERIENCES OF MANAGERS FROM DOMESTIC VIOLENCE AND SUBSTANCE MISUSE SERVICES

Managers working in domestic violence services and substance misuse services reported that it is not general practice to routinely refer dependent children living with their clients, to children's social care. Referring a case to children's social care depends on the practitioner's assessment of the extent to which the parenting issues are impacting on the children.

> Referrals are made to social services departments when concerns grow that any domestic violence may be directly impacting on the child or the parent's ability to parent/protect the child. (Domestic violence manager – Metropolitan Borough 2)

> The needs of the child and how serious they were. It would depend on the specifics of the cases. (Substance misuse service manager – Metropolitan Borough 1)

> Risk factors; what supports the family already have, client's views, response of social services. (Substance misuse service manager – London Borough 1)

> The best interests of the child/unborn child: these are always paramount and we would act according to the current criteria set by social services re child protection/child in need. (Substance Misuse Manager – Metropolitan Borough 2)

At the time of the research there was no nationally agreed Assessment Framework for carrying out such assessments. The new Common Assessment Framework (CAF), launched in April 2005 and expected to be fully operational by March 2008, provides an easy-to-use assessment for practitioners in all agencies to use when there are concerns that children may have additional needs (HM Government 2006b).

SYSTEMS FOR RESOLVING ISSUES REGARDING CONFIDENTIALITY

Managers were asked if there was a clear and effective system for resolving issues of confidentiality between services when cases involved children living with domestic violence or parental substance misuse. Table 3.6 shows that just over half the managers reported that no clear system was in place for resolving issues of confidentiality within their agency or organisation.

Table 3.6 Do effective systems exist for resolving confidentiality issues?

Managers' opinions	Cases involving substance misuse (n = 66)	Cases involving domestic violence (n = 62)
Yes	39%	44%
No	53%	52%
Don't know	8%	5%

Note: Substance misuse managers were only asked to comment on cases of parental substance misuse and domestic violence managers were only asked to comment on cases involving parental domestic violence.

The findings suggests that the lack of information sharing protocols and guidance, which include substance misuse services and domestic violence services, is having a negative impact on inter-agency working (see Chapter 6 for detailed information about information sharing protocols). In each local authority the same worrying trend has been identified – over three-quarters of managers reported that issues over confidentiality hamper effective inter-agency working in substance misuse and domestic violence cases, and only some 40 per cent reported that they were aware of any clear, effective systems to resolve these problems.

The findings point to a real need for senior managers in children's social care to develop information sharing protocols with their colleagues in domestic violence services and substance misuse services. Without such protocols it is the responsibility of middle and line managers to try and resolve conflicts over confidentiality on a case by case basis.

Lack of resources

Time, workload, cost, and particularly staff shortages were all quoted as factors that hinder inter-agency working. Recruiting and retaining staff in children's social care has been identified as a national problem for some years and recent research suggests that vacancy rates (posts not filled by a permanent staff member) are on average 22 per cent (Cleaver *et al.* 2004a).

> Very difficult to get hold of each other with so many staff shortages. (Health manager PCT – London Borough 1)

> Some workers (stressed – overworked) are discourteous and rude on the telephone. Don't cancel appointments or meetings; just don't turn up and waste our workers' time and effort. (Health manager PCT – Shire County 2)

> Due to staff shortages social services are sometimes slow to communicate and information has to be chased by repeat phone call. (Health manager PCT – Shire County 1)

Lack of trust

Managers within domestic violence services and substance misuse services reported that children's services do not always trust agencies where the adult is the primary client, and this has a negative affect on inter-agency working.

> Social services mistrust of agencies seen as working with 'perpetrators'. (Substance misuse manager – Shire County 1)

> There is unfortunately a high level of mistrust within both the voluntary and statutory sectors in this area. This leads to unproductive disputes between agencies and really affects the levels of services which are provided. (Domestic violence manager – Metropolitan Borough 2)

Practitioners in children's services believe that colleagues in services primarily for adults frequently hesitate in referring children within the family to children's social care. The perception is that practitioners in these services are reluctant to refer to children's social care because they fear that making a referral would alienate their client and destroy the therapeutic relationship (Kroll and Taylor 2003).

Multi-agency training can help build mutual trust through developing a better understanding of the roles and responsibilities of different agencies and organisations.

> Logic and reason suggest that training people together to undertake this work (child protection) helps in building positive relationships based on mutual respect, and also enables lessons to be learnt from past failures in collaboration. (Hendry 2000, p.1)

Preconceptions of parents

> I didn't want to tell anyone because I was afraid of what social services might do. (Child quoted in Brisby *et al.* 1997, p.14)

Practitioners tend to focus on the needs of their specific client and advocate vigorously on their behalf (Cleaver *et al.* 1999; Kroll and Taylor 2003). This may result in polarised views which block effective inter-agency working.

Managers in services for domestic violence and substance misuse reported that some practitioners in children's services held prejudicial attitudes towards the parents they worked with. Such attitudes were seen as hampering effective multi-agency working.

> Negative prejudicial attitudes towards substance using parents. (Substance misuse manager – Metropolitan Borough 2)

The importance of taking a non-stigmatising approach to working with the children of problem drug users is stressed in the Advisory Council's Inquiry report on the misuse of drugs (Home Office 2003). This stresses that services working with parents and their children should:

- see the health and well-being of the child as being of paramount importance

- be accessible, welcoming and non-stigmatising to problem drug users who have children

- be able to share information with other agencies and professionals on a 'need to know' basis when it is in the interests of the child to do so.

(Home Office 2003, pp.72–73)

Training on substance misuse and domestic violence is needed, for practitioners working in children's services, to increase their understanding of the varying effects these issues have on children and families (see Chapter 7 for more details). Inter-agency training which includes professionals from both adult and children's services can provide opportunities to develop inter-agency networks, increase levels of trust, and provide insights into the philosophy and work of each others' organisations. Practitioners in substance misuse services and services for domestic violence want to feel confident that their colleagues in children's services will respect the people they work with and take an open and unprejudiced approach to assessment, decision-making and of provision of services.

Summary points

- The extent to which managers were aware of, and would involve, local agencies that provide services to families experiencing domestic violence or substance misuse varied between and within each local authority.

- The services least likely to be involved were support organisations such as Surestart, counselling services, and housing.

- The findings suggest managers' awareness of services is related to staffing levels and the quality of management. The introduction of service directories should help raise awareness of service provision within an authority.

- Managers classified their relationships with most of the relevant agencies as generally very good or fairly good. Only 8 per cent were classed as poor.

- Working relationships with housing and substance misuse services were much poorer. Inter-agency working relationships were affected because focusing on different client groups resulted in different priorities and different timescales for service provision.

- Managers identified the following eight factors as supporting good inter-agency working:
  - understanding and respecting the roles and responsibilities of other services
  - good communication
  - regular contact and meetings
  - common priorities
  - joint training
  - knowing what services are available and who to contact
  - clear guidelines and procedures for working together
  - low staff turnover.

- Managers reported that confidentiality, a lack of resources, a lack of trust and preconceptions of parents were factors that hindered multi-agency working.

Chapter 4

Families' Experience of Referral and Assessment

The original aim of the in-depth study was to interview 42 families, seven from each participating local authority. However, gaining access to families proved difficult and cases were lost to the research at all stages in the accessing process (see Appendix I). This chapter and Chapter 5 are based on the interviews with parents, their social workers and any other key worker in 17 cases. Cases were identified from the case file study and drawn from the six participating local authorities.

Parents' experiences of being referred to children's social care because of concerns about their child's safety and welfare that were related to either domestic violence or parental substance misuse, are explored and particular focus is given to the following issues:

- characteristics of the families
- issues that led to the referral
- the referral process
- the assessment process.

The circumstances of the families interviewed are extremely varied as are their experiences of contact both with children's social care and other agencies (see Appendix II for a brief description of each family). One family has been chosen as a case study and is used throughout this chapter and the next, to highlight issues encountered by the group of families as a whole.

The children had been on the child protection register in London due to Mum's drinking, serious domestic violence and the emotional abuse of the children. They were taken off the register when the family moved to this area. They did not immediately come to our attention but very soon did. (Caine social worker: domestic violence and alcohol abuse by mother)

The family have been involved with social services since the birth of their first child [now age 13]. They have moved to several authorities and then returned here. (Sheridon social worker: domestic violence, alcohol abuse by mother, both parents learning disabled)

Previous contact with children's social care can result in preconceptions, both positive and negative, being formed which can affect future involvements (Cleaver and Freeman 1995). However, none of the interviews in this study allude to any prejudice due to prior involvement either on the part of the parents or the practitioners.

Issues that led to the referral

Case Study: Jackie's family
Referral

Jackie was referred to children's social care by her aunt without her mother's agreement. At the time the mother was depressed and she and her partner were taking a mixture of amphetamines, heroin and cocaine.

> I was not in touch with reality. I used drugs to block out feelings of depression. Because I was using drugs I didn't see the effect it was having on Jackie. (Mother)

Jackie's home was regularly used by other drug users whose presence presented a danger to Jackie and her four-year-old half brother Morgan. The health visitor's report shows why she became concerned about Jackie and her brother.

> There was a downward slide in her caring for the child – she was missing important appointments and I was not getting access to the home. I was concerned about Jackie not getting the regular treatment she needed. I contacted the school and found that Jackie was not attending regularly. It was the sudden deterioration that concerned me. Mum had been OK for a long time and then suddenly the situation deteriorated. (Health visitor)

> The social worker was also aware of the situation.
>
> > The children were being left to their own devices. Jackie was left in the bedroom alone and unsupervised with drug using men in the house. She was at risk of anything. They could have abused her. They were high on drugs. Morgan was also left unsupervised. (Social worker)
>
> Jackie was badly affected by her mother's drug use. She was caring for herself and Morgan which affected her school work and friendships. Medical appointments were being missed and the family were ostracised.
>
> > She had no friends; they were not allowed to come to the home because of the known drug users that were frequently there. There was also a lack of extended family support as they had in effect given up on Mum. They had been isolated from all normal areas of society. There was no routine, no regular meal times and no food in the cupboards. (Health visitor)

Problems the families were experiencing at time of referral

In less than a quarter of cases (23.6%) the parent identified only one major problem affecting their family at the time of referral. In three cases this was domestic violence and in one substance misuse.

> I was in a bad relationship, my partner was battering me black and blue, it started when I was pregnant. (Harding mother: domestic violence)

> I was pregnant and a drug addict. (Cossins mother: drug abuse by mother)

The other 13 families were experiencing a multitude of chronic problems including, for example, substance misuse, domestic violence, mental illness, physical disability, unsuitable housing, prostitution, learning difficulties and debt.

> I was drinking and there had been a lot of violence from my husband – he beat me up and he caused me a miscarriage by sticking his fist up me. He also forced me into prostitution. (Caine mother: domestic violence and alcohol abuse by mother)

> I had a history of postnatal depression and psychosis. I was taking crack, alcohol, dope – medicating myself to survive. (Hammond mother: domestic violence, drug and alcohol abuse by both parents, mother has post natal depression)

> Drinking too much, unsuitable housing and lifestyle... Was moved to a small hotel as temporary accommodation. (Pine father: alcohol abuse by father)

The majority of families had been experiencing the identified problems for over two years.

Parents' and social worker's perspectives of the problems

When parents and practitioners hold a common perspective about the difficulties facing the family research suggests it is associated with better outcomes for children (Cleaver and Freeman 1995).

In the majority of cases parents and social workers held a similar perspective of the strengths and difficulties families were experiencing at the time of the referral. However, in two cases views differed. In one the social worker highlighted additional issues which the family had not mentioned during their interview.

> Parent's view: I was drinking heavily. There were concerns over neglect and leaving the children at home alone during the evening. We could not control the children. (Sheridon mother: domestic violence, alcohol abuse by mother, both parents learning-disabled)

> Social worker's view: Neglect. Concerns over aggressive behaviour between the parents in front of the children – domestic violence. Parenting skills. Mum was sometimes under the influence of alcohol. (Sheridon social worker)

In the other case, although there was broad agreement about the difficulties facing the family, the mother expressed anger, believing she was wrongly accused of drug taking. This perception was not supported by the social worker who did not identify drug misuse when discussing the reasons why children's social care was working with the family.

> Parent's view: They also thought I was on drugs. I wasn't. (Peel mother: domestic violence and alcohol abuse by mother)

> Social worker's view: Police were concerned about Mum's drinking and her leaving the children alone. There was also violence going on in the house. It had been going on for a number of years – before she moved to XXX. (Peel social worker)

Although sometimes difficult, it is vital that the parents and social workers agree on the full range of problems facing the family. If the social worker and the parent hold a common perspective on the family's strengths and difficulties, it is more likely to result in appropriate services being provided and a better take-up of those services (Cleaver and Freeman 1995).

The effects on the children

> Through violence in the home, children may suffer emotional and psychological damage. The very young may show physical signs of distress such as bedwetting, stomach-aches and disturbed sleep. Older children can become withdrawn and exhibit problematic behaviour, such as misusing alcohol or drugs. (Webster, Coombe and Stacey 2002, p.3)

Twelve families in this in-depth study were experiencing domestic violence at the time of referral, in an equal number one or both parents had a drug or alcohol problem and in seven cases there was evidence of both parental substance misuse and domestic violence.

Three of the parents with very small children felt infancy had protected their children from the effects of the domestic violence and/or the substance misuse.

> It didn't affect him he was only a baby, it affected me, I was scared. (Harding mother: domestic violence)

> Alice was only 6 or 7 months at the time, too young to be affected. (Reed father: drug and alcohol abuse by both parents, father mentally ill)

In eight cases, where older children were involved, the parents felt that their problems *had* affected their child's behaviour. Nearly all these families were experiencing domestic violence, and in some families substance misuse was also a problem.

> The children [aged 7, 11 and 13 years] were always fighting, very violent to each other, very disruptive in the home, breaking furniture and belongings, they were also aggressive towards us. (Sheridon mother: domestic violence, alcohol abuse by mother, both parents learning disabled)

> She [daughter aged 6 years] was behaving bad, her insecurities about Mummy and Daddy fighting. Us shouting and yelling, she would say 'stop it' and cover her little ears. (Booth mother: domestic violence by father, allegation of father's sexual abuse made by the daughter)

> He [son aged 8 years] was out of control. He hit a teacher and the social worker. He was barred from school but then went back. He would hit me and fight with me. He was in care for a bit but the foster people could not handle him so he came back home. (Caine mother: domestic violence and alcohol abuse by mother)

> We didn't notice Jenny's [aged 8 years] difficulties at first. We noticed with her brother – he was aggressive with her, copying his dad. (Murch mother: domestic violence, mother physically disabled)

> He [son aged 11 years] was unhappy at school and stopped going. (Peel mother: domestic violence and alcohol misuse by mother)

My eldest son [aged 9 years] is very quiet. He hides his feelings and is very protective towards me. (Hendy mother: domestic violence)

He [son aged 8 years] was very insecure and he still is – won't sleep on his own, at one time he couldn't go upstairs to the loo without all of us going up. He didn't want to leave me to go to school he was scared we would bump into his father whenever we went out. Rachel [aged 4 years] was younger. She acted more aggressive and her behaviour got worse. (Davis mother: domestic violence and alcohol misuse by father)

The older children, like Jackie, were also suffering in more subtle ways because they had to look after themselves and in many cases, younger siblings.

He [son aged 10 years] was having to behave like a much older child, he had to look after himself, take responsibility for getting to school and to generally care for himself because of his dad's serious drinking. The son and his father had in effect changed roles – he had become the carer with dad the dependant person. (Pine social worker: alcohol misuse by father)

The referral process

> **Case Study: Jackie's family**
> The referral process
> Jackie's mother became aware of the referral to children's social care when she received a visit from a social worker. Jackie's aunt had made the referral because she was concerned about the mother's drug use and because she thought Jackie and Morgan were being neglected.
>
> At this time, Jackie's mother was already receiving a range of help from her health visitor, the mental health support team, housing and the community drug team. Jackie herself was also getting some additional support from her school.

How the families had been referred

In most cases (13/17) families were aware that a referral had been made; a rate similar to that found in previous research (Cleaver *et al.* 2004a). This finding reinforces the suggestion made in the earlier research, that in most cases professionals talk to families about their concerns before referring them to children's social care.

The families were split between those who had either asked for help themselves ($n = 4$) or agreed to the referral being made ($n = 4$) and those, like Jackie's, who were referred without their agreement ($n = 5$) or knowledge ($n = 4$).

> I asked for help. I was neglecting the children, I couldn't protect them – I wasn't protecting myself so I just couldn't protect them. (Hammond mother: domestic violence, drug and alcohol abuse by both parents, mother has postnatal depression)

Referrals came from a number of different sources – police, family members, schools, domestic violence services, neighbours, health visitors, other social services departments and the prison service.

Neighbours accounted for three of the four cases where the family was referred without their knowledge and in the remaining case the mother reported that the school and the health visitor had contacted children's social care without her knowledge.

> They were concerned about Glen's temper [husband] and how he might smash up on the kids. They weren't bothered if he smashed the place up. (Murch mother: domestic violence, mother physically disabled)

Some of those who were referred without their agreement or knowledge were, not surprisingly, angry that a referral had been made.

> My mum phoned social services and the police. I was annoyed that Mum had told social services, I was angry with her. She always sticks her beak in. (Thomas mother: domestic violence and alcohol abuse by father)

> I went to a solicitor... It was horrendous. She arranged for me to see a domestic violence organisation. I was bulldozed into everything – I was on my own there was no choice. They [the domestic violence agency] got onto social services and the police child protection. (Booth mother: domestic violence by father, allegation of father's sexual abuse made by the daughter)

How children's social care first made contact

In nearly all cases (15/17) contact was first made by a visit from the social worker which was sometimes, although not always, preceded by a phone call or letter.

> The social worker came round with a letter saying she was coming. (Murch mother: domestic violence, mother physically disabled)

> I got a letter off social services saying they wanted to see me over concerns for Jimmy [aged 18 months]. I went to see them. (Harding mother: domestic violence)

> We had a phone call saying could they visit – we made an appointment over the phone. (Cossins mother: drug abuse by mother plus history of imprisonment)

One mother described her anger and fear when a social worker and a police officer from the child protection team arrived unexpectedly on her doorstep one night to demand her husband left immediately. She phoned her solicitor who agreed to be present.

> I felt very bullied and threatened and didn't know what would happen if I refused to co-operate. I feared Hannah [aged 6 years] would be taken away. Once they knew the solicitor was coming they said they would go and come back another time. (Booth mother: domestic violence by father, allegation of father's sexual abuse made by the daughter)

When professionals who are perceived as having the power to remove children arrive unannounced and raise concerns about the safety and welfare of the children, families find the experience frightening and humiliating. Parents feel trapped and fear that everything they say will be given a hostile interpretation. If children's social care are to work collaboratively with families and develop plans and provide services acceptable to parents, to safeguard and promote the welfare of the children, they must not lose sight of how violating to families are accusations of and enquires about child abuse.

> Social workers and others must display extreme sensitivity, tolerance and awareness at the point of confrontation because it is the moment when parents' operational perspectives crystallise in a form that may colour the case during subsequent months. (Cleaver and Freeman 1995, p.89)

The importance of professionals respecting and working as sympathetically as possible with families, who they have to confront with suspicions of child abuse, is explained in the government's guidance on assessment.

> The quality of the early or initial contact will affect later working relationships and the ability of professionals to secure an agreed understanding of what is happening and to provide help. (Department of Health *et al.* 2000, p.13, paragraph 1.47)

Agencies involved with the families at the point of referral

In nearly all cases (15/17) professionals from agencies other than children's social care were involved with the family at the time the referral was made. The number of agencies working with the family ranged from two to seven and included a range of services. Most commonly involved were the police (11), health visitors (11), schools (8) and housing (5). Other, less frequently involved services included GP (4), educational welfare (1), probation (3), hospitals (2), a solicitor (1), and mental health (1). In two cases the family was already involved with a domestic violence organisation; two families were receiving services for alcohol misuse and three for drug misuse.

The assessment process

Case Study: Jackie's Family
The social worker's assessment

Jackie's mother felt she had been fully involved during the assessment process. She knew that an assessment had been carried out and that a plan had been put together which stated what was expected of her and what services would be provided. She felt that the social worker had discussed most of the issues she felt were important and had specifically addressed her drug problem and what help she wanted. However, Jackie's mother felt that her underlying problems of depression had not been explored.

> The social worker asked me all about my drug problem, my partner's drug problem and about how we were living… It would have helped if she had talked about my feelings of depression. I started using the drugs to block the depression. (Jackie's mother)

She had a good relationship with the social worker and felt able to be honest about the family's difficulties, even though she was worried that her children might be taken from her.

> I was very honest with the social worker, I told her everything. I could only get the help I needed if I told the truth. She was easy to talk to. I knew she could help me. I was scared I would have my kids taken off me. (Jackie's mother)

This rosy picture of co-operation was not fully endorsed by the social worker. At times she had found Jackie's mother difficult to work with.

> Initially she would not engage. She went to XXX a seaside resort during the assessment and this made things difficult. (Social worker)

But despite this, Jackie's mother felt that she had been fully involved in the assessment process. She reported having seen a copy of the assessment record and had been able to discuss what had been written about her family with her social worker. She felt it was accurate and honest. She also remembers receiving a copy of the plan.

The families' awareness of the assessment and plans

> Gathering information and making sense of a family's situation are key phases in the process of assessment. It is not possible to do this without the knowledge and involvement of the family. It requires direct work with children and with family members, explaining what is happening, why an assessment is being undertaken, what will be the process and what is likely to be the outcome. (Department of Health 2000b, p.38, paragraph 3.32)

Explaining what an assessment is and providing information to families is essential to successful working relationships. Local authorities are increasingly providing families with easily accessible information brochures and leaflets explaining the purpose and process of assessments (Cleaver *et al.* 2004a).

Practically two-thirds (64.7%) of families had the same experience as Jackie's family; they knew at the time that an assessment of their child and family circumstances was being carried out. This level of awareness is rather lower than found in previous research (Cleaver *et al.* 2004a) where over three-quarters of parents were aware of the assessment having taken place.

> She came round, it was like an interview, she ticked things off a list and had a look round. We did it as a family – she talked to us all together. (Cossins mother: drug abuse by mother)

> The process was explained and an assessment carried out. I was contacted by phone after the assessment to check I had fully understood what had taken place and discuss details I was unsure of. There were meetings every 6–8 weeks. I was phoned after these to check I had understood the points made. (Hendy mother: domestic violence)

Six families were not aware at the time that the social worker was carrying out an assessment. However, three of these families realised with hindsight that an assessment had been undertaken. This lack of initial awareness may reflect the poor mental state, possibly aggravated by domestic violence or substance misuse, of many parents at the time of the assessment.

> I now realise that an assessment was completed but at the time it was not explained clearly. I feel I was told what was needed rather than issues being discussed. (Pine father: alcohol abuse by father)

> I did not realise that an assessment had taken place. It wasn't explained although now I realise an assessment was carried out. (Sheridon father: domestic violence, alcohol abuse by mother, both parents learning-disabled)

One mother did not feel that an assessment had been carried out as she had not seen any written record.

> He did get the background and history of the situation but nothing formal or written down that I saw. (Davis mother: domestic violence and alcohol abuse by father)

Parents were not always aware that a plan had been developed as a result of the assessment. Only seven of the 11 families who knew that an assessment had been carried out were aware of the subsequent plan; two parents were uncertain and two were sure no formal plan had been developed. Interviews with the social workers in these cases revealed that formal plans had been made in every case. This disparity in the reports of parents and social workers gives increasing weight to the notion that problem drug and/or alcohol use may impair parents' capacity to retain and recall information. It underlines the need for social workers to allow sufficient time to explain carefully the plan to parents in the first place and to reiterate the key points on later visits.It follows that the seven families who were aware of the plan were the only ones who felt they had been fully involved throughout the whole process of assessment and planning.

The extent to which families thought the important issues had been discussed

> In the process of finding out what is happening to a child, it will be critical to develop a co-operative working relationship, so that parents or caregivers feel respected and informed, that staff are being open and honest with them, and that they in turn are confident about providing vital information about their child, themselves and their circumstances. (Department of Health *et al.* 2000, p.13, paragraph 1.43)

Most families that had been aware of the assessment felt fully involved in the process. For example, three-quarters of these parents felt their social worker had asked them about all the relevant things that were happening in their family, and had asked specifically about the difficulties they were experiencing with alcohol, drugs and/or domestic violence. They also thought that social workers had discussed what help they felt their family needed.

> They asked about me drinking and said I should not drink as much and they asked about the violence. He [partner] was really violent. (Caine mother: domestic violence and alcohol abuse by mother)

> He went through what services could have been helpful. (Davis mother: domestic violence and alcohol abuse by father)

In contrast, there were three families who had known that an assessment was being carried out but felt that important issues had not been discussed and they had not been asked what help they needed.

> I told them what they wanted to know. They did not want to know anything about me. No one was on my side. They were only interested in the children. (Peel mother: domestic violence and alcohol abuse by mother)

Five of the six families who had not known that an assessment had been carried out felt the circumstances of their family and particularly the difficulties they were experiencing with substance misuse or domestic violence were not explored during the assessment and did not inform the social workers' decisions. These parents felt they had not been listened to and that their views and wishes had not been taken into account.

> I was never asked what was important to me and what help I felt would benefit me. (Pine father: alcohol abuse by father)

> Nobody seemed to want to listen. (Krausse mother: domestic violence, alcohol abuse by mother, mother with learning difficulties)

> No one talked to me about my feelings. I could not tell anyone how I felt. I did not feel able to talk openly about myself. (Thomas mother: domestic violence and alcohol abuse by father)

Involving families in the assessment process has been found to be associated with a greater take-up of services (Cleaver 2000; Farmer and Owen 1995; Jones and Ramchandani 1999). Families should be involved in planning the process of the assessment, unless to do so would place the child at increased risk of significant harm. For example, families need to know where and when the assessment will take place, who will be involved, what issues will be discussed and why. Parents need to be empowered to talk about the things they feel are important in their family, and be reassured that their views and ideas will be listened to and valued.

Most parents, confronted with concerns about the safety and welfare of their children, fear they will lose their children. When faced with such accusations parents react in different ways, for example, some may become defensive and react aggressively towards practitioners, while others become filled with self-doubt and lose confidence in all aspects of their parenting.

> I felt a bit worried about if I was doing anything wrong and they might take my child away. (Fox mother: domestic violence)

Relationship between children's social care and the family

The relationship between parents and social workers was influenced by how the family came to the attention of children's social care. Parents who requested help themselves or agreed to a referral being made were more likely to have a good relationship with their social worker than when the referral had been made either without their consent or without their knowledge. Five of the eight parents who had agreed to the referral reported that their relationship with the social worker was good compared with three of the eight where the referral had been made either without their consent or knowledge. This link between the way referrals were made and parental satisfaction with children's social care has been identified by previous research (Cleaver 2000). How families become involved with children's social care does not necessarily foretell the quality of the relationships and research shows how perspectives can change when practitioners and families meet or when new information comes to light (Cleaver and Freeman 1995).

Level of agreement on the quality of the parent/social worker relationship

There was complete agreement between the social workers' assessment of the quality of their relationship and parents' views. The cases were split half and half between those who, like in Jackie's case, viewed the relationship as positive and those who did not.

> Mum worked with us well, we had a good relationship – that was a real positive. (Fox social worker: domestic violence)

> They say I cannot see the kids if I have had a drink, well that's fair enough but they also say I must not smoke when I am with them, but she [social worker] smokes and that is not right – they are just as fucking bad as me. They are full of shit, fucking shit, I am angry with them. (Caine mother: domestic violence and alcohol abuse by mother)

> I am upset at the way I am made to feel at core group meetings – the social worker is patronising, unfriendly and has a poor attitude. I would like social services to be more approachable, explain things in more detail and to have a better attitude when talking to me. (Pine father: alcohol abuse by father)

Parents' experience of the relationship

The parents' perception of their relationship with the social worker affected the extent to which they felt able to reveal the true extent of the difficulties their family was experiencing. Seven of the eight parents who reported a good relationship with the social worker said they had been honest when discussing their problems compared with five of the nine who felt their relationship was poor.

> I could tell the social worker the truth. I had no problem with being truthful, I knew it would be best to be honest. (Hendy mother: domestic violence)

The importance of the relationship is reinforced by the reports of parents who did not feel they could be totally honest about what was happening in their families. Parents resented social workers whom they felt did not treat them with respect and talked down to them. When this happened parents were not prepared to trust them.

> I didn't feel I could be honest as I was always made to feel like a naughty child. One social worker once said 'come on I can see right through you'. I always tried to put my view forward but felt I was never listened to. (Krausse mother: domestic violence, alcohol abuse by mother, mother with learning difficulties)

> I wouldn't speak to them at first. I felt they spoke to me as if I was a kid, they wouldn't believe that I wasn't with my ex-partner anymore. I was angry. I felt I was being punished for something I hadn't done. (Harding Parent: domestic violence)

Interviews with the social worker in these two cases substantiate the breakdown in trust. In each case the social workers reported that she found the mother to be unreliable and untrustworthy.

> During the assessment when she was supposed to have left her husband we got word that she was with him… Mum was at this time very unreliable and we could not believe her. (Krausse social worker)

> Difficulty involving Mum due to her inconsistent approach and her need to keep the truth from us. (Harding social worker)

Involving families in the process of assessment, listening to what they say and showing respect for them as individuals is an essential ingredient to developing an honest and open working relationship.

However, parents' behaviour in very stressful situations (and being suspected of child abuse is extremely stressful) can often be misleading. Parents may cope with the emotions that are aroused, by what they perceive as an accusation, by denial and disbelief (Cleaver and Freeman 1995). For example, one mother on reflection felt that she had not been totally honest with her social worker because at the time her mental state and substance misuse meant that she was not able to acknowledge the extent of the family's problems.

> Not really 'cos I couldn't be honest with myself. I really didn't know what was going on. (Hammond mother: domestic violence, drug and alcohol abuse by both parents, mother has postnatal depression)

Social workers' experience of the relationship

The quality of the relationship between parents and social workers will also be affected by the problems the family are experiencing.

> They may be resistant because of the nature of their own difficulties, such as psychiatric illness or problems of alcohol and drug misuse, or because of allegations being made against them. Whatever the reasons for their resistance, the door to co-operation should be kept open. (Department of Health *et al.* 2000, p.40, paragraph 3.35)

In 12 of the 17 families one or both parents had problems with alcohol and/or drug use. In seven cases, social workers had experienced difficulties in engaging parents in the assessment process. The findings suggest that the difficulties one or other of the parents' were experiencing with alcohol and/or drugs was a key factor.

> Dad was very hostile and angry and difficult to effectively engage… Mum was not very cooperative but I think this was under the influence of dad, he was intimidating her. She was hiding things, not being very truthful, not being open. (Thomas social worker: domestic violence and alcohol abuse by father)

> Some difficulties involving Dad as he frequently said he was not well and I think this was at least partly a way of avoiding issues. He was however quite ill as a result of his serious drinking. (Pine social worker: alcohol abuse by father)

> There were difficulties involving dad – in some meetings he would come in glaze-eyed as if he was on drugs. He could be threatening and aggressive. (Fox social worker: domestic violence)

> Mum was problematic, she would forget the conferences and meetings and when she did attend she would tend to slag off others. Not very constructive. When drunk she could be very difficult. (Caine social worker: domestic violence and alcohol abuse by mother)

> Mum went missing for a few months so was not all that much involved. (Peel social worker: domestic violence and alcohol abuse by mother)

Substance misuse, aggression and, as with Jackie's mother, going missing, were all factors which hampered the development of a positive working relationship between the social worker and the family.

The relationship between parents and social workers was linked to the ability of social workers to engage families in the assessment process. When the relationship was assessed by both the social worker and parent as good, social workers reported that parents were more ready to collaborate and work with them during the assessment. It is difficult to know whether a poor relationship resulted in a lack of engagement or *vice versa*. Indeed, perhaps both are the effects of assumptions and pre-judgements that each party holds of the other, which in turn impacts on the ability to develop a working relationship that is built on mutual respect and trust.

Changes in social worker

> Whenever it occurred, a key moment in an abuse inquiry was a change of social worker. There was little neutrality, they [the parents] liked them or they didn't like them, and they liked them better if they could relate to them as struggling parents like themselves, as survivors of a difficult childhood or as fellow travellers on a rocky road. (Cleaver and Freeman 1995, p.117)

In four cases the family experienced a change of social worker; in one case because the family moved to live in another authority. A change of worker can have unexpected consequences to the process of assessment, planning and intervention. It offers an opportunity for both parties to reassess the situation and to adopt different approaches. Although the findings suggest that relationships between practitioners and families have much to do with individual personalities, nonetheless the importance of practitioners being transparent, open and honest is reinforced. Some families found the change in social worker beneficial while others experienced the change as a personal loss.

> The first two social workers were like friends. The next one wasn't so good, the one we've got now is brilliant. (Murch mother: domestic violence, mother physically disabled)

> The different social worker we have now has made things better. This one is straight up and honest and doesn't beat around the bush. She doesn't make a judgement. She's polite and has manners – is respectful. (Booth mother: domestic violence by father, allegation of father's sexual abuse made by the daughter)

> I saw Lorraine my other social worker who has now left – she saw me in the street and I told her that they had taken my children off me. She said she would not have done that. She said she would never go back as a social worker. That's what she thinks. (Caine mother: domestic violence and alcohol abuse by mother)

Numerous changes in social worker can be frustrating because issues have to be revisited and new relationships developed. A challenge not only for the adults involved but also the children.

> They should stop giving you so many social workers – the children won't talk to them and then the social workers wonder why. We should be able to choose the social worker. (Murch father: domestic violence, mother physically disabled)

Offering families a choice of social worker would be one aspect of empowering parents when working in partnership with children's social care to safeguard and promote the welfare of their children (Thoburn *et al.* 1995). The principle of client choice would undoubtedly garner agreement in principle. However, the difficulties of staff recruitment and retention experienced by local authorities in England mean that changes in worker are driven by staffing arrangements not parental choice.

Parents' access to written records

The concept of partnership between children's social care and the family, where parents need help in bringing up their children, is at the heart of child care legislation (Department of Health *et al.* 2000). True partnership, which involves equal power being held by both parties, may not be possible. Nonetheless, involving and consulting parents in the process of assessment and planning is fundamental to understanding children's circumstances.

> ...the family is generally the first and most important source of information about the child and the family's circumstances. (Department of Health 2000b, p.45, paragraph 3.46)

One aspect of involving parents in the process of assessment and planning is to enable them to know what has been recorded about their family. Allowing parents access to records about them can result in inaccurate and misleading information being amended and the views of parents and young people being recorded.

However, social workers will need to allow sufficient time to discuss what has been written about the family, simply showing parents and older children a copy of the assessment record and plan is not enough. Parents and young people who have problems with literacy will need to have the contents read to them. Similarly, parents who speak English as an additional language may want help to fully understand what practitioners have written about their family.

> I can't read very well, they didn't show it to me and they didn't read it to me. I don't know what it said. (Caine mother: domestic violence and alcohol abuse by mother)

Finally, the stress and distress that parents and children are experiencing may make concentration difficulty and many will appreciate having a sympathetic social worker to discuss the findings of the assessment and subsequent plan. Only 10 of the 17 families reported having seen a copy of the assessment, eight of whom had had a chance to discuss it with their social worker.

Knowing what has been written about them is a priority for most families. For example, a mother who had not realised at the time that an assessment was being carried out and information about her family formally recorded, sought the help of her solicitor to gain access to the documentation.

> Once I got a solicitor I gained access to documentation and any reports that had been completed. (Krausse mother: domestic violence, alcohol abuse by mother, mother with learning difficulties)

Of those who had seen a copy of their assessment record, six thought that what had been written about them was, on the whole, accurate and honest. However, four parents thought there were many mistakes and inaccuracies, which they had not always had the opportunity to correct.

> There were a lot of mistakes and errors. I didn't always get the opportunity to say the reports weren't accurate before meetings. On one occasion I only received a

copy of the assessment the day before the meeting. I was unwell and unable to attend the meeting so the mistakes were never changed. (Pine father: alcohol abuse by father)

It was a bit long and stupid – didn't seem to fit our family. (Murch father: domestic violence, mother physically disabled)

It wasn't accurate, totally inaccurate and it wasn't helpful. (Hammond mother: domestic violence, drug and alcohol abuse by both parents, mother has postnatal depression)

Agencies involved in the assessment process

The interviews with social workers confirm the findings from the scrutiny of the social work process (discussed in Chapter 2); health, education and the police service are the agencies most frequently contacted by social workers when carrying out an initial assessment on children living with domestic violence and/or parental substance misuse. At this stage social workers rarely made contact with specialist agencies providing services for domestic violence or substance misuse. For the 17 cases included in this in-depth study, social workers reported that they had involved a domestic violence service provider in one case and a service for substance misuse in another.

In carrying out a core assessment, which is a much more detailed exploration of the child's needs and circumstances, a greater number of agencies were involved in the assessment. For example, in 14 of the 17 cases the health services (GPs, HVs, school nurses, or paediatricians) were involved, and in 10 cases the education service (schools, nursery or education welfare service), the police were involved in 12 cases, and housing in 7 cases.

There was also an increased involvement of specialist services for domestic violence and substance misuse. However, the trend found from studying the social work case files (see Chapter 2) is again evident. Services for substance misuse are more likely to be involved in the core assessment and the subsequent plans than services for domestic violence. A substance misuse service was involved in 9 of the 12 cases where there was evidence of substance misuse, and a service for domestic violence in only 2 of the 13 cases where there was evidence of domestic violence.

There appeared to be a number of reasons to account for social workers not involving services for domestic violence in the core assessment.

Domestic violence services not seen as relevant

In some cases social workers had decided that the involvement of a specialist domestic violence service was not relevant.

The reason for referral was domestic violence primarily, there were some concerns about the children, emotional damage to Billy and Rachel. The father was not in the family home but was seeing the children there. The issues of domestic violence were affecting both of the children and Mum's ability to protect the children around the times of contact. She didn't have much control at all over when Dad saw them – he still had keys, etc. At the time there was no agreed contact order or residence order, they were going through the divorce at the time. (Davis family centre social worker: domestic violence and alcohol abuse by father)

Although a local voluntary domestic violence service was working with the mother at the time of the assessment, the social worker decided not to involve them in the assessment.

A social worker carried out the assessment in discussion with the health visitor. XXX [a voluntary domestic violence agency] didn't seem relevant. (Davis family centre social worker: domestic violence and alcohol abuse by father)

The findings suggest that in cases of domestic violence social work practitioners tend to see the solution to recurring difficulties as lying with the parents themselves and with the law, as the following cases illustrate.

The mother does meet all the children's needs. However, she needs to prioritise her children's needs over her own and ensure their safety and welfare are paramount at all times. In order to ensure this, she must inform the police if her husband presents himself at the family home, causing any upset to herself and the children. Although she agrees to undertake this task, it is unclear if this relationship is in fact over for good and if it is not this is going to raise further concerns to social services department. (Davis family: extract from the Parenting Assessment attached to Core Assessment Record).

After the core assessment there was also a probation report undertaken on the father regarding the domestic violence. (Booth social worker: domestic violence and accusations of sexual abuse against father)

A lack of resources

In some cases a lack of resources within children's social care appeared to have affected the social workers' response.

Domestic violence has not really been addressed as the main issue, it was not treated as a priority – its resources again. (Murch social worker: domestic violence, mother physically disabled)

A perceived lack of local services

A lack of available local services for domestic violence was an issue raised by a number of social workers. The findings from the interviews suggest that the expertise of workers from these services would have been valued but social workers were not always aware of a local agency.

> May have been helpful to discuss the findings of the assessment with a domestic violence group but there is none here. (Caine social worker: domestic violence and alcohol abuse by mother)

Summary points

- Seventeen families and the relevant professionals, from six local authorities, took part in the in-depth study.

- For most families domestic violence or substance misuse did not exist in isolation; families were also experiencing poor mental or physical health, learning disability, housing, debt and prostitution.

- In most cases parents and social workers held a common perspective of the difficulties facing families.

- Although parents of very young children thought they were not affected by the family's difficulties, parents were very aware of the impact on older children's behaviour and welfare.

- Only 4 of the 17 families were unaware that their child was being referred to children's social care; five were referred without their consent.

- Most social workers notified parents before visiting them. Unannounced visits were deeply resented by parents.

- Two-thirds of families were aware of the assessment. Parental ability to remember and recall the assessment may be impaired by parents' poor mental health, a state exacerbated by the effects of domestic violence or substance misuse. Social workers need to ensure parents understand what is taking place.

- Most parents who were aware of the assessment were satisfied that the social worker had understood the difficulties facing their family. Nonetheless, nine parents were either unaware that an assessment had been undertaken or felt key issues, particularly the problems they were experiencing personally, had not been discussed.

- In half the cases parents and social workers rated their working relationship as good.

- Parents valued social workers who treated them with respect, listened to what they had said and involved them in the assessment.

- Social workers found parents with whom they had a good relationship were more likely to cooperate with plans for children. Parents' personal difficulties with drugs, alcohol and violence affected their relationship with practitioners.

- Changes in social worker were an opportunity for reappraisal and rapprochement.

- Parents valued the opportunity to learn what had been written about their family and to correct inaccuracies and mistakes.

- In carrying out core assessments social workers frequently involved the following services: health, education, police and substance misuse.

- Domestic violence services were not routinely involved and may be the result of: social workers not seeing their involvement as relevant, a lack of resources, or insufficient local services.

Chapter 5

Families' Experience of Services

This chapter continues to explore the experiences of the 17 families who make up the in-depth study group. It takes up where Chapter 4 left off, and examines parents' views about the services provided to them, following the children's social care assessment. In particular it explores the:

- services families received

- outcomes for families

- what helped or hindered the families' situation.

Once again the experiences of Jackie and her family are used to illustrate key issues.

Services families received

Case Study: Jackie's Family
Services received
As a result of the assessment Jackie's mother felt she had received most of the services she needed. For example, she was helped to move house in order to separate from her partner who also used drugs. The drug and alcohol team continued to work with her to help reduce her drug dependency. She attended parenting classes to improve her confidence and skills in looking after her children. Eight-year-old Jackie received regular help with her medical condition because her mother became more aware of the importance of keeping appointments. Jackie also received support from a young carers' project.

However, Jackie's mother was also experiencing bouts of depression which she felt was a major contributor to her substance misuse.

> I used drugs to block out feelings of depression… I wanted counselling or therapy of some sort, and although this was offered it was never set up.

Overall, Jackie's mother was satisfied with the services she had received. She felt that children's social care had helped her realise what was important in life and that she had been helped in becoming a better parent. She had been supported in giving her children a more stable life with greater security and better routines.

She also considered that the agencies who had provided services had worked well together. On the whole she thought she had been given choices about most of the services. Although she felt there had been no choice over attending parenting classes, on reflection she acknowledged their value.

What services did the families receive?

Every family reported that as a result of the assessment they had received some support or help. This ranged from advice and support provided by the children and families' team, to a range of co-ordinated service provision. The services that families received included those aimed at helping parents to sort out their own problems, such as services for domestic violence, anger management, or alcohol or drug addiction. Other services were specifically aimed at supporting children and included, support workers, counselling, specialist health care, and after school clubs. More still were aimed at helping the family as a unit, for example, support from family centres, help with housing and finance, parenting courses, and childcare.In half the cases where children were exposed to domestic violence the assessment resulted in services for domestic violence being provided and/or a place on an anger management course. A lack of local services for victims of domestic violence was one reason given by social workers to explain why such services were not always forthcoming. This issue was not confined to a particular local authority.

> The SAFE agency is 40 plus miles away and so has limited support to offer… The main issue for me is the lack of local resources. This limits the work we can do with people in her position. (Thomas social worker: domestic violence and alcohol abuse by father)

Families experiencing substance misuse were more likely to be provided with appropriate services. In two-thirds of cases where children were exposed to parental substance misuse the assessment led to the relevant parent being provided with services to help with drug addiction or alcoholism. However, planned services could not be guaranteed to materialise as the following case illustrates. The family were referred to children's social care because the parents were unable to control their children, both parents were very stressed, the mother was drinking heavily and the two older children were aggressive and violent towards both parents. The plan was to:

> …give all family members support. Family support worker to visit family daily, support parents with parenting skills, Mum to attend alcohol support service. At this point all children were living with the father and Mum was visiting regularly. (Sheridon social worker: domestic violence, alcohol abuse by mother, both parents learning-disabled)

However, the mother reported that the support she wanted to help her control her drinking had not been provided.

> I wanted advice and information on how to stop drinking. I did not get any. (Sheridon mother)

This breakdown in the plan was acknowledged by the social worker.

> Due to the learning difficulties of both parents they were only able to cope effectively with family support. The children have been removed from the parents' care and are not likely to return. (Sheridon social worker)

Families' satisfaction with the services

The degree to which families were satisfied with the services they received was associated with: being involved in the assessment process, being consulted over the type of services that can be provided, and having some choice over the service provider.

Parental satisfaction with the services is dependent on having insight into the difficulties within their family and a willingness to engage with services. Some parents did not acknowledge any problems and children's social care were seen as unnecessarily intruding in their lives.

> Support was offered because they felt I had issues I needed to deal with – I haven't. I wanted to be left alone. I stopped attending the counselling as it was not helping…the whole process was very stressful. I just wanted my life back. I want help to re-locate, I have asked but they can't help me. (Hendy mother: domestic violence)

> I didn't want any services I wanted to be believed when I told them [children's social care] I was no longer with my partner... I have attended the sessions [with domestic violence agency] as it may help me get my son back... I asked to be re-housed, social services said they couldn't help me with this... I don't feel I need social services to be involved, I just want to be able to live my life. (Harding mother: domestic violence)

Other families may find their situation so overwhelming that they are unable to see how children's social care could help.

> I don't know what help I needed. I wasn't in a position to know. They did offer for me to go away for rehab and to a refuge but I didn't have a clue what to do. I just didn't know what to do... The rehab was helpful and I'm clean. (Hammond mother: domestic violence, drug and alcohol abuse by both parents, mother has postnatal depression)

In the majority of cases ($n = 12$) parents were aware of the difficulties they were experiencing and held definite views on the type of services they thought would help their family. Of these, five thought that the plan following the assessment had resulted in relevant services.

> I wanted them to help me with my partner's aggression... Things have improved for us, for me and Glen [partner] definitely, also for Jenny [aged 8 years] – she's happier. Daniel [aged 11 years] is different; some things have had a good effect but it's difficult with him. (Murch father: domestic violence, mother physically disabled)

> I wanted help to stop us arguing. And I wanted help in how to look after Sasha and do it right... The childcare helps me a lot... The time apart from him [father] has helped him, he wants to change and come back. (Fox mother: domestic violence)

An equal number of families ($n = 5$) reported receiving some of the services they thought were needed. Although the services that had been forthcoming were generally seen as beneficial, parents were left feeling that some serious difficulties had not been addressed. The reasons why parents thought their family problems had not been fully addressed fell into three categories: long waiting lists; helpful services being stopped prematurely; and parents wanting additional help.

Long waiting lists

> The parenting course and the anger management both improved things. The parenting was very helpful. It made you aware of what you're doing wrong and how it could be better... but we are still awaiting family therapy. (Booth mother: domestic violence by father, allegation of father's sexual abuse made by the daughter)

Services stopped prematurely

When the family centre were helping us things were much better. The children started to eat properly; they went to bed at a decent time and did not fight as much. They were good in the house and stopped swearing at us. They went for days out and it was much better. I was not drinking as much as I felt better, less stressed... But this support stopped and we then had support from another team which was not helpful. The children began to be aggressive again and I began to drink again. (Sheridon mother: domestic violence, alcohol abuse by mother, both parents learning-disabled)

Additional help wanted

The clinic was a waste of time. They were supposed to help with a withdrawal programme but they've got a bad attitude. We've made a complaint... We've got two bedrooms for four adults but they haven't offered us anything. (Cossins mother: drug abuse by mother)

In four cases social workers judged that the family's problems were so severe that short-term service provision would not bring about sufficient change to enable children to remain safely at home. The trauma of children having to leave home tended to overshadow parental perspectives of the interventions that had been provided. For example, in one case the mother had requested practical support to help her look after her children. However, the core assessment revealed chronic problems that affected the safety of her 8-year-old son and 3-year-old daughter, and resulted in her son becoming looked after.

Mum was a chronic alcoholic and was in self-destruct mode. There was a very poor prognosis. We offered support in the home and Mum to attend Drink Sense; we also arranged respite care for the children, but Tom's behaviour was so difficult that we returned the children home... Eventually we had to remove the children to their grandparents. (Caine social worker: domestic violence and alcohol abuse by mother)

The mother felt she had not been provided with the services she needed.

If they thought I could not look after the kids they could have helped me. They didn't do anything for me they just moved the children. I went to Drink Sense and they talked about drinking but I stopped going – I don't go now... It has not helped at all. The kids are away from me with my mum...they [social workers] didn't seem interested in me. (Caine mother)

In other cases, where children became looked after, the mothers had wanted someone to listen to them and provide them with advice and information about childcare. However, even though services to support the parent had been provided, parents felt that their personal problems had not been adequately addressed, and having children accommodated left them feeling bereft. The following two examples illustrate this point.

EXAMPLE 1

They said John [aged 11 years] had to be in care...there was nothing for me...someone to be on my side. I was referred to the drug and alcohol team but they were not much help. I felt alone... They have not helped me. (Peel mother)

The social worker was aware of the mother's need for psychiatric help, but found it difficult to organise because of long waiting lists.

Some psychological support for Mum would have been helpful but there is a very long waiting list of about two years. (Peel social worker)

EXAMPLE 2

I found DASH very supportive and useful at the beginning until my support worker left. I found it difficult to build a relationship with the new support worker so stopped attending the centre...

If he [her 8-year-old son] can't be with me at home then this placement is the best place for him... I can see that he gets consistency of care and has routine in his life which is important... I feel worse, very depressed and have gone downhill. I want to blame social services for the way I feel... I want to be treated like a human being as well as a mother. I've got needs and would like social services to realise this. (Krausse mother)

The eight-year-old, learning-disabled boy in this case was accommodated because of the mother's deteriorating mental health.

Child was not removed immediately but only after other inputs had failed, and after Mum had taken a serious overdose, an apparent serious attempt at suicide. (Krausse social worker: domestic violence, alcohol abuse by mother, mother with learning difficulties)

Finally, in some cases parents were angry because they felt the assessment and subsequent plan had failed to provide any of the services their family needed. For example, the following mother had wanted someone to talk to, financial help and to keep her children with her.

The social worker wanted to take Nicky away and put him in care but he was allowed to stay at Mum's... I needed financial help. Andrew [partner] had punched a hole in the door and window and he sold the TV. He ruined the house. It took £4500 to repair all the damage and I had to pay that. I borrowed and am still paying back. No one gave me any financial help... Support was not given and I feel peed off about it... Nothing social services has done has helped...they

> seem to blame me for what happened. (Thomas mother: domestic violence and alcohol abuse by father)

The social worker's explanation for the lack of services draws attention once more to the importance of available local services, and the managers' role of ensuring practitioners have a comprehensive knowledge of all resources within their authority.

> We are short of resources in this area. For instance, the family centre is miles away, and although they gave out-reach support it may have been helpful if Mum could have attended the centre. There may be other services available that would have been useful but I am not aware of them. (Thomas social worker)

The findings show the importance of working in partnership with families. Parents wanted to be listened to, they wanted their views to be taken into account, they wanted to be involved in the choice of service, to be informed when there were waiting lists, and kept up to date about developments. Satisfaction with the outcome of the assessment was linked with these factors. For example, 80 per cent of families who thought they received *all* the services they needed felt they had been fully involved in the assessment and planning process, compared to only 40 per cent of those who only received *some*, and 33 per cent of those who had received *none* of the services they thought they needed.

Families' views on how well services worked together

The difficulties these families were experiences meant that in most cases more than one agency was providing a service. For example, children's social care may be providing direct support, or a place at a family centre, while at the same time the parent is attending a clinic for alcohol or drug addiction, and housing are trying to re-house the family. In these circumstances agencies need to collaborate and dove-tail their services to ensure the best outcomes for children and their families.

Practically all (14/17) the families involved in this in-depth study received a service from more than one agency. Half the parents thought that the agencies had worked well together.

> My support worker from DASH attended meetings with social services and I found this very supportive. They communicated effectively with each other. (Krausse mother: domestic violence, alcohol abuse by mother, mother with learning difficulties)

The other half felt there was much room for improvement, highlighting difficulties in co-ordination and breakdowns in communication.

> At times we felt overwhelmed and then there would be nothing for a while, then all of a sudden another lot of people would be involved. (Murch mother: domestic violence, mother physically disabled)

> Nobody was aware of what everyone else was doing. It was very bad. (Hammond mother: domestic violence, drug and alcohol abuse by both parents, mother has postnatal depression)

In cases where parents identified agencies as having difficulties in collaborating and working together, social workers also acknowledged the problem. Social workers identified four issues that hampered collaboration (issues that have been explored in greater depth in Chapter 3).

The primary focus of the service provider

Agencies providing services for alcohol or drug problems concentrate on the needs of adults and may not identify the needs of children within the family.

> The drug and alcohol agency tend to focus on the adult and not take in the whole family. (Peel social worker: domestic violence and alcohol abuse by mother)

> With the drug workers the adult is the customer. It is a different approach. They sometimes do not take the impact on the children on board. (Linden social worker: drug abuse by both parents and depression of mother)

Different timescales

Services for adults tend to work over a longer timescale which may not be appropriate for children whose health and development is being negatively affected.

> The timescales between agencies are really very different. The drug team work at a much slower pace and they do not understand our timescales. This makes working together difficult. (Linden social worker: drug abuse by both parents and depression of mother)

Confidentiality and information sharing

Agencies working with very vulnerable adults may be reluctant to share information with children's social care, fearing that to do so would destroy the therapeutic relationship.

> The only agency I found any difficulty with was the Women's Aid, they worked extremely effectively with the mother but on occasions were reluctant to share information with me. I had to remind them of their legal obligations relating to the child's welfare. (Harding social worker: domestic violence)

> Communication is not always good between the drug workers and us. They do not always tell us things. I think they feel they should not betray a trust – that's

alright but there are times when they need to tell us things and they don't always do it. (Linden social worker: drug abuse by both parents and depression of mother)

A possible solution identified by the health visitor in this case was to develop

...more robust agreements between these services and child care services. (Linden health visitor: drug abuse by both parents and depression of mother)

A failure to attend meetings

Voluntary agencies providing services for adults may not always recognise the value of attending meetings about children.

...non-attendance by alcohol support worker, this was to support mum... It would have been helpful to have had more intense involvement with the alcohol support agency. (Sheridon social worker: domestic violence, alcohol abuse by mother, both parents learning-disabled)

When families felt that different agencies had worked well together and provided a co-ordinated response, they were more likely to be satisfied with the outcome. For example, five of the seven families who thought that services had worked well together were satisfied with the services in contrast to two of the six families who thought services were unco-ordinated.

Outcomes for the families

Case Study: Jackie's Family
Outcomes

Life improved for Jackie, Morgan and their mother. They were still together but had separated from mother's partner who was also addicted to drugs. The mother had her drug use under control.

Mum is now on controlled drug replacement methadone treatment, she is in a new home, the children are fine, there is now a good routine and proper medical supervision. (Health visitor)

Jackie's life was far more stable and she was receiving full-time education again. Jackie's mother acknowledged the positive impact children's social care has had on her family.

They gave my life a purpose... Although it was difficult at times things have improved for all of us. I realised my children are the most important thing in my life. (Jackie's mother)

The social worker agreed that Jackie's mother had changed her life around and the family was doing well.

> Mum has improved a lot… she really is a good mum when she is using drugs in a managed way. She has started a hairdressing course. Her childcare is much better and we have reduced accordingly the level of support. (Social worker)
>
> Jackie's mother was worried that support had been curtailed too early in her rehabilitation. She felt she was still vulnerable and worried that the reduced support would not be sufficient and her problems would overwhelm her once again. She knew she could call her social worker when she wanted advice but felt she needed a greater level of support. She would have liked someone to talk things through with.

Families' views on the intervention

Families held very different views about the impact of children's social care on their lives. Like Jackie's family, eight families thought their situation had improved as a result of the intervention and the services they had received.

> Life is better for both me and Ian. We now have a better quality of living. (Pine father: alcohol abuse by father)

Two families felt that their situation had not changed.

> No change really, my ex-partner leaving was only a matter of time. (Hendy mother: domestic violence)

A further two families felt their situation had deteriorated since being referred to children's social care.

> Our situation is worse. We receive very little communication from social services about our sons, which makes me angry. If we knew how our children were and were kept informed of events then we would be a lot happier. (Sheridon father: domestic violence, alcohol abuse by mother, both parents learning-disabled)

Finally, four families felt the intervention had had a mixed effect on their lives; while some things had improved others had not.

> I don't know if I will ever get back John [aged 11 years]. I am not strong enough yet to ask that question. I am frightened of the answer. However, I'm not drinking as much and things are better in some ways. I'm getting my life back together again. (Peel mother: domestic violence and alcohol abuse by mother)

As has been shown earlier, the extent to which families were satisfied with the services they receive was associated with their willingness to engage with agencies and the extent to which they are involved in the assessment and planning process. This trend continues; families who felt that their situation had improved tended to be those who had received all the services they felt their family needed. All six of the families who thought they had received and were satisfied with the services they got, felt their situation had improved. This is in stark contrast to the finding that none of the families who had not received any of the help they wanted and were dissatisfied with the services they had received, felt that their situation had improved.

Families' changed circumstances

Although numbers are small, differentiating cases where there was evidence of domestic violence from those where there was evidence of parental substance misuse provides some insight into how interventions impact on families' circumstances. Families were grouped into the following categories:

- domestic violence $n = 5$
- domestic violence and parental substance misuse $n = 7$
- parental substance misuse $n = 5$.

Domestic violence

Five families were experiencing domestic violence and there was no evidence of parental substance misuse. As a result of the assessment, plan and subsequent intervention two mothers remained with their partners and their children continued to live with them. In both cases the social worker felt that as a result of the work that had been done the domestic violence had ceased.

> Mum felt more supported. No more reports of domestic violence. (Murch social worker: domestic violence, mother physically disabled)

> Dad is more focused in managing his own feelings and will find alternate ways of dealing with his anger... I think the domestic violence has stopped. (Booth social worker: domestic violence by father, allegation of father's sexual abuse made by the daughter)

Both mothers felt that the situation had improved for their children and themselves, as a result of the intervention.

> The children are happier now that they're going to after-school club. They are off the register now. Things have improved for me and Glen [partner] definitely, also for Jenny [aged 8 years] – she's happier. (Murch mother)

> The parenting course and the anger management – both improved things. (Booth mother)

The three other mothers had separated from their violent partners, two of whom kept their children with them. In all cases the mothers felt the removal of their violent partner had reduced the violence they and their children were exposed to.

> The time apart from him [father of child] – it's helped him, he wants to change and come back with me and be with Sasha. (Fox mother)

This mother was satisfied with the outcome and felt her situation had improved.

However, the view of some parents was that separating from a violent partner was not always the result of the intervention from children's social care.

> ...anything that has made life better I have done by myself, I have had my ex-partner prosecuted and have an injunction against him. (Harding mother)

> I would sooner have been left alone. If the police had done their job in the beginning it wouldn't have happened. (Hendy mother)

In both these cases the mothers were not satisfied with the outcome of the intervention. In the first case (the mother who prosecuted her husband for assault) the mother found the intervention of children's social care extremely stressful.

> The whole process was very stressful. I felt I lost my life. It seemed to revolve around meetings with the social worker, core meetings or court appearances. I just wanted my life back. (Harding mother)

The other mother had mixed feelings, welcoming being able to live without fear, but deeply regretting the loss of her child. She wanted her child returned and felt that she was blamed for being a victim of domestic violence.

> I am no longer living with my partner and thought I could be left alone. All I wanted was to have my child back to live with me and to get on with my life. They wouldn't believe that I wasn't with my ex-partner anymore. I felt I was being punished for something I hadn't done. I'm in limbo, I have to do everything social services ask me to do so that I can have my son home to live with me. Wherever possible they should keep the child and mother together. Don't punish the mother because she has been a victim of domestic violence. (Harding mother)

The social worker's report provides a rather different perspective on events.

> After a short while she [mother] returned, with child to live with the child's father. The violence began again... this was very unstable for Jimmy [aged 18 months] and a danger for him living in such a violent environment. (Harding social worker)

This was the only case where a child had been removed because of continuing exposure to domestic violence.

Domestic violence and parental substance misuse

In seven cases there was evidence of domestic violence *and* parental substance misuse. In two cases the mother continued to live with her violent partner; in the other cases the mother and her partner separated. In only two cases did the children continue to live with one or other of their parents. In both instances the children remained with their mothers who had no history of substance misuse and the fathers, who were violent and had serious alcohol problems, left the household. In both cases the mother was satisfied with the outcome of the intervention, having found the support helpful.

For example, in one case the father served time in prison for his violence and did not return to live with the family on his release.

> The fact that Ian [husband] isn't living here helps. Things have improved for me – more confident, the children are a lot better and more relaxed around the house. (Davis mother: domestic violence and alcohol abuse by father)

In the other case the father's drinking and violence had resulted in an arrest and being bailed to a hostel. The mother was relieved not to be living with violence anymore but had reservations about the long-term outcome.

> He is not around to hit me and shout and scream, but also Nicky does not now have a dad… He was threatening to set fire to my house and was threatening me in the street. He got involved in car offences and he broke my fingers in the street. He then disappeared and there is an arrest warrant out for him now. He comes round to the house sometimes and I have told the police but they do nothing. He is not supposed to come to the house and they are supposed to arrest him. (Thomas mother: domestic violence and alcohol abuse by father)

In the remaining five cases social workers felt that the only way to safeguard the children was to remove them from their parents' care. The primary reason for the decision to accommodate the children was the mother's continued substance misuse; the domestic violence of her partner meant he could not be allowed to safely assume the parenting role.

> Reasons for this included mother drinking heavily, concerns over neglect and leaving the children at home alone during the evening… (Sheridon social worker: domestic violence and alcohol problems of mother)

The parents' views of intervention when children had been removed were mixed. For example, in one case parents felt the intervention had helped them to some extent despite the fact that their children were living away from home.

> I've got more understanding of myself and Billy [partner]. I think we've both grown together. We've got rid of the baggage and we feel we can get on with it now… You have to get yourself ready and then convince them [children's social care] that you are ready [to have the children back]. (Sheridon mother)

In the other four cases, where children were looked after, parents' perception of the intervention was generally negative, and the long-term outcome looked bleak.

> I am angry with them – things are worse now, much worse, and it is their fault. I don't have the kids and I don't trust them [children's social care]. I was not a bad mum but they said I was not looking after them. I am trying to deal with the drink, but it is hard, and now that I am with Andy [new partner] there is no violence and he's working and I am living with him in his house. But I am not getting anywhere with the social worker. (Caine mother: domestic violence and alcohol abuse by mother)

In this case the social worker thought the children were unlikely to return to live with their mother.

> Unless Mum would accept treatment – this would involve about 18 months for detox and rehabilitation. The advice from the consultant psychiatrist suggests Mum is not able to cope with this. Her prognosis is very bleak. (Caine social worker)

Substance misuse

In five cases the primary reason for the intervention of children's social care was parental substance misuse. In every case the plan following an assessment was for the children to remain living with a parent. It is of interest that in all cases the parents had separated. In three cases the children lived with their father, in one with their mother, and in one with their mother and her own parents.In three cases both the parent and social worker thought that the addiction was under control. For example, in Jackie's family the mother received help to move away from her drug-using partner, and with the help of a specialist service was managing her drug use. Her perception of the intervention was very positive.In the remaining two cases the parent continued to have problems with drugs or alcohol. In some cases parents and practitioners held a similar perception of the parent's continued drug use.

> Nothing's really changed or moved on. Still taking drugs, still living here [own parents' home], which isn't working for any of us. (Cossins mother)

> This mother has actually got to do something herself, she is aware of the services available. (Cossins social worker)

However, a shared perspective on substance misuse was not always found. For example, one father felt that he had his drinking under control.

> I am receiving support and have managed to control my drinking… I have done everything social services have asked me to do and have recognised my problems

and am making an effort to deal with them. I am frustrated that social services don't appear to share the same view. (Pine father)

The social worker's perception of this father's drinking was very different.

We were very concerned about the impact of chronic and very serious alcoholism on Ian's [aged 10 years] life. Dad is very ill, the alcohol has affected both his physical condition and his mental condition. He has problems walking with a very unsteady gait, and his short-term memory is seriously affected. He will probably be dead within a short period. His condition is deteriorating and yet he is unable to stop drinking. (Pine social worker)

Much research has shown that a co-morbidity of problems, particular the presence of domestic violence, has more negative effects on children's safety and welfare than being exposed to a single issue (Cleaver *et al.* 1999). This is reflected in the social workers' decision-making in this in-depth study of families. Children exposed to domestic violence *and* parental substance misuse, were more likely to be accommodated than in cases where these issues did not coexist.

Factors that hamper the impact of services

Social workers identified a number of factors that hampered the ability of families to change their situation when experiencing domestic violence and/or parental substance misuse. Some issues related to the ability of parents to fully engage with the service providers.

Mum was referred to the drug clinic but only attended on a few occasions and then went back on to drugs. (Reed social worker: drug and alcohol abuse by both parents, father mentally ill)

Mum was quite difficult to engage…the community drug team were on her case but she wasn't engaging. (Cossins social worker: drug abuse by mother)

It was a constant struggle, Mum was reluctant to work with us at all, she never worked with real honesty. Services have been imposed on her so she has been reluctant to work with people and agencies. (Harding social worker: domestic violence)

We encouraged Mum to attend Drinksense but she did not really take this up very seriously. (Caine social worker: domestic violence and alcohol abuse by mother)

Other factors were service driven and included: a lack of local services and difficulties in getting specialist service providers to collaborate.

Housing – they didn't turn up to the case conference which gave a message to the family that they weren't valued. (Cossins social worker: drug abuse by mother)

Adult services should be involved to help mum but this is not happening... Adult services do not wish to get involved in this type of case. Some psychiatric input would be helpful. I think that attitudes need to change towards the victims of alcoholism. There are not sufficient support services available. It is difficult to get adult services involved. I think that the prospects for Mum are very bleak... she really needs a separate adult worker to work supporting her. (Krausse social worker: domestic violence, alcohol abuse by mother, mother with learning difficulties)

At one point we did consider referring to the adult mental health team, but ultimately we did not. My experience with the mental health team is that as soon as they know there is a child protection issue they do not want anything to do with the case. They say it is our responsibility. (Pine social worker: alcohol abuse by father)

The difficulties adult psychiatry and children's services experience in working collaboratively has been highlighted in earlier research (Darlington *et al.* 2005; Göpfert, Webster and Seman 1996; James 1994) and the reports of these social workers suggest professional perspectives remain largely unchanged.

Parents' views of what helped and what hindered their family's circumstances

Case Study: Jackie's Family
Learning points

Jackie's mother thought that her family would have benefited if the intensive support she was given could have continued for longer. Her social worker's report reflects this view.

There are not enough resources for families where a parent misuses drugs to this extent. We need a different approach – working with drug misusing parents is a long term issue... There was pressure to close the case but I have managed to keep the case open as she really does need continued support. (Social worker)

Jackie's mother's desire to change her situation and her willingness to engage with the practitioners were key factors to her improved self-image and the outcome for her children.

I think we were extremely fortunate in this case. Mum was very co-operative. She recognised the harm of the situation she was in. She was very co-operative, not deceitful and was honest and open.

> She wanted to get away from the situation and she was motivated towards the children, at least once she had started to get the drugs under control. She was driven by wanting to help her children. We 'harassed' her into believing that we thought she could do it. In the end she really did believe that we, social services, health and the drugs worker really did believe in her. She responded well to our help. She improved considerably and has now got her life under control. (Health visitor)
>
> The intensive, targeted services provided by the various agencies following the social worker's assessment were identified by Jackie's mother as being the things that really helped to bring about the necessary changes. However, she expressed fears that she would be 'deserted' by the service providers now that she had made some progress in getting her drug addiction under control.

What families found most supportive

Not all parents thought the intervention of children's social care had helped their family. For example, four families felt that the referral to children's social care and the social worker's assessment and plan failed to result in any helpful services being provided. Three of these families had not sought the help of children's social care and resented their involvement in their lives.

> It's worse because they have taken the kids and I am not allowed to see them without the social worker there and they have said they are letting me see less of them in the future. They only told me that yesterday and I got angry and I kicked the door down – they really got me upset. (Caine mother: domestic violence and alcohol abuse by mother)
>
> Nothing social services has done has helped us. They have done nothing. (Thomas mother: domestic violence and alcohol abuse by father)
>
> They [children's social care] were not any help to me... I wanted someone to sit down with me – someone who I felt was on my side. I got no support at all. It was really difficult where I was living. They were interested in the children and not me. (Peel mother: domestic violence and alcohol abuse by mother)

The social worker interviews show that social work assessments and plans mobilised strengths within the wider family that proved supportive. However, parents did not always attribute this help to the intervention of children's social care.

> Getting the involvement of grandmother was very helpful as was the help of the sister. (Thomas social worker: domestic violence and alcohol abuse by father)

We identified good support from the extended family, especially from paternal grandfather and an aunt. (Pine social worker: alcohol abuse by father)

Nonetheless, the majority of families referred to children's social care believed the assessment and plan had resulted in services which had helped their family. Parents valued both the practical and emotional support they had received.

Practical support

Parents expressed their satisfaction with the practical help they had got. They valued the advice they had been given about parenting, the help they had received to control their alcohol or drug addiction, help to re-house, the anger management courses, financial help and childcare arrangements.

The childcare – it was very quick and very helpful. Really efficient. (Cossins mother: drug abuse by mother)

The childminding – we can spend more time together and sort things out. (Fox mother: domestic violence)

The parenting was very helpful. It made you more aware of what you're doing wrong and how it could be better. Very practical. (Booth mum: domestic violence by father, allegation of father's sexual abuse made by the daughter)

The practical support from the family centre was really helpful. (Sheridon father: domestic violence and alcohol abuse by mother)

Anger management courses helped him [partner], also moving house helped us. (Murch mum: domestic violence, mother physically disabled)

I found DASH [alcohol service] helped me sort out my alcohol problems. (Pine, father: alcohol abuse by father)

Mike [aged 8 years] can't be with me at home then this placement is the best place for him, he tells me he is happy there if he can't be with me. They are lovely people who care for Mike. I can see Mike gets consistency of care and has routine in his life which is important. (Krausse mother: domestic violence, alcohol abuse by mother, mother with learning difficulties)

Emotional support

Many parents also valued the emotional support given by their social workers.

The social worker helping me through the process. (Hendy mother: domestic violence)

It is nice to talk to someone who's like a friend. (Murch mother: domestic violence, mother physically disabled)

The reassurance from the social worker. (Davis mother: domestic violence and alcohol abuse by father)

The way the social worker read everything out and planned everything out. (Reed father: alcohol and drug abuse by both parents, father mentally ill)

Issues that hampered families engaging with service providers

The parents identified a number of issues that made working with service providers difficult. The most common problems were insufficient communication from children's social care, the perceived attitudes of social workers, unannounced visits, inaccurate social service reports and too frequent changes in social worker.

Lack of supportive communication and the stress the situation has caused. (Harding mother: domestic violence)

The initial confrontational approach and threats. It felt like intimidation. (Booth mother: domestic violence by father, allegation of father's sexual abuse made by the daughter)

Not being treated like a person, nobody appearing to listen, not asking what I needed or wanted. (Krausse mother: domestic violence, alcohol abuse by mother, mother with learning difficulties)

Unannounced visits. (Hendy mother: domestic violence)

When the social worker sent a report to me – what I had said was not in it. It was only what he wanted in it. (Thomas mother: domestic violence and alcohol abuse by father)

Changing social worker all the time. (Murch mother: domestic violence, mother physically disabled)

Most complaints were set at the door of children's social care. Only one mother reported dissatisfaction with the response of other service providers; she had expressed very positive opinions of the work of children's social care.

Housing – lack of response. Drug team unfriendly and unbelievably rude. (Cossins mother: drug abuse by mother)

Parents' views of how intervention could be improved

A few families had not sought or wanted professional help. These families rejected and negated the services they had been offered and believed any improvements to their family circumstances had been brought about by themselves.

I just got myself together a bit. They [children's social care] were not any help to me. (Peel mother: domestic violence and alcohol abuse by mother)

Anything that has made life better I have done by myself. (Harding mother: domestic violence)

The areas where parents felt improvements could be made to the way children's social care and other agencies work with families like theirs echoed the areas of practice which they had found least supportive. Families identified the following aspects of intervention as areas where improvements could be made:

- Communicating with families.

- Practitioners' attitudes to families.

- Listening and taking account of parents' wishes and feelings.

- Access to services.

- Longer-term service provision.

- Improved co-ordination of services.

Communicating with families

Half the families felt that communication between children's social care and themselves could be improved. For example, eight families expressed a wish that children's social care had kept them better informed throughout the process of assessment, planning and intervention, and explained things more clearly to them.

At all stages of the process it should be explained exactly what is happening. (Pine father: alcohol abuse by father)

Discuss what is happening or is going to happen with plenty of warning. (Krausse mother: domestic violence, alcohol abuse by mother, mother with learning difficulties)

They should have kept me informed and given me information. (Peel mother: domestic violence and alcohol abuse by mother)

If advice had been given and options I could choose from, e.g, to move away with Jimmy [aged 18 months] then life would be so different. (Harding mother: domestic violence)

Practitioners' attitudes to families

Four families felt that social workers held negative and prejudicial attitudes towards families such as theirs.

Approach from the social worker – need training to help him be polite, caring, gentle and understanding. (Pine father: alcohol abuse by father)

Other families thought their social worker had not treated them with respect or been sufficiently honest with them.

> If social services had been honest with me and treated me with respect, even if I'm not going to like what they say then it would be a lot better, I would not get so angry with them. I try not to, but when they don't tell me anything until they have to, it gets me angry. (Sheridon father: domestic violence, alcohol abuse by mother, both parents learning-disabled)

> They should be honest to people and they are not. (Caine mother: domestic violence and alcohol abuse by mother)

Raising sensitive issues with families requires great skill. Social workers have to balance confronting parents about aspects of their lives in a forthright and honest manner, with the parent's capacity to 'hear' the message. When under considerable stress parents may need much support to enable them to acknowledge the issues in their lives that are negatively impacting on their children's safety and welfare. For example, the practitioner working with the father who felt his social worker needed to be trained to be 'polite, caring, gentle and understanding' felt that his honest approach had resulted in this father taking offence.

> Dad did not like me being honest with him. I believe that parents should be told the truth about our concerns and I was very frank with him – this he did not like. He tried to deny how much he was drinking and when I said I did not believe him he got quite unpleasant. (Pine social worker: alcohol abuse by father)

Listening and taking account of parents' wishes and feelings

Six families felt that social workers did not devote sufficient time to understanding the circumstances of their family and failed to listen and take account of their views and opinions. As a result these parents felt social workers did not have a comprehensive understanding of the situation their family was facing.

Parents generally acknowledged that social workers need to identify the children's needs and provide them with services, but felt that their own needs were often disregarded. Some social workers were perceived as unable to empathise or indeed understand the lives of families such as theirs. This echoes the findings that will be explored in Chapter 7 which show that a third of social service managers had received no recent training on domestic violence and approximately half no training on parental substance misuse.

> They could listen to us and try to understand what is going on and how it feels to be like we were. No one seemed interested in me. (Thomas mother: domestic violence and alcohol abuse by father)

I was never asked what I wanted or what would help with the situation I was in... Take time to find out what the parent needs and wants. (Harding mother: domestic violence)

They think we are to blame when we get hit by men. They do not understand. (Thomas mother: domestic violence and alcohol abuse by father)

Access to services

Families wanted greater access to specific services such as housing, independent advisors, and specialist services.

Help me re-locate, I have asked but they can't help me. (Hendy mother: domestic violence)

Re-house me. (Harding mother: domestic violence)

Lack of service from housing has stopped things changing... Housing priorities should be changed. They don't know what is going on in our home, they don't really know how difficult it is. (Cossins mother: drug abuse by mother)

Useful to have a guide or advocate through the process – so you know what's going on. (Hammond mother: domestic violence, drug and alcohol abuse by both parents, mother has postnatal depression)

An independent body to go to – that you can talk to in confidence and sort yourself out. (Booth mother: domestic violence by father, allegation of father's sexual abuse made by the daughter)

They should have more courses to help people like me. (Thomas mother: domestic violence and alcohol abuse by father)

The difficulty of working in partnership with housing has been mentioned in previous chapters. The importance of housing for the outcome of these families was acknowledged by social workers.

Housing could help improve the situation further – Mum desperately needs to be re-housed. (Cossins social worker: drug abuse by mother)

Other parents felt their family would have benefited from an increase in the services they were already receiving; others thought that access to specialist services should be easier and more timely.

The domestic violence unit could help me more and give me more support. (Hendy mother: domestic violence)

It was quite difficult to get access. The health visitor didn't hold out much hope of social services providing anything. She advised me to contact XXX [voluntary agency working with survivors of domestic violence] and hoped that would be enough, which it wasn't. It would be good if you were able to ring up and ask for

> help and get it, more resources and more accessible. (Davis mother: domestic violence and alcohol abuse by father)

> Get the family therapy sorted quickly. (Booth mother: domestic violence by father, allegation of father's sexual abuse made by the daughter)

Longer-term service provision

Other families and practitioners thought that the services that were provided to families ended too prematurely. Many parents and social workers thought that the family would have benefited from the service being provided for longer.

> Don't give us something [practical support] and then take it away without helping us. (Sheridon father: domestic violence, alcohol abuse by mother, both parents learning-disabled)

> Long-term support. (Linden mother: drug abuse by both parents and depression of mother)

Improved co-ordination of services

Some parents thought that the help their family received would have been improved if services from the different agencies had been more co-ordinated.

> Services need to be more co-ordinated and linked together. (Hammond mother: domestic violence, drug and alcohol abuse by both parents, mother has postnatal depression)

> If agencies didn't pull out after doing a specific piece of work whether finished or not, it would help. (Sheridon social worker: domestic violence, alcohol abuse by mother, both parents learning-disabled)

The views of this group of parents poignantly illustrate issues identified in previous research that have been shown to be associated with good working relationships between parents and practitioners (see for example, Cleaver *et al.* 2004a; Freeman and Hendy 1998; Thoburn, Wilding and Watson 2000).

Summary points

- Services were provided to all 17 families following a social work assessment and plan. The planned services did not always address all the problems families were experiencing. The main reasons that hampered service provision were long waiting lists, services ending prematurely, and relevant services not being available.

- Parental satisfaction with the outcome of the assessment and plan was associated with being able to acknowledge the problems their family was experiencing, being willing to engage with services, being fully involved in the assessment and planning process, and being kept informed about developments.

- The co-morbidity of issues meant that in most cases more than one agency was providing a service to the family. In half the cases the approach was co-ordinated. When families felt that agencies worked well together they were more likely to be satisfied with the services they received.

- Parents held very different views on how the services had affected their families. Half ($n = 8$) thought their family life had improved, a further quarter had mixed feelings, and in two cases, where children had been accommodated, parents felt their situation had deteriorated. The remaining families felt that their situation had not changed.

- Parents were more likely to be satisfied with the outcome of the assessment where domestic violence was not associated with parental substance misuse. In most cases the service provision either reduced the violence and the family were able to stay together or the parents separated and the children remained with the non violent parent.

- A similar outcome was found when parental substance misuse was not associated with domestic violence. As a result of the plan following an assessment and service provision children continued to live with a parent, approximately half of whom had gained some control over their drug or alcohol problem. These parents were satisfied with the outcome.

- In cases where domestic violence and parental substance misuse coexisted the outcome was less positive. In five of the seven cases children were removed from home. Parents held negative or mixed views of the outcome when children were accommodated.

- Social workers identified the following issues as impeding positive outcomes for families: parents not fully engaging with the service provider, a lack of local services, and difficulties in getting access to specialist services.

- Parents valued services that provided both practical help and emotional support. The practical help included advice about parenting, respite child care, specialist help to control alcohol or drug addiction, anger management and re-housing. Parents were also grateful for the emotional support their social workers gave them.

- Parents identified a number of issues which they felt could improve the way children's social care and other agencies work with families like theirs. These included:
  - ○ more effective communication
  - ○ practitioners taking a more honest, open and respectful approach to families
  - ○ listening and taking account of parents' wishes and feelings
  - ○ greater access to specific services
  - ○ longer-term service provision
  - ○ improved co-ordination of the service.

Chapter 6

Plans, Procedures and Joint Protocols

To understand inter-agency collaboration and working, in cases where there are concerns about the safety and welfare of children living with domestic violence or parental substance misuse, each participating local authority was asked for copies of current relevant local plans, procedures and joint protocols. This resulted in a wide range and volume of documentation being made available to the research team. The documents were reviewed and logged indicating their organisational source, title, date, main purpose and whether they were relevant to child protection, domestic violence or parental substance misuse.

The purpose of collecting this documentation was to:

- identify what was currently available to managers and practitioners (within relevant agencies) to guide and support inter-agency collaboration in this area of work

- compare documents across local authorities to identify good and innovative practice

- explore the relationship between the range, quantity and quality of written information and managers' awareness of the materials, their confidence in collaborative working, and their awareness of the services available to help children and families where these issues are present (discussed in earlier chapters).

In order to review the documentation, factors known to be associated with good practice were identified and the documents assessed against these criteria. For example, the documents were examined to find out whether there was evidence of appropriate and clear ownership of the document, if it was readily accessible (was it written in a clear and concise way and well circulated), whether it was reviewed and dated, and the level of inter-agency involvement. As a result essential or primary documents, such as Area Child Protection Committee (ACPC) annual reports, Domestic Violence Forum plans, and drug and alcohol service plans, were reviewed using the following criteria:

- Dated (and up-to-date) and reviewed regularly.
- Evidence of ownership from senior management and frontline practitioners across relevant agencies.
- Evidence-based/research-based where appropriate.
- Clear, concise, accessible language for the target audience.
- Evidence of availability/access to all relevant members of staff/volunteers/carers.
- Relates to other policies, procedures, guidance and plans – and this is clearly stated.

In addition to using these criteria to establish a baseline of good practice, the submitted plans, procedures and protocols were examined for evidence of information sharing and joint working between children's social care and domestic violence and substance misuse services.

Plans

The following plans were scrutinised:

- ACPC Annual Report/Business Plan.
- Domestic Violence Forum Annual Report/Business Plan.
- Drug Action Team/Drug and Alcohol Action Team Annual Report/Business Plan.
- Crime and Disorder Reduction Strategy/Community Safety Plan.
- Children and Families' Service Plan.
- Training Plans (covered in Chapter 7).

ACPC Annual Report/Business Plan

At the time of the research local authorities were still working with Area Child Protection Committees; these would be replaced by Local Safeguarding Children Boards in 2006.

> Each ACPC should produce an annual business plan, setting out a work programme for the forthcoming year, including measurable objectives; relevant management information on child protection activity in the course of the previous year; and progress against objectives the previous year. ACPC plans

should both contribute to and derive from the framework of the local children's services plan and should be endorsed by senior managers in each of the main constituent agencies. (Department of Health *et al.* 1999, p.37, paragraph 4.19)

Using the base-line criteria to review the ACPC annual report/business plan shows considerable variation between the six participating authorities (see Table 6.1). For example, in five of the six authorities the plan was dated and regularly reviewed, it was written in an easily accessible language, and the relationship with other relevant policies, procedures, guidance and plans was clearly stated. In contrast, in only two authorities was there either evidence of ownership from senior management and frontline practitioners, or that the plan was readily available to all relevant persons. In no authority was there evidence that findings from research or inquiries had been influential in developing the plan.

Table 6.1 Research assessment of the ACPC Annual Report/Business Plan

Feature	Metro-politan Borough 1	Metro-politan Borough 2	Shire County 1	Shire County 2	London Borough 1	London Borough 2
Dated/ reviewed	Yes	Yes	–	Yes	Yes	Yes
Ownership	Yes	Yes	–	–	–	–
Evidence-based	–	–	–	–	–	–
Accessible language	Yes	–	Yes	Yes	Yes	Yes
Availability	–	Yes	Yes	–	–	–
Relates	Yes	Yes	Yes	Yes	Yes	–

All local authorities are expected to have an annual report/business plan for their multi-agency work on safeguarding children – currently this is the responsibility of the ACPC but will become the responsibility of the Local Safeguarding Children Boards (introduced by the Children Act 2004). The annual report/business plan should emphasise the multi-agency nature of the work, set out how progress will be made during the next 12 months and review past performance. Any important local or national policies or guidance should also be referenced within this document.

THE EXTENT TO WHICH ACPC BUSINESS PLANS COVER CHILDREN AND FAMILIES AFFECTED BY DOMESTIC VIOLENCE OR PARENTAL SUBSTANCE MISUSE

The 2002–2003 ACPC business plans in three of the six local authorities addressed the issue of children living in families where there was evidence of domestic violence and/or parental substance misuse. The authorities differed in their approaches. For example, in London Borough 1 the ACPC plan showed a commitment to effective inter-agency working, indicated links with the domestic violence forum were ongoing and improving, and similar links with the local drug action team were planned. The importance of inter-agency working was underpinned by information relating to the proportion of children on the child protection register affected by domestic violence or parental substance misuse. In Shire County 2 the ACPC plan made reference to the development of a domestic violence protocol to be used across the county, and to improving information systems to identify the links between child protection, domestic violence and parental substance misuse. Finally, in Metropolitan Borough 2 the ACPC business plan indicated that services for children and parents, subjected to domestic violence, were being developed. Priority was given to: monitoring cases where children are living with domestic violence or parental substance misuse; developing links with the local drug and alcohol team; and reducing the number of children on the child protection register where parental substance misuse is an issue. Once again statistics on the proportion of children experiencing domestic violence or parental substance misuse were used to justify the changes.

In the other three authorities the ACPC business plan did not contain objectives specifically aimed at working with children whose families are affected by domestic violence or parental substance misuse. However, in Metropolitan Borough 1 the ACPC plan suggested that the association between domestic violence and child protection had been covered in their training courses.

Domestic Violence Forum Annual Report/Business Plan

> It is equally important, though, that any forum has clearly stated aims, objectives and action plans against which it can be easily evaluated. Without this there is a risk that the multi-agency forum could become a 'smokescreen' behind which some agencies might be able to hide – for example, by saying that their response to domestic violence was to participate in the forum. The purpose of a forum is to improve the overall approach to addressing domestic violence and the level of service to survivors. Agencies co-operating in the forum must have actual domestic violence policies and practices which they can co-ordinate. (Home Office 2000, paragraph 3.6)

Applying the base-line criteria showed that most domestic violence annual reports/business plans were dated, regularly reviewed, and written in a clear, concise and accessible language (see Table 6.2). There was also evidence that findings from research had been used to inform policy and planning in four of the six authorities. However, in only half the participating authorities was it clear how the plan related to other relevant guidance and plans, and in only two authorities was there evidence of ownership from senior management and frontline practitioners. Finally, in none of the authorities was there evidence that the plan was available or accessible to all relevant members of staff and volunteers.

Table 6.2 Research assessment of the Domestic Violence Forum Annual Report/Business Plan

Feature	Metro-politan Borough 1	Metro-politan Borough 2	Shire County 1	Shire County 2	London Borough 1	London Borough 2
Dated/ reviewed	Yes	Yes	Yes	–	Yes	Yes
Ownership	–	Yes	–	Yes	–	–
Evidence-based	–	Yes	Yes	Yes	–	Yes
Accessible language	Yes	Yes	Yes	Yes	–	Yes
Availability	–	–	–	–	–	–
Relates	–	Yes	Yes	Yes	–	–

Because of the Government's emphasis on reducing and preventing domestic violence (*Safety and Justice* – the Government's proposal on domestic violence, Cm 5847 2003; Domestic Violence Crime and Victims Act, Home Office 2004) most authorities now have strategies, policies and some form of planning and reviewing system concerning domestic violence. However, the range of provision and emphasis given to domestic violence was variable across the six authorities.

THE EXTENT TO WHICH DOMESTIC VIOLENCE FORUM PLANS INCLUDE CHILDREN AND CHILD PROTECTION ISSUES

The domestic violence forum plans in five of the six local authorities specifically addressed the issue of children living in families where there was evidence of domestic violence. The plans ranged from well-researched, comprehensive documents covering effective working with families affected by domestic violence through to a brief table of objectives (London Borough 1). For example, the domestic violence forum plan in Metropolitan Borough 2 included extensive action plans, local research, national research findings, and useful resources. It also included a number of objectives for working with children and families such as reviewing and developing direct services for children, improving preventative work with young people, and improving provision for the protection of families. However, although most domestic violence forum plans contained detailed targets, they did not always specify who was responsible for the work required to meet the targets, or when these targets should be met.

The importance of collaborative working between different professional groups and organisations was highlighted in most domestic violence forum plans, as was the provision of guidance for practitioners. For example, in Shire County 2 the plan emphasised the importance of multi-agency planning across the children's services sector and included a number of accompanying documents which indicated the recent prioritisation of domestic violence within the authority. Similarly, the domestic violence strategy in London Borough 2 included focused plans, an updated protocol for multi-agency working and good practice guidance for all staff. In addition background information and current research was used to illustrate the needs of children and young people living with domestic violence.

In some authorities, the domestic violence forum plan also included initiatives to raise public awareness of domestic violence and its impact on children, or examples of innovative practice to support children and young people exposed to domestic violence. For example, the domestic violence forum plan in Metropolitan Borough 1, in addition to implementing a large-scale, multi-agency strategy, also included the appointment of a children's development worker, the introduction of an awareness raising project in several local high schools, plus the publication of articles on domestic violence in the local youth newspaper. Another example of innovative practice was found in Shire County 1 where the domestic violence forum plan established a programme for perpetrators of domestic violence with a concurrent support group for children. The plan also included ACPC multi-agency training on domestic violence and showed how police data were starting to include reference to the number of children in households where domestic violence was reported.

In addition to domestic violence forum plans some authorities provided reports from other organisations that addressed domestic violence. For example, London Borough 1 provided their 'Domestic Violence Working Party Report' April 2004 which was an extensive, thoroughly researched document identifying gaps in the provision of services for children affected by domestic violence. Metropolitan Borough 2 provided an annual report (2002–2003) from a local domestic violence voluntary organisation that receives much of its funding from social services. The report made reference to existing good inter-agency links, shared priorities and plans. It included information concerning the safety of children in families affected by domestic violence and provided a specific counselling service for children. This organisation was part of the local community safety strategy with links to the domestic violence executive (a multi-agency, decision-making body) and to other voluntary sector agencies also providing services for needy families.

Drug Action Team and Drug and Alcohol Action Team Plans

> Each DAT should have a strategic plan for preventing drug misuse and reducing drug-related harm in its area. In some areas the remit of the DAT has been widened to cover alcohol and tobacco. However, it appears that relatively few DATs have as yet given the children of problem drug users more than passing attention. (Home Office 2003, p.72, paragraph 7.2)

Applying the base-line criteria shows that in most Drug Action Teams/Drug and Alcohol Action Teams, plans were dated and regularly reviewed, and written in a clear and concise language. The relationship of the plan with other relevant plans was clearly stated (see Table 6.3). Half the plans showed that research had been used to drive and substantiate the planning. However, only one of the plans (Metropolitan Borough 1) provided evidence of ownership by key staff, and none indicated whether the plan was accessible to all relevant staff and volunteers.

Table 6.3 Research assessment of the Drug Action Team and Drug and Alcohol Action Team Plans

Feature	Metro-politan Borough 1	Metro-politan Borough 2	Shire County 1	Shire County 2	London Borough 1	London Borough 2
Dated/ reviewed	Yes	Yes	Yes	Yes	Yes	Yes
Ownership	Yes	–	–	–	–	–
Evidence-based	Yes	Yes	Yes	Yes	–	–
Accessible language	Yes	Yes	Yes	–	Yes	Yes
Availability	–	–	–	–	–	–
Relates	Yes	–	Yes	Yes	Yes	Yes

The DAT (Drug Action Team) or DAAT (Drug and Alcohol Action Team) plan is the requirement for each local authority to annually review and plan in line with national requirements to reduce the misuse of drugs and alcohol in the community. Within this remit there is a Community Plan, a Treatment Plan, a Young People's Plan and an Availability Plan (dealing with drug supply). The DAT or DAAT plan is essentially a monitoring and planning tool for professionals. The National Drug Strategy does not include specific targets in terms of reducing the effect of parental substance misuse on children. Consequently it was rare to find reference to parental support or support for children and young people whose parents misuse drugs or alcohol among the plans we reviewed. On the whole the Community Plan and the Young People's Plan were the most relevant to this study. However, most plans focused on young people at risk of, or currently misusing drugs or alcohol; planning to meet the needs of children and young people of substance misusing parents are featured infrequently.

THE EXTENT TO WHICH DAT OR DAAT PLANS COVER CHILDREN WHO LIVE WITH PARENTS WHO MISUSE DRUGS AND/OR ALCOHOL

The Community Plan

Four of the six local authorities were able to provide the research team with a copy of their Community Plans. Only one of these four Community Plans dealt with parental substance misuse (London Borough 2). This plan included the funding of a parental substance misuse project offering specific support to parents to encourage treatment and help prevent relapse. In the other three authorities (Shire County 2, London Borough 1, Metropolitan Borough 1) the Community Plans did not refer to the needs of children affected by parental substance misuse. One plan included reference to a young people's service; however, it was not clear whether this service included support for children of drug users as well as young people who were currently drug users.

Young People's Plans

Four local authorities provided the research team with a copy of their Young People's Plan (Shire County 1, Metropolitan Borough 2, London Borough 1, Metropolitan Borough 1). The main focus of the plans was the needs of drug-using young people. Nonetheless, three of the plans made some provision for the needs of children of substance users. For example, the plan in Shire County 1 included specific aims and objectives to support the needs of children and young people affected by parental substance misuse. The plan in Metropolitan Borough 2 recognised that services needed to target 'at risk' groups such as the children of drug using parents. Similarly the 'young people's planning grid' provided by Shire County 2, which was a lengthy table of actions, included several related to improving support for drug using parents and their children. However, as with the Young People's Plans the vast majority of actions applied to young people who were at risk or currently using drugs/alcohol unsafely.

Crime and Disorder Reduction Strategy/Community Safety Plan

A strategy shall include: (a) objectives to be pursued by the responsible authorities, by co-operating persons or bodies or, under agreements with the responsible authorities, by other persons or bodies; and (b) long-term and short-term performance targets for measuring the extent to which such objectives are achieved. (Crime and Disorder Act 1998, S6.4)

Applying the base-line criteria shows that all the Crime and Disorder Reduction Strategy/Community Safety Plans were dated and regularly reviewed and all but one were written in a clear, concise and accessible language, using research findings to drive strategies and plans (see Table 6.4). In four cases there was evidence that the strategy/plan was readily available to the relevant people. Half the strategies/plans evidenced the links with other key policy and plans, but in only two cases was there evidence of ownership from relevant staff.

Table 6.4 Research assessment of the Crime and Disorder Reduction Strategy/Community Safety Plan

Feature	Metro-politan Borough 1	Metro-politan Borough 2	Shire County 1	Shire County 2	London Borough 1	London Borough 2
Dated/reviewed	Yes	Yes	Yes	Yes	Yes	Yes
Ownership	–	Yes	–	Yes	–	–
Evidence-based	Yes	Yes	Yes	Yes	–	Yes
Accessible language	Yes	Yes	–	Yes	Yes	Yes
Availability	Yes	Yes	Yes	–	–	Yes
Relates	–	Yes	Yes	–	–	Yes

The government's aim is that all local authorities will bring together relevant agencies and organisations in Crime and Disorder Reduction Partnerships. These partnership bodies (local authorities, police, health services etc) will carry out an annual audit and develop a local strategy for tackling crime and disorder and drug problems locally; the community safety plan or crime and disorder reduction strategy. The Crime and Disorder Reduction Partnerships are expected to work closely with the drug and alcohol teams.

THE EXTENT TO WHICH CRIME AND DISORDER REDUCTION STRATEGIES AND COMMUNITY SAFETY PLANS COVER CHILDREN WHO LIVE WITH DOMESTIC VIOLENCE OR PARENTAL SUBSTANCE MISUSE

The Crime and Disorder Reduction Strategy/Community Safety Plan embodies a local authority's strategy for tackling crime and disorder and drug problems within their area. In the two Shire Counties, different safety plans were drawn up for the different regions (five in Shire County 1 and four in Shire County 2).

The plans generally included objectives and targets aimed at reducing domestic violence and drug availability and use. However, the needs of the children and young people within the families affected by these difficulties were rarely covered. This emphasis is understandable given the core of the Crime and Disorder Reduction Strategy/Community Safety Plans which is the criminal nature of domestic violence or substance misuse and its effect on local crime rates rather than the impact of these issues on children and family welfare.

Most of the plans included objectives relating to the support of female victims of domestic violence. For example, the targets in London Borough 1 were to be achieved through, among other things, the Community Safety Unit providing support and ensuring women fleeing domestic violence can access a refuge place the same day. However, in only two local authorities (Shire Counties 1 and 2) did the plans make mention of children within the family. In both authorities children were highlighted when reference was made to the support planned for those affected by domestic violence.

None of the Crime and Disorder Reduction Strategy/Community Safety Plans developed by the participating local authorities included objectives that related to supporting the 'victims' of problem substance users, either adults or children.

In two authorities (Metropolitan Borough 1 and Shire County 2) the Community Safety Plan included reference to innovative multi-agency developments. For example, in Metropolitan Borough 1 the target was to appoint a children's development worker; a specialist nurse service within the authority was funded by the community safety partnership and provided support and clinical services to those affected by domestic violence (no specific reference, however, is made to children within the family). In Shire County 2 the Community Safety Plan in one region referred to obtaining sufficient finances to fund a full-time domestic violence co-ordinator and a family support worker for families affected by drug use.

Children's Services Plan

The Children's Services Plan was replaced by the Children and Young People's Plan in 2005 (HM Government 2005b).

> Each local authority with social services responsibilities is required to produce a children's services plan which should bring together all aspects of local services for children. Plans should look widely at the needs of local children, and the ways in which local services (including statutory and voluntary services) should work together to meet those needs. (Department of Health *et al.* 1999, p.34, paragraph 4.7)

Applying the base-line criteria shows that all available Children's Services Plans were dated, regularly reviewed and clearly evidenced the links with other relevant plans (see Table 6.5). In all but one of the Children's Services Plans there was evidence of research being referred to; in two cases there was evidence of how key staff had been involved in its development, but in only one authority was there evidence that the plan was readily available to all relevant staff.

Table 6.5 Research assessment of the Children's Services Plan

Feature	Metro-politan Borough 1	Metro-politan Borough 2	Shire County 1	Shire County 2	London Borough 1	London Borough 2
Dated/ reviewed	Yes	Yes	Yes	Yes	–	Yes
Ownership	Yes	–	Yes	–	–	–
Evidence-based	Yes	–	Yes	Yes	–	Yes
Accessible language	Yes	Yes	–	–	–	Yes
Availability	–	Yes	–	–	–	–
Relates	Yes	Yes	Yes	Yes	–	Yes

Note: London Borough 1 had no Children's Services Plan after 2000.

The Children's Services Plan, and its replacement the Children and Young People's Plan (HM Government 2005b), should include the overarching themes and priorities for all services involved with children in the local authority. Mention of parental substance misuse or of domestic violence would indicate that such issues were integrated into planning and provision for children and families.

THE EXTENT TO WHICH CHILDREN'S SERVICES PLANS COVER CHILDREN LIVING WITH DOMESTIC VIOLENCE AND/OR PARENTAL SUBSTANCE MISUSE

Planning for families rather than just the victim of domestic violence was included in three of the five authorities' Children's Services Plans made available to the research team. For example, Shire County 1 had a comprehensive, multi-agency document that brought together the objectives of all linked and relevant plans. It included reference to the Community Safety Plan, Young People's Substance Misuse Plan, ACPC Business Plan and the Domestic Violence Strategy. Objectives included reducing the impact of domestic violence, supporting victims and improving accommodation for victims, as well as developing practice guidance and training specific to families affected by domestic violence. Another example was the Children's Service Plan in Metropolitan Borough 1 which incorporated a detailed action plan which included improving the co-ordination of services for families affected by domestic violence. London Borough 2 was the third authority's whose plan made reference to the needs of families affected by domestic violence, detailing how these were being met.

In contrast, planning for families (i.e. children) living with substance mis-using parents was included in only one authority's Children's Services Plan (London Borough 2). This authority provided evidence of creative inter-agency work to develop innovative programmes to support children affected by domestic violence *and* substance misuse. The Children's Fund programme was financing work with children affected by domestic violence and the Health Improvement Programme funded a project specifically addressing parental substance misuse. However, these government funding sources have a limited life and the initiatives will need to be incorporated into core funding arrangements if they are to survive.

Procedures

Effective interventions to support children living with domestic violence or parental substance misuse depend on ensuring that practitioners have access to guidance and procedures that cover both issues.

ACPC procedures

A key objective of ACPC procedures was to ensure practitioners in one agency understand the roles and responsibilities of those in other agencies, and provide guidance to assist the recognition of child abuse and the legal framework in which practitioners must act. All members of the ACPC would have access to these procedures including any representatives from domestic violence services and agencies working with substance misuse. However, in most authorities although a member of the committee commonly represented domestic violence, substance misuse was less frequently championed.

The introduction of Local Safeguarding Children Boards (LSCBs) has put the roles and responsibilities of current ACPCs on a statutory footing since 1 April 2006. LSCBs widen the range of Board partners and the government guidance makes specific mention of the need to engage with Domestic Violence Forums, drug and alcohol misuse services and Drug Action Teams because of their particular role in service provision to children and families, and their role in public protection (HM Government 2006a). These changes should help to ensure that all agencies providing services for domestic violence or substance misuse will have access to the LSCB procedures. Moreover, since the data were collected for this study, the government has published comprehensive guidance for practitioners working in the statutory or independent sector that explains:

> …what you should do if you have concerns about children, in order to safeguard and promote the welfare of children, including those who are suffering, or at risk of suffering, significant harm. (Department of Health 2003, p.1)

A scrutiny of the ACPC procedures found that in all six participating authorities they were clear and written in an easily accessible language (see Table 6.6). Half the procedures were dated and regularly reviewed and half gave clear information about how they linked with other relevant procedures. In only two cases were findings from research used to inform the procedures and in only one instance was there evidence that all pertinent staff had been involved in their development.

Table 6.6 Research assessment of ACPC procedures

Feature	Metro-politan Borough 1	Metro-politan Borough 2	Shire County 1	Shire County 2	London Borough 1	London Borough 2
Dated/reviewed	–	Yes	–	–	Yes	Yes
Ownership	Yes	–	–	–	–	–
Evidence-based	Yes	–	Yes	–	–	–
Accessible language	Yes	Yes	Yes	Yes	Yes	Yes
Availability	–	–	–	–	–	–
Relates	–	–	Yes	–	Yes	Yes

THE EXTENT TO WHICH ACPC PROCEDURES ADDRESS DOMESTIC VIOLENCE AND PARENTAL SUBSTANCE MISUSE

ACPC procedures did not always cover domestic violence and parental substance misuse adequately. For example, the two London Boroughs followed the London Child Protection Procedures; these included a short section concerning families affected by domestic violence and another covering parental substance misuse. The sections were not able to cover the issues in any depth and there was no reference to research findings.

In the other four authorities the ACPC procedures or separate linked documents, provided sound information on the implications of domestic violence for children in the family and linked this with the child protection process. These included:

- A 3-page chapter within the ACPC procedures (Metropolitan Borough 1).

- A 13-page guidance document with sections aimed at staff from each of the main statutory bodies, with specific guidance in cases where domestic violence is suspected or evident (Shire County 1).

- A separate 15-page document covering domestic violence and child protection, with detailed guidance and information for staff (Shire County 2).

- A procedures manual focusing on supporting children and young people living with violence or abuse produced by an inter-agency group, sponsored by the ACPC and regeneration money. This provided clear, user-friendly and evidence-based guidance for staff in the authority (Metropolitan Borough 2).

ACPC procedures rarely covered children living in families where a parent was a problem alcohol or drug user. In only one authority (Metropolitan Borough 1) did the ACPC procedures include information about parental substance misuse. In this authority both domestic violence and parental drug and alcohol misuse were prioritised in that they were highlighted in the opening chapter covering the recognition of child abuse. The procedures also contained a 4-page chapter for practitioners dealing with parental substance misuse, and as noted earlier a similarly detailed chapter on domestic violence.

Procedures addressing domestic violence provided by individual agencies

Three authorities provided the research group with procedures and guidance when working with families affected by domestic violence that had been developed by a specific agency.

In Metropolitan Borough 1 the domestic violence forum had obtained funding from the Community Safety Partnership to produce step-by-step guidance for all practitioners when working to support women living with domestic violence. It included reference to relevant legislation and pointers to local resources.London Borough 1 had produced extensive procedures and background information for housing staff working with families affected by domestic violence. This provided legal information, emergency and safety procedures and background to domestic violence.

In Metropolitan Borough 2, the police officers when dealing with domestic violence work to regional policy guidance. This policy document provided suggestions when dealing with domestic violence and made reference to children's safety and protection. It pointed out that within each division there is a 'domestic violence officer' who takes the lead in such cases. The authority had also developed a short practical guide for members of the public who want to keep safe when living with domestic violence. The guide was devised by the local Community Safety Partnership, the regional police force and a local voluntary domestic violence service. It included a self risk-assessment, a document entitled *Preparing to leave and safety planning for parent and child*, plus tear-off cards with safety and emergency information.

Procedures addressing parental substance misuse provided by individual agencies

No additional procedures developed by specific agencies, that addressed parental substance misuse were submitted to the research team.

Domestic violence agency procedures that cover child protection

All six authorities were asked to provide the research team with any procedures used by local domestic violence services that covered working with children or the child protection system. Although domestic violence services in five of the six participating authorities provided copies of their procedures in most cases how to deal with concerns about children, was not addressed.

Nonetheless, there were some examples of innovative practice. For example, in Metropolitan Borough 2, a local refuge had produced a number of very helpful procedural documents for staff and residents. One of these guides staff through issues of child protection and how to deal with them. It is a clear and user-friendly document which should go towards ensuring that the child is not forgotten in the process of working with the parents.

Drug team and drug agency procedures that cover child protection

A similar request was made to drug action teams and agencies working with substance misuse for any procedures they had which related to working with children or child protection. Drug services from three local authorities provided examples of their procedures.In one authority (Shire County 1) procedures from a voluntary agency providing services for local substance misusers and their families were clear and concise and referred specifically to working with substance misusing parents. The procedures contained a chapter linking drug and alcohol work with the child protection system. They emphasised the importance of inter-agency working and provided detailed guidance on information sharing and communication with other relevant professionals.

Another authority (London Borough 1) provided a joint protocol between their Adult Substance Misuse Service and their Children and Families Division. The protocol included detailed procedures for staff working with parental substance misusers where there were possible child protection issues.

The third authority (Shire County 2) provided a document for use by health practitioners, many of whom are responsible for identifying children living with substance misusing parents. It provided clear and concise instructions for assessing parents and families, and advised practitioners to seek advice from social services when appropriate.

Joint protocols for information sharing and confidentiality

Joint protocols for information sharing and confidentiality of client information across agencies were commonly found. These were not specific to parental substance misuse or to domestic violence within families. Most were helpful in clarifying and reassuring staff of their duties and responsibilities in obtaining and sharing information concerning children and young people who might be in need of protection. This study did not deal with the detail of these protocols; suffice it to say that they were helpful and appropriate to the families we were looking at where privacy, secrecy and safeguarding personal information are usually a high priority.

Focusing specifically on domestic violence and parental substance misuse revealed that joint protocols for information sharing did not routinely cover these issues and when they did, all relevant agencies and organisations were rarely included.

For example, some protocols for sharing information in relation to children living in violent families had been developed between two or three agencies such as the police, probation and children's social care while other seemingly relevant services such as health had not been included. In one authority (London Borough 2), police and probation had agreed a protocol which clarified information sharing in relation to protecting women and children from domestic violence offenders who joined the Domestic Violence Pathfinder Programme. Part of the

Pathfinder initiative also included a written agreement between the Probation Area and the Social Services Department which clarified the co-ordinated and informed response of both parties when working with offenders and their families.

Similarly, some protocols for sharing information when there is evidence of parental substance misuse are restricted to a single adult service provider and children social care. For example, one authority (London Borough 1) provided a joint protocol between adult substance misuse services and children's social care. It provided step-by-step guidance for both services when dealing with possible child protection issues and parental substance misuse. It covered not only information sharing but the procedure and decision-making process during assessment and care planning.

However, two authorities had produced joint protocols for information sharing, which covered many relevant agencies and organisations such as: the local authority, the police, local voluntary services, the health trust, the probation service and the magistrates' court services. For example, the domestic violence protocol in London Borough 2 provided guidance for staff coming into contact with women and children experiencing domestic violence. It included a section specifically concerned with protecting children. In the other authority (Metropolitan Borough 2) a guide to sharing personal client information in different circumstances and within different agencies had been developed. Although the main focus of this document was dealing with anti-social behaviour, it also covered child protection issues, domestic violence and the misuse of drugs and alcohol.

Summary points

- A range of plans, procedures and joint protocols were scrutinised to identify what was available to support inter-agency working and identify innovative practice.

- The plans, procedures and joint protocols were generally dated and regularly reviewed (90% of cases); the relationship with other relevant policies, procedures, guidance and plans was clearly stated in 70 per cent of cases, and they were written in easily accessible language in 76.7 per cent of instances. Just over half (56.7%) showed evidence that findings from research or inquiries had been influential in developing the plan. However, less than a third (30%) showed evidence of ownership from senior management and frontline practitioners and in only 23.3 per cent of cases was the plan readily available to all relevant persons.

- The ACPC business plan in only three of the six authorities addressed the issue of children and families affected by domestic violence or parental substance misuse. These authorities differed in their approach. One was working to improve the links between children's services, the domestic violence forum and the drug action team. Another had developed a shared domestic violence protocol and was working to improve information systems to identify links between child protection, domestic violence and parental substance misuse. The third authority was working towards developing more services to support children living with domestic violence or parental substance misuse.

- The domestic violence forum plan in five of the six local authorities specifically addressed the issue of children living in families where there was evidence of domestic violence. A number of the plans highlighted innovative initiatives aimed at, for example, raising public awareness, or establishing specific projects to support children exposed to domestic violence.

- The drug and alcohol team plan includes four separate plans: a Community Plan, a Treatment Plan, a Young People's Plan and an Availability Plan. Although the Community Plan and the Young People's Plan are the most relevant for children living with parental substance misuse only one of the four Community Plans, and two of the four Young People's Plans (available to the research team) covered the issue. The Community Plan that covered children living with substance misusing parents offered an example of innovative practice with the development of a substance misuse project that provided specific encouragement to parents to engage with treatment and help to prevent relapse. The primarily focus of local authorities' Young People's Plans is young drug users although two included aims to support the needs of children affected by parental substance misuse.

- The primary focus of the Crime and Disorder Reduction Strategy/Community Safety Plan is tackling crime and disorder and drug problems. Although most included objectives related to supporting victims of domestic violence, few made specific reference to children and/or covered children living with parental substance misuse. The Children's Services Plan (replaced in 2005 by the Children and Young People's Plan) were more likely to make provision for children living with domestic violence, than those living with parental substance misuse. Three plans covered domestic violence whereas only one covered parental substance misuse. Innovative use of short term Government funding was found in one authority; one Government initiative was used to finance innovative work with children affected by domestic violence and another

Government initiative to develop work with children living with substance misusing parents. However, these initiatives will need to be incorporated into core funding arrangements to survive.

• ACPC procedures did not always cover domestic violence and parental substance misuse adequately. Three ACPC procedures dealt with each of these issues very briefly. In the other three local authorities the ACPC procedures or separate linked documents provided sound information on the implications for children of domestic violence and linked this to the child protection process. In only one authority did the ACPC procedures include information on parental substance misuse.

• In half the authorities procedures and guidance for practitioners working with children and families affected by domestic violence have been developed by a specific organisation or group of organisations such as the Domestic Violence Forum, or jointly by the local Community Safety Partnership, the regional police force and a local voluntary domestic violence service. There was no evidence of similar guidance and procedures in relation to children living with parents with problem alcohol or drug use having been produced.

• The procedures produced by domestic violence services and drug and alcohol services did not routinely cover how to deal with concerns about children's safety and welfare. Nonetheless, there were individual examples of innovative practice. For example, a local women's refuge in one authority had produced a number of helpful procedural documents for staff and residents. In another local authority a voluntary drug service provided staff with clear and concise procedures that refer specifically to working with substance misusing parents ensuring links are made with the child protection system.

• Joint protocols for information sharing did not routinely cover domestic violence and parental substance misuse. When joint protocols were developed for working with children living with domestic violence or parental substance misuse they were generally restricted to a few specific agencies and rarely included all relevant services.

Chapter 7

Training

Policies, procedures and practice guidance alone will not result in the desired changes to professional practice unless they are underpinned by a comprehensive training programme.

> Professionals who work primarily with children may need training to recognise and identify parents' problems and the effect these may have on children. Equally, training for professionals working with adults should cover the impact parental problems may have on children. Joint training between adults and children staff can be useful. (Department of Health *et al.* 1999, p.11, paragraph 2.26)

This chapter explores the confidence with which managers and practitioners approach working with children and families where there is evidence of domestic violence or parental substance misuse. Particular attention is given to the impact of training and how training could be improved.

The findings are based on data from three sources: the Area Child Protection Committee (ACPC) annual training plans, manager questionnaires, and trainer questionnaires. These data are used to explore:

- training plans
- training opportunities
- the impact of training on knowledge
- knowledge of child protection procedures
- barriers to training
- supporting training.

Managers from a range of services in all six local authorities and trainers from three authorities returned questionnaires to the research team. The number from each authority and professional group are shown in Table 7.1.

Table 7.1 The number of questionnaires broken down by authority and professional group

Authority		Professional group	(n = 82)
Metropolitan Borough 1	10	Police managers	5
Metropolitan Borough 2	12	Health managers	22
Shire County 1	19	Substance misuse managers	17
Shire County 2	20	Housing managers	3
London Borough 1	13	First line children's social care manager's	5
London Borough 2	8	Senior children's social care managers	13
		Domestic violence managers	12
		Trainers	5

The trainer group included three ACPC trainers, one child care trainer and an education child protection trainer. All the trainers had been involved in training practitioners on domestic violence and three had also been involved in substance misuse training during the past three years.

Training plans

> The ACPC is responsible for taking a strategic overview of the planning, delivery and evaluation of the inter-agency training that is required in order to promote effective practice to safeguard the welfare of children. (Department of Health *et al.* 1999, p.98, paragraph 9.9)

The ACPC (now Local Safeguarding Children Board) training plan is by its nature a multi-agency document and should reflect this in the range of subjects covered and trainers used. The research team was given access to training documents in the six authorities. These documents included brief timetables of courses as well as extensive and strategic training plans. The aim of the scrutiny was to identify whether training plans covered domestic violence and parental substance misuse, as well as the multi-agency nature of the training.

The extent to which local authority ACPC training plans cover domestic violence and parental substance misuse

Local authorities in their ACPC training plans for 2002–2003 took different approaches to providing training about the impact of domestic violence and parental substance misuse on children within the family. Some plans suggested the issues had a high profile within the authority while others indicated that they were not currently a priority.

DOMESTIC VIOLENCE

The ACPC plans in four of the six local authorities included training on domestic violence. In the other two authorities the training plans for 2002–3 did not make mention of any training on these issues.

When ACPC training plans included training on domestic violence the amount of training differed between the authorities; ranging between 4.5 days' to 1 day's training. For example, Metropolitan Borough 1 provided 4 days of multi-agency training on domestic violence every year. In addition, the domestic violence forum in this authority made a considerable contribution through providing in-house specialist packages of training, holding regular road show events on domestic violence, and routinely contributing to the ACPC training events.

In two other local authorities the ACPC training plan also indicated considerable time had been devoted to multi-agency training on domestic violence. For example, in Shire County 1, the plan indicated that a two-day course had been held twice during the study year and in Metropolitan Borough 2, a two-day course and two half-day courses were included in the plan.

The ACPC training plan in the fourth authority (London Borough 2) showed that a one day course focusing on Domestic Violence and the Welfare of Children had been planned. In addition, the Children and Families Service training programme aimed at children's social care managers, included a one-day policy forum concerning domestic violence.

PARENTAL SUBSTANCE MISUSE

Three of the ACPC training plans that included domestic violence also planned for training on substance misuse and one authority (London Borough 1) provided training on substance misuse, though none was provided on domestic violence.

Although domestic violence and substance misuse were issues covered by the same number of local authorities' ACPC training plans, domestic violence received more extensive training. For example, no ACPC training plan provided for more than a two-day course on substance misuse. The ACPC training planned on substance misuse in Metropolitan Borough 2 was two days, in London Borough 2 two half-day courses, and in London Borough 1 a single half-day course. Moreover, in Metropolitan Borough 1 training on substance misuse was not included in the training plan each year.

The ACPC plans also indicated that local authorities took different app-roaches to the delivery of multi-agency training. For example, some authorities utilised the skills of professionals working in specialist services. For example, the ACPC plans in two authorities (Shire County 1 and Metropolitan Borough 2), make reference to using a range of professionals to underpin the multi-agency aspect of their training including representatives from health, education, proba-tion, children's social care, the local authority legal department, services for sub-stance misuse and for domestic violence. In other authorities a different approach was taken and ACPC plans indicate that training was provided by a multi-agency trainer.

Training opportunities

The experience of managers from services other than substance misuse and domestic violence (n = 35)

Managers were more likely to attend training on domestic violence and child pro-tection procedures than on parental substance misuse and child protection proce-dures. More than two-thirds of managers (68.6%) from police, health, housing and first line children's social care reported having received training on domestic violence and child protection procedures during the past four years, compared with approximately half (54.3%) having received training in relation to parental substance misuse and child protection procedures. This reflects the difference in emphasis found within the ACPC plans on providing training on substance misuse. Managers thought the most effective way of ensuring practitioners understood the issues and their impact on children, and the roles and responsibil-ities of other services was through joint training.

> The purpose of training for inter-agency work is to help develop and foster the following, in order to achieve better outcomes for children and young people:
> o   a shared understanding of the tasks, processes, principles, and roles and responsibilities outlined in national guidance and local arrangements for safeguarding children and promoting their welfare
> o   more effective and integrated services at both the strategic and individual case level
> o   improved communication between professionals, including a common understanding of key terms, definitions and thresholds for action
> o   effective working relationships, including an ability to work in multi-disciplinary groups or teams
> o   sound decision making based on information sharing, thorough assessment, critical analysis and professional judgement.
>
> (HM Government 2006a, pp.91–2, paragraph 4.3)

The reports from managers and the ACPC training plans suggest that most of the training had been open to all relevant agencies, a decision appreciated by managers.

> Training should be multi-agency on methods of how to work with children affected by domestic violence or parental substance misuse. (Senior children's social care manager – London Borough 2)

Except for children's social care line managers, all of whom had recently received training on child protection procedures, those managers who had not undertaken such training came from a range of services. For example, three of the five police, half the health managers, and two of the three housing managers had received no recent training on child protection procedures.

These are matters that should be addressed urgently by the newly introduced Local Safeguarding Children Boards. All managers from relevant agencies should receive training on child protection procedures because they are crucial to the effective implementation of good systems, and of monitoring and supervising the work of practitioners. The importance of ensuring not only managers but also their teams receive the relevant training is reinforced by managers from the health and police services reporting that, to their knowledge, only a proportion of their staff group had attended training during the past 4 years on domestic violence and child protection procedures (40%) or parental substance misuse and child protection procedures (30%).

The experience of managers from substance misuse and domestic violence services (n = 30)

Well over three-quarters (84.6%) of domestic violence managers said they had received training on the impact of domestic violence on children's development and just over two-thirds (69.2%) had attended training on child protection procedures in the past four years.

Training for managers of substance misuse services was not as prevalent. Practically two-thirds (64.7%) of substance misuse managers reported that they had received training on the impact of parental substance misuse on children's development and approximately half (52.9%) reported having received training on child protection procedures.

The disparity between the training received by managers of these specialist services was reflected in the training provided to their staff group. Managers of services for domestic violence reported that to their knowledge practically half (46.2%) of their team had received training regarding the impact on children's development and well over three-quarters (85.7%) on child protection procedures. A similar mirroring of managers' experiences was found within substance misuse services, managers reporting that to their knowledge 44.4 per cent of their team had received training on the impact on children of parental substance misuse but only 58.8 per cent had received training on child protection procedures.

As would be expected managers and staff from these specialist services are more likely to receive training on the impact of parental substance misuse and domestic violence on children, than managers in services that have a wider remit, such as health, education and the police.

The amount of training

When managers had received training on the impact of parental substance misuse or domestic violence on children's development, this was generally no more than one or two days. Managers attended less training on the impact of parental substance misuse on children's development than domestic violence. For example, half the managers reported attending only one day's training on parental substance misuse compared with 29 per cent whose training on domestic violence was done in a single day. This reflects the greater emphasis ACPC training plans gave to domestic violence than to parental substance misuse, both in relation to holding a course at all and the length of the training.

When significantly more training had been received this was associated with attending degree courses or with managers themselves being involved in the delivery of training. For example, two managers, one from a substance misuse agency and the other from a domestic violence agency, had helped to deliver the training courses.

> Delivering training ensures that one is up to date with most issues. (Domestic violence manager – Metropolitan Borough 2)

Another manager, from a domestic violence agency, had been taking an MA module which had included training on the impact of domestic violence on children.

All the managers expressed satisfaction with the training they had received with practically three-quarters reporting that they found it very useful.

Consistent with local policy and best practice

It is important that training is consistent with local policies, procedures and best practice. Twenty-seven managers provided information on this issue. Most managers (70.6%) reported that the training they had received on parental substance misuse and domestic violence had been consisted with local policy and best practice. The majority of the remaining managers thought the training had been consistent to some extent and only three thought it had been totally inconsistent with local policy and best practice. A scrutiny of the local authority and the type of agency these managers came from revealed no trends.

Training linked to a specific initiative

The introduction of new initiatives, procedures or guidelines can be accompanied by specific training events. The managers' reports suggest that the launch of new initiatives etc was responsible for a third (35.7%) of the training on parental substance misuse and 44.4 per cent of the training they had attended on domestic violence.

The initiatives to which training had been linked related to safeguarding and promoting the welfare of children, working with domestic violence, or to tackling the rise in illicit drug use:

- Launch of our authority's domestic abuse forum.

- ACPC policy and procedures.

- Assessment Framework and new procedures.

- Launch of 'safeguarding and promoting the welfare of children in need' in the authority.

- The first local clinical guidance for domestic violence.

- Inter-agency strategy for tackling substance misuse in response to influx of crack in area.

- Assessment Framework and update training. Half-day all agencies.

These illustrations suggest that there have been few new initiatives with linked training events directly related to working with children who live with substance misusing parents.

The impact of training on knowledge

Managers were asked to describe their understanding of the impact of parental substance misuse and domestic violence on children's development. They rated their understanding as either (a) good, they had received sufficient training; (b) adequate, they would find more training helpful; or (c) poor, they felt that more training was necessary.

Managers of services other than domestic violence or substance misuse

Table 7.2 shows how police, health, housing and first line children's social care managers rated their understanding.

Table 7.2 Managers' levels of understanding of the impact of parental substance misuse and domestic violence on children's development

	Impact of parental substance misuse	Impact of domestic violence
Good – sufficient training	45.5% (15/33)	60.6% (20/33)
Adequate – some more training helpful	45.5% (15/33)	33.3% (11/33)
Poor – some more training necessary	9.1% (3/33)	6.1% (2/33)

The figures show that managers thought they had a better understanding of the impact of domestic violence on children's development than they had of substance misuse; 60.6 per cent of managers felt they had sufficient training on the impact of domestic violence compared with only 45.5 per cent for substance misuse. This difference reflects the greater emphasis ACPC training plans gave to domestic violence, and the higher proportion of managers who had attended training on domestic violence.

A detailed scrutiny of the data gives additional weight to the notion that training is key to managers' knowledge and confidence in working with these cases. For example, in two authorities (Metropolitan Borough 2 and Shire County 1) the ACPC training plan indicated that 2 days' training was provided on domestic violence; in these authorities a greater proportion of managers rated as good their understanding of how domestic violence impacts on children (90%). The obverse was also true. In one authority (Shire County 2) ACPC training plans indicated no training on domestic violence and in this authority only 27.3 per cent of managers rated their understanding of domestic violence as good, over half (54.5%) thought more training would be helpful, and 18 per cent rated their understanding as poor.

Given the connection between alcohol misuse, domestic violence and child protection it is of concern that over half the managers (54.5%) wanted more training on parental substance misuse, and 39.4 per cent wanted more training on domestic violence; over a third of managers (36.4%) wanted more training on both issues. This finding has particular significance for line managers, given their critical role in implementing policy, monitoring practitioners' work, identifying training needs, and supporting inter-agency working.

These findings suggest that the recommendations that arose from the Advisory Council Inquiry Report to the Home Office (2003) have yet to be fully implemented. The report recommends appropriate training for staff in a range of agencies, including health, education, police and children's social care in relation to problem drug and alcohol use and its impact on children. For example, in relation to maternity services the report is robust about the need for training.

> The medical, midwifery, social work and other staff involved in the woman's care require accurate knowledge about and appropriate attitudes to drug use and its consequences for the pregnancy and the future child. They also need sufficient training and experience to do the right things well. (Home Office 2003, p.73, paragraph 7.8)

The amount of training provided in particular local authorities was reflected in practitioners' awareness and understanding of the subject. Managers of services for domestic violence in two authorities reported that practitioners from other agencies were not adequately trained on the complexity of domestic violence and this affected inter-agency working; in these authorities the ACPC training did not cover domestic violence or was very brief – one day.

> Inter-agency working is helped when practitioners have an 'awareness of the complex issues surrounding domestic abuse'. (Domestic violence manager NSPCC – Shire County 2)

> Inter-agency working is helped when practitioners have 'some understanding of domestic violence and risk issues and that victims are not doing it for a laugh'. (Domestic violence manager probation – London Borough 2)

However, even when ACPC training plans indicate multi-agency training is provided this may not always achieve its aim. A range of factors, which are discussed later in this chapter, may prevent staff from attending. The difficulty of meeting the needs for training is highlighted by the report from a substance misuse service manager in an authority where the ACPC training plan indicated a two-day course was provided on substance misuse.

> Other agencies need to have a better knowledge and understanding about our client group and the process of drug treatment services. (Substance misuse manager – Metropolitan Borough 2)

Managers from domestic violence services and children's social care thought that training needed to be more robust in highlighting the links between domestic violence, substance misuse and the safeguarding and welfare of children within the household.

> It is not sufficiently recognised that domestic abuse really always means child abuse – it is seen separately. Domestic abuse in itself is child abuse and also where a women is being abused it is probable that the children are also – a violent

household – this is not recognised sufficiently. (Domestic violence manager probation – Shire County 2)

There needs to be more integration of health and social services and education recognising the effect and risks that domestic violence has on children. There is a risk of the effect of domestic violence on children being mis-diagnosed. (Domestic violence manager – Shire County 1)

There is a correlation between child welfare and abuse and drugs, alcohol misuse and domestic violence. Need to tackle these issues collectively and not in isolation. (Senior children's social care – Metropolitan Borough 2)

Managers of services for domestic violence and substance misuse

Overall, managers working in agencies providing services for domestic violence or substance misuse reported a better understanding of how the problems of their client group impacted on children within the household; a finding that reflects the greater emphasis on training on this subject in these specialist services. For example, all the managers of domestic violence services, involved in the research, assessed their understanding of how domestic violence impacted on children's development as good. It can be recalled that 84.6 per cent reported that they had attended training on these issues.

The impact of training is also found for managers in substance misuse services. Practically two-thirds (64.7%) thought they had a good understanding of how parental substance misuse impacts on children's development – the same group who reported having attended recent training that covered these issues. Over a third of substance misuse managers wanted more training on this issue. The tendency to focus less on the children of parents with problem drug or alcohol use when training on substance misuse reflects the traditional focus of substance misuse services – providing a confidential service that focuses on the needs of adult users. The impact of substance misuse on children and other family members is not generally addressed, and the commitment to confidentiality can create difficulties for information sharing when there are concerns about the welfare of children in the household (see Chapter 3 for more detailed findings on confidentiality).

The lack of appropriate training and resources for workers from specialist drug agencies was highlighted in the Advisory Council Inquiry report *Hidden Harm: Responding to the Needs of Children of Problem Drug Users* (Home Office 2003).

Although 75 per cent of the specialist drug agencies said they had contact with pregnant drug users, and inevitably all would have at least some clients with

> children, only about half offered services that were specifically designed to help pregnant women or drug users with children, and less than one-third offered any form of service for the children themselves. This seems far from satisfactory. Only about a third of agencies offered any training for staff about clients' pregnancy or children. This suggests that very few agencies have the know-how to understand these issues, let alone the resources to address them. (Home Office 2003, p.55)

The report goes on to recommend:

> The training of staff in drug and alcohol agencies should include a specific focus on learning how to assess and meet the needs of clients as parents and their children. (Home Office 2003, p.84)

The findings from the current study would suggest that these recommendations need to be addressed. In establishing the Local Safeguarding Children Boards local authorities have an opportunity, under s13 (5) to include representatives of drug and alcohol services on the Board.

> A Local Safeguarding Children Board established under this section may also include representatives of such other relevant persons or bodies as the authority by which it is established consider, after consulting their Board partners, should be represented on it. (Children Act 2004, s13 (5))

Knowledge of child protection procedures

> At training courses it becomes obvious that various agencies are unsure of the procedure to follow when there are child welfare concerns. (Domestic violence manager – Metropolitan Borough 2)

Managers were asked to describe how well they understood the use of child protection procedures in cases involving parental substance misuse or domestic violence. They rated their understanding as either (a) good, they had received sufficient training: (b) adequate, they would find more training helpful; or (c) poor, they felt that more training was necessary.

Managers of services other than domestic violence or substance misuse

The responses from police, health, housing and first line children's social care managers are shown in Table 7.3.

The data show no difference in how managers classed their understanding of child protection procedures for cases involving domestic violence or parental substance misuse.

Table 7.3 Managers' understanding of child protection procedures

	In cases involving parental substance misuse	In cases involving domestic violence
Good – sufficient training	69.7% (23/33)	69.7% (23/33)
Adequate – some more training helpful	27.3% (9/33)	27.3% (9/33)
Poor – some more training necessary	3.0% (1/33)	3.0% (1/33)

Only one manager (housing) felt that his or her understanding of the use of child protection procedures in cases involving domestic violence and parental substance misuse was poor and more training was essential. However, it is of concern that practically a third (30%) of managers thought more training would be helpful or necessary. All but one of the six children's social care line managers reported that they had a good understanding of how child protection procedures related to children in cases of domestic violence and parental substance misuse; the remaining line manager wanted more training specifically in relation to parental substance misuse.

The extent to which managers understood the use of child protection procedures reflects the amount of training they had received. Those who had attended recent training reported their understanding of how to apply child protection procedures in cases involving parental substance misuse or domestic violence was good.

A good understanding of child protection procedures is essential to managers working in these areas. A key aspect of the manager's role is to supervise their staff and make decisions of what to do when there are concerns about the safety and welfare of children. Although Government Guidance (HM Government 2006d) is available, nonetheless training on child protection procedures is essential to ensure managers and practitioners have the knowledge and confidence to act appropriately when concerns about children arise.

Managers of services for domestic violence or substance misuse

Managers of domestic violence services were more aware of child protection procedures, than managers of substance misuse services. The findings show that 83.3 per cent of domestic violence service managers classed their understanding of using child protection procedures as good compared with 58.8 per cent of managers in services for substance misuse.

Generally, those managers who felt they had a good understanding of the impact of parental substance misuse or domestic violence on children's development also felt they understood the use of child protection procedures in their work, and the opposite equally applied. Moreover, a greater proportion of managers in substance misuse services reported a need for additional training in relation to children than did managers in domestic violence services. This reinforces the recommendation of the Home Office (2003) to ensure staff in drug and alcohol services are adequately trained so that they are able to assess the needs of children. The findings also go some way to substantiating the experience of children's social care that substance misuse managers are not always fully engaged with child protection and welfare issues.

> Drug workers rarely attend child protection conferences. There are issues around prioritising children's welfare above adults. (Senior children's social care manager – Metropolitan Borough 1)

Barriers to training

The reports from managers and trainers about the issues that stood in the way of training could in the main be categorised under three headings:

- Time to attend training.
- Availability of training.
- Funding.

Time to attend training

Not being able to take time off from their day-to-day tasks to attend training was a reason given by a number of managers to account for practitioners' non-attendance.

> Due to work commitments in my previous role as a health visitor I was unable to attend workshops on domestic violence. I have attended training on substance misuse. (Health manager – Shire County 2)

> It is difficult getting staff to attend courses, they are not being allowed or can not take time off to attend due to staff shortages and work pressures. (Domestic violence manager – Shire County 1)

Some managers, whose work commitments prevented them attending specific training events, attempted to keep themselves up to date on emerging research findings and new policies and guidance through other means.

I have not attended any training specific in these two areas but have read every-thing that has crossed my desk and visit the internet every week seeking information related to child protection e.g. *Hidden Harm.* (Health manager – Shire County 2)

Availability of training

The other most frequently given reason why managers and practitioners had not attended training was a lack of available courses. In some authorities the ACPC plans indicated that training was not provided on domestic violence or substance misuse. As a manager in one of the authorities, where courses on substance misuse were not part of the ACPC training plan reported:

Specific training should be given but has not yet been developed. (Health Manager – Shire County 1)

The lack of suitable training opportunities to learn about domestic violence and parental substance misuse was raised by managers from a range of different agencies.

I would have welcomed some training in these issues but I am not aware of any being offered. (Housing manager – Shire County 2)

There is never enough training in domestic violence or substance misuse to meet all health staff requirements. (Health manager – London Borough 2)

More places should be made available to those not working within social services. (Domestic violence manager – Metropolitan Borough 2)

The wish for more training should be seen within the wider context. Reports from trainers suggest that they experience difficulty in putting on training events because of a shortage of trainers specialising in parental substance misuse.

It would be useful if information could be provided about good quality trainers who combine both an expertise about the subjects as well as excellent presenta-tional skills. It has been particularly difficult to find anyone to fit this bill re: sub-stance misuse. We have not re-run this course, despite an identified need because we were not able to find a skilled trainer. (Trainer – Shire County 1)

Funding

Managers providing services for domestic violence and substance misuse felt insufficient funding was being ear-marked for training on their area of work.

It is a vital part of a professional person's life to receive adequate domestic violence training. This is important irrespective of their discipline, for example line managers have a responsibility to staff to be aware. This area of training is grossly under funded. (Domestic violence manager – Metropolitan Borough 2)

The local training is co-ordinated and we are asked to provide free training for a range of staff. It is impossible for alcohol agencies to do this work without funding... Not sustainable...limited by capacity in alcohol services. On occasion social services have used non-specialist trainers and I do not feel this answers the need. (Substance misuse manager – Shire County 1)

Resources, funding and statutory agencies' attitudes sometimes get in the way of them accessing training from the independent sector. (Domestic violence manager – Shire County 2)

Supporting training

Senior children's social care managers and trainers suggested a number of ways staff awareness and knowledge about substance misuse and domestic abuse could be improved.

Ensuring sufficient time and resources

In line with the views of managers from other services, senior managers in children's social care stressed the importance of ensuring practitioners and line managers were enabled to attend and reflect on what they had learnt, and that sufficient resources were in place to provide the relevant training.

Time for staff to take part in training. Time for staff reflection. (Senior children's social care manager – Shire County 1)

Social workers not accessing training due to turnover, caseloads, absence and vacancy rates. (Senior children's social care manager – London Borough 1)

There is a gap here but our business plan includes the development of training on substance misuse. (Senior children's social care manager – Metropolitan Borough 1)

Our training section has been broken up – there is no training section now... There is some basic training going on with very few people to do it. (Senior children's social care manager – Shire County 1)

Domestic violence – working with fathers/perpetrators we've neglected this. (Senior children's social care manager – London Borough 1)

Linked and joint training

A further suggestion to improve staff awareness and increase training provision was to link different training initiatives together.

It should and could be linked with other training initiatives i.e. child abuse training – and both linked to each other. (Senior children's social care manager – Metropolitan Borough 2)

Senior managers thought that joint training for practitioners working in adult and children's services would improve their understanding of each others' roles and responsibilities and support working relationships.

> Must be joint with adult services. Significantly different perspective to cover – adult and child. (Senior children's social care manager – London Borough 1)

> Should be done jointly with adult services where possible and other council divisions such as housing. (Senior children's social care manager – London Borough 1)

It is important when considering which agencies to include in child protection training events that all relevant services for adults are included; the remit needs to be wider than adult social services and include, for example, housing, probation as well as services for domestic violence, drugs and alcohol.

Targeting training

The reports from trainers suggest that some agencies are more difficult to engage in multi-agency training events than others. In particular practitioners from the health service such as GPs, housing, education, police and adult social services are less likely to attend training than are practitioners from children's social care and health visiting. For example, a multi-agency training course focusing on domestic violence and child protection procedures, run by one trainer was attended by 35 staff from children's social care, 30 from health visiting, 25 from the voluntary sector, five each from education, housing and the police, and no one from adult social services, drug and alcohol services, YOT or probation.

Trainers tried a number of different approaches to draw in these 'hard to engage' services; some were found to be more successful than others. For example, one trainer had moved the training to outside office hours but found this had little effect.

> Medical staff are a problem – reluctant to attend. Police often not released from their duties. Education same to a lesser extent. We offered evening and weekend courses to these people but they still did not attend. (Trainer – Shire County 1)

Another initiative was to directly target an agency.

> Directly invite housing managers to send staff. Encourage managers from other statutory agencies to 'lobby' housing to attend. Statutory requirement for training would also help. (Trainer – Shire County 2)

> Offer more courses funded by domestic violence forum. Offer single agency 'Roadshows' as 'tasters'. Ensure trainers are well prepared and co-ordinated. Create info. 'flyers' explaining what this issue has to do with target group. Target

> officer/decision makers to inform them of training opportunities. Offer 'tailor made' courses at a negotiated time/place. (Trainer – Metropolitan Borough 1)

> Higher priority promoting courses within specific agencies. (Trainer – Shire County 1)

The report of one trainer suggests that direct targeting and single agency training can be successful.

> The course was intended primarily for education staff. We were happy with the uptake. (Trainer – Shire County 1)

To combat low attendance some managers thought that training on domestic violence and substance misuse should be mandatory for practitioners working in key organisations.

> Domestic violence training should be made mandatory for social workers (very low turn out on the yearly ACPC course). The course also has a low turnout of teachers – they need to be more inclusive. (Domestic violence manager – London Borough 2)

> Training should be two-way, for example social care staff need training re substance misuse. I have provided this in the past on a number of occasions but feel the input should be managed so that it is mandatory and consistent rather than ad hoc and reactive. (Substance misuse manager – Shire County 1)

Auditing and monitoring

Finally, senior managers in children's social care recognised the need to improve their processes of auditing and monitoring training.

> It has become quite apparent from talking to you that we need to know what there is in our authority, what is available, what it does, how effective it is and if there is enough of it. We need a sort of audit of training. It is difficult to know if people's practice has changed. You can write all of the policies and strategies but unless you go out and monitor and audit people you do not know how effective it is. (Senior children's social care – Shire County 1)

The audit of training requirements should be an integral part of managers' responsibilities, and not left to sometimes remote training sections which have little connection with operational processes. The findings from auditing and monitoring the training practitioners receive should inform future training plans. Managers need to work in partnership with training sections to ensure the training meets the needs of practitioners.

Whatever the reason for some of the managers and staff not having received training *Working Together to Safeguard Children* (HM Government 2006a) clearly states that it is the responsibility of employers to resource and support training, including giving employees time off to attend.

Employers also have a responsibility to identify adequate resources and support inter-agency training by:

- providing staff who have the relevant expertise to support the Local Safeguarding Children Board (LSCB) e.g. by sitting on an LSCB training sub-group, and/or contributing to training)
- allocating the time required to complete inter-agency training tasks effectively
- releasing staff to attend the appropriate inter-agency training courses
- ensuring that staff receive relevant single-agency training that enables them to maximise the learning derived from inter-agency training, and have opportunities to consolidate learning from inter-agency training; and contributing to the planning, resourcing, delivery and evaluation of training.

(HM Government, 2006a p.92, paragraph 4.6)

The reports from managers and trainers suggest that training on domestic violence and parental substance misuse is given a relatively low priority in terms of resource allocation, and is perceived as an adjunct to service delivery as opposed to an integral part of providing a quality service. Training should be seen as part of a continuing process of practitioners' and managers' professional and operational development. It should become embedded into the culture of every relevant organisation.

Summary points

- ACPC training plans provided more training on domestic violence than on parental substance misuse.

- A significant proportion of managers (excluding services for domestic violence and substance misuse) had not recently attended training on domestic violence or substance misuse. Attending training on domestic violence was more common than on substance misuse.

- Practitioners in services for domestic violence were more likely to have attended training on how the issues their clients experience affect children's development and specific training on child protection, than practitioners in alcohol or drug services.

- Managers' understanding of the impact of domestic violence and parental substance misuse on children's development was associated with the whether their authority provided relevant training. Managers who had a good understanding of the subject were from authorities where ACPC training plans had included this in their training calendar. Of concern was the finding that over half the managers, from services other than domestic violence or substance misuse, wanted more training on parental substance misuse and over a third wanted more training on domestic violence.

- All the managers in services for domestic violence reported that they understood how domestic violence impacted on children. However, a third of managers in alcohol and drug services wanted more training on how parental substance misuse affected children.

- Two-thirds of managers (excluding services for domestic violence and substance misuse) understood how child protection procedures were to be applied in cases where children lived with domestic violence or parental substance misuse. Most managers in services for domestic violence also classed their understanding as good. However, many managers in services for substance misuse wanted more training on child protection procedures. Again managers' understanding was found to be linked to training.

- Barriers that hampered staff training, included: time to attend the training, availability of the courses, and funding.

- Training was supported by: ensuring sufficient time and resources were available, providing linked and joint training (multi-agency and joint adult and children's services training), targeting training on practitioners from agencies that are 'hard to engage', and auditing and monitoring training. Auditing and monitoring training enables gaps to be identified and future training to be better targeted to meet the needs of practitioners.

- Training on the impact of domestic violence and parental substance misuse on children's development and training on child protection procedures should be given a higher priority. It should be seen as an integral part of the professional and operational development of practitioners and managers.

Chapter 8

Conclusions and Implications for Policy and Practice

There is a considerable body of research which shows the vulnerability of children who live with domestic violence and/or parental alcohol or drug misuse. Not only are children's health and development likely to be negatively affected, but the problems parents themselves experience influence their capacity to meet the basic needs of their children. Moreover, domestic violence and parental substance misuse are often associated with difficulties in family functioning, housing, income and social integration. This multiplicity of problems will frequently require different agencies, from both children and adult services, to collaborate in order to provide a co-ordinated approach to the provision of services.

Unfortunately, when children experience serious injury or death innumerable government inquiries have shown a failure of agencies to work together; an issue forcibly raised in the 2003 *Victoria Climbié Inquiry Report* (Cm 5730). In response the Government introduced The Children Act (2004) and a suite of accompanying guidance to support better inter-agency collaboration.

The study on which this book is based was commissioned under the Government's *Quality Protects* research programme, Objective 2 *Protection from Significant Harm*. The focus of the research is children referred to Children's Social Services (which became Children's Social Care after the implementation of The Children Act 2004) where there are concerns of domestic violence and/or parental substance misuse. The report describes the extent to which services work together, identifies factors that support collaborative working, and explores what aspects of the services provided to families parents find helpful. In undertaking the work a number of methods have been applied including a scrutiny of the protocols, policies, and working practices used by relevant agencies, a survey of practitioners working in these agencies, a study of social work case files, and interviews with a small group of parents and their key workers.

Conclusions

Source of the referral

To understand the response of children's social care when children are referred because concerns for their safety and welfare are linked with domestic violence and/or parental substance misuse, 357 relevant social work case files were examined.

This exercise showed that children's social care became aware of the children and their families in a variety of ways. For example, children were referred by professionals such as health visitors or the police, or the child or parent themselves asked for help. In over a quarter of cases the referral had originated from more than one source, such as the health visitor *and* the police, or a nursery worker *and* the parent, both making a referral because of similar concerns.

Non-professionals, such as the child, parent or neighbours were partly or wholly responsible for bringing a quarter of cases to the attention of children's social care, but in most instances children were referred by professionals. Although referrals emanated from a variety of agencies, the police were responsible for half of all cases included in the sample. Many police forces when called to attend an incident of domestic violence where a child is present, automatically notify children's social care. As a result local authorities felt they were in danger of being overwhelmed by the number of police notifications relating to domestic violence.

Parents were not always aware that their child had been referred to children's social care. Government guidance is clear that practitioners who have concerns about a child's welfare should discuss these with the child (taking into account their age and understanding) and their parents and seek their consent to making the referral to children's social care, unless to do so would place the child at risk of significant harm (HM Government 2006d). In over half the cases (57.2%) practitioners had discussed their concerns with parents before referring the child to children's social care. The apparent reluctance of practitioners in practically half the cases to raise concerns with parents about their children before making a referral may reflect the need for more training on child protection procedures identified by managers.

The response of children's social care

The way the sample was selected meant that referrals to children's social care must have been acted on to get included in the study; it is of interest that practically half were re-referrals. As a result of the current referral three-quarters resulted in an initial assessment, a quarter in a core assessment, approximately a fifth in a strategy meeting, a fifth in s47 enquiries being undertaken, and a third in an initial child protection conference.

The case files suggest that in carrying out their duties children's social care did not always follow government guidance (Department of Health *et al.* 2000; Department of Health *et al.* 1999). For example, all cases resulting in an initial child protection conference should have been preceded by s47 enquiries (the purpose of which is to decide whether the authority should take any action to safeguard or promote the child's welfare) and a core assessment (which is the means by which a s47 enquiry is carried out).

The records held on the case files, however, showed that in some cases there was no evidence that a core assessment had been started at the point the s47 enquiries were initiated or indeed by the time an initial child protection conference was held. A scrutiny of the findings for individual authorities showed great variation ranging from one authority where all s47 enquiries were accompanied by a core assessment to another where a core assessment was found on only 16 per cent of cases where s47 enquiries were made. At the time of the research the participating authorities were at different stages in their implementation of the Assessment Framework. The findings suggest government guidance is more likely to be adhered to once the Assessment Framework has become embedded into day to day practice.

The scrutiny of the social work case files provided valuable insights into the circumstances of children living with domestic violence and/or parental substance misuse. For example, three-quarters of children had unmet needs in at least one area of their development, 85 per cent were living with parents who were not able to undertake all key parenting tasks, and the wider family and environment were having a negative impact on most children (87.5%). Indeed, a fifth of cases were classified by the research team as *multiple-problem* (that is children had severe needs in relation to all three domains: developmental needs *and* parenting capacity *and* family and environmental factors).

A key factor in their vulnerability was the co-morbidity of issues confronting the family. Many families experienced a combination of domestic violence, parental alcohol or drug misuse, mental illness and learning disability. Domestic violence and parental substance misuse rarely existed in isolation. A quarter of children were living in families where there was evidence of both domestic violence and parental substance misuse, a further quarter where parents had poor mental health, and in 10 per cent of cases a parent had physical or learning disabilities. When domestic violence and parental drug or alcohol misuse coexisted the effect on all aspects of children's lives was more serious.

With the extent and intensity of children's needs being revealed by the initial assessment, it is reassuring to find that in three-quarters of cases the initial assessment led to some form of action being taken. In cases that resulted in no further action ($n = 62$) the findings from the initial assessment did not always appear to justify the decision. For example, 38 of the 62 children (61.3%) were shown to have severe needs in relation either to the child's development, parenting capacity or family and environmental factors; two of which had severe needs in all three domains. This raises the question of whether children identified by children's social care as 'in need' being left unsupported and unmonitored in families who are unable to adequately safeguard or promote their welfare.

The co-morbidity of the difficulties facing many families means that a number of different agencies will need to work together in order to understand and provide effective services to address children's needs and their families' circumstances. The findings suggest that services for domestic violence and alcohol and drug misuse are not routinely involved at any stage in the child protection process. For example, there was little evidence that social workers consulted colleagues working in these specialist services to inform their decision-making. At the initial assessment stage colleagues in services for domestic violence were consulted in 4 per cent of cases where children were living with domestic violence; colleagues in services for substance misuse were consulted in 15.9 per cent of cases where children were living with a parent with problem substance misuse. Similarly, when an initial child protection conference was held services for domestic violence were represented in only 5 per cent of cases and services for substance misuse in 18.2 per cent of cases, despite the fact that domestic violence was an issue in 72.7 per cent of cases and parental substance misuse in 60.3 per cent of cases.

The involvement of substance misuse services increased somewhat at the planning stage, being involved in a quarter of plans following a core assessment. However, this level of involvement did not apply to services for domestic violence who were involved in only 8.1 per cent of plans following a core assessment. The interviews with social workers suggest this lack of involvement may have a number of roots. For example, involvement may be not seen as relevant because the violent partner had left the family home, or because responsibility for addressing the violence was assumed to reside with a different organisation such as the police. In other cases a lack of resources within children's social care or insufficient local services appeared to have affected multi-agency working.

The agencies working with domestic violence and substance misuse were more involved in providing services to families than in contributing information to inform social work assessment and decision-making. Following an initial assessment a fifth of cases where there was evidence of domestic violence were referred to a domestic violence service provider, and over a quarter of cases (27.8%) where there was evidence of parental substance misuse were referred to services for substance misuse. Although this increased level of inter-agency collaboration is to be applauded, nonetheless, it remains surprising low given that in every case there was evidence of domestic violence and/or parental substance misuse.

Knowledge of relevant organisations

The extent to which agencies collaborate in cases which involve children living with domestic violence or parental substance misuse depends on managers' and practitioners' knowledge of and willingness to work with each other. Reports from the managers in the six participating local authorities (including: police, children's social care, health, education, domestic violence, substance misuse, housing, voluntary support, and probation) showed that their awareness of the agencies and organisations that provide relevant services varied both between and within authorities. For example, children's social care managers within the same authority did not always have a similar awareness of the services for domestic violence and substance misuse available within their authority. It is the managers' role to ensure that they have a comprehensive knowledge of local services that support children and families and to ensure that this information is kept up to date and made available to all relevant staff. The government requirement for local authorities to introduce a local service directory, providing information on local providers, eligibility criteria, geographical location and referral procedures (Cm 5860, p.102), should help to ensure managers and practitioners have ready access to this information.

Managers' reports indicate a high degree of inter-agency collaboration when working with families experiencing domestic violence or parental substance misuse. For example, over 70 per cent of managers reported that they would contact and involve the following services: children's social care, police, substance misuse, and domestic violence and nearly two-thirds reported that they would involve the health service. This reported level of inter-agency collaboration with services for domestic violence and substance misuse is at odds with the evidence found on the social work case files which showed these services were rarely involved. Reports from managers and social workers suggest this disparity may be due to a lack of available services, long waiting lists, and high thresholds for adult services such as those for mental health problems, drug and alcohol misuse or domestic violence.

Inter-agency collaboration may also be affected by the perceived quality of the relationship between the agencies and organisations. Relationships between key services, such as the police, children's social care, health, domestic violence, substance misuse, and housing were rated by managers as generally good or fairly good. However, working relationships with housing and substance misuse services were more fraught. The findings suggest that adult services such as substance misuse focus mainly on the needs of adults (their clients) whereas children's services have children as their primary focus. This difference in emphasis can result in an erosion of trust, difficulties in information sharing and confidentiality, and the application of different timescales. These differences may have been exacerbated because existing Area Child Protection Committee (ACPC) plans and procedures and inter-agency training did not always cover the link between child protection and parental substance misuse.

Managers working in the key agencies commonly identified the following factors as those necessary to support good working relationships:

- understanding and respecting the roles and responsibilities of other services
- good communication
- regular contact and meetings
- common priorities
- joint training
- knowing what services are available and who to contact
- clear guidelines and procedures for working together
- low staff turnover.

The converse was also true, with managers identifying additional issues which hampered good working relationships such as no clear systems to resolve issues of confidentiality, insufficient resources including time, workloads, costs and staffing, a lack of trust, and negative preconceptions of parents with problem alcohol or drug use.

Families' experiences of referral and assessment

Gaining access to families who had come to the attention of children's social care because of child protection concerns that were related to parental substance misuse and/or domestic violence, proved particularly difficult. Although the original aim had been to interview 42 families the research team only managed to gain access to 17. The reasons for this rate of attrition were varied and included closed cases, social workers deciding an approach was not appropriate, and families disappearing or declining to be interviewed.

The stories of those parents who were interviewed, and the reports from social workers, strongly reinforce the picture that has been revealed from the scrutiny of social work case files. For most families domestic violence or substance misuse did not exist in isolation; families were also experiencing poor mental or physical health, learning disability, poor housing, debt and prostitution.

The family's difficulties affected all members and parents realised that unless children were very young they could not shield them from what was happening. Concerns about their children led half the parents to seek the assistance of children's social care themselves or agree to an agency making a referral; the other half were either unaware that a referral had been made or had not given their consent.

Involving parents and children in the assessment is key to gaining a comprehensive understanding of children's needs and circumstances. Two-thirds of parents knew a social worker had carried out an assessment of their child's developmental needs and circumstances. To ensure parents are involved in assessments is always a challenge because most parents experience high levels of anxiety and stress when children's social care enter their lives; emotions which affect the relationship. Moreover, the ability to remember and recall events can be impaired by poor mental health, a state exacerbated by the effects of domestic violence or substance misuse.

Most parents who knew that an assessment had been carried out felt they had been involved in the process and thought it had resulted in social workers understanding the difficulties facing their family. Nonetheless, parents in 9 of the 17 families were either unaware of the assessment or felt key issues, particularly the problems they were personally experiencing, had not been discussed.

The relationship between parents and social workers is influenced by how children's social care had become involved with the family. For example, voluntary involvement was linked with positive relationships, with the reverse also being broadly true. In half the cases parents and social workers rated their working relationship as good. Parents felt the quality of their relationship depended on social workers treating them with respect, being honest and open in their approach, listening to what they had to say, and involving them in the assessment. The quality of the relationship also affected the social work process; positive relationships led to greater parental co-operation during assessment and planning. Relationships, however, were not set in stone but changed, sometimes for the better and sometimes not, with the departure and arrival of new workers.

One aspect of showing respect to families and ensuring their views and experiences inform the assessment and planning is to enable parents to know and comment on what has been written about their family. Simply allowing parents access to the records was not enough. Parents and young people appreciated sympathetic social workers who took time to read, explain and discuss with them the assessment, decisions and plans.

Families' experiences of services

Every family reported that they had received a service following the social worker's involvement. The services that had been provided ranged from advise and support from children's social care to a range of services from different agencies to address both the children's and parents' needs. The extent to which parents felt satisfied with the services they had been offered was associated with them being able to acknowledge their family difficulties, being fully involved in the assessment and planning process including being consulted and offered some choice over the service provider, and being kept informed of what was going on. When services were provided by different agencies parents were more likely to be satisfied with services when they had been well co-ordinated.

The planned services, however, did not always address all the problems families were experiencing. Half the parents thought the services had improved their family life, a further quarter had mixed feelings, and in two cases, where children had been accommodated, parents felt their situation had deteriorated. The remaining families felt that their situation had not changed. Parents identified a number of reasons why some of the problems their family was experiencing had not been fully addressed. The reasons fell into three broad groups: long waiting lists for specialist services, services such as family support ending prematurely, and relevant services not being locally available.

Parents were more likely to see their situation as having improved as a result of the intervention, when domestic violence and parental substance misuse did not coexist, (it should be recalled that many parents also experienced other difficulties that hampered their parenting, such as poor mental health or a childhood in care). In cases where domestic violence and parental substance misuse did not coexist, 6 out of 10 parents were satisfied with the outcome. For example, when there was only domestic violence ($n = 5$) in most cases the referral to children's social care either coincided with parents separating and the children remaining with the non-violent parent, or the service provision resulted in a reduction in violence and the family being able to stay together. In the five cases where there was only parental substance misuse, the children continued living with a parent and in three cases the parental addiction was brought under control.

In cases where domestic violence and parental substance misuse coexisted, parents were less likely to express satisfaction with the intervention and children were more likely to be accommodated. In two of the seven cases the mother was pleased with the outcome. In both cases the child's father was the problem substance user and the perpetrator of the violence. As a result of the intervention he left the household and the children continued to live with their mother. In the remaining five cases the mother was experiencing the alcohol or drug problem and the father's violence and/or substance misuse meant he was not able to provide safe care for the children who had to be accommodated.

The reasons why some families were less able to improve their circumstances was complex, and social workers identified a number of key factors. For example, some parents were less able to engage with the service providers and devote the time and energy needed to bring about the necessary changes. In other cases, however willing parents were to take up services, progress was hampered by long waiting lists and high thresholds for specialist services.

When parents expressed satisfaction with the outcome of the intervention they pointed out that services were of most value when they provided both practical help and emotional support. Examples of practical help included advice about parenting, respite child care, specialist help to control alcohol or drug addiction, anger management and re-housing. The emotional support was generally provided by the social workers themselves and included support, empathy, advice and reassurance.

Finally, parents were also able to identify issues they felt could improve the impact of services to families like their own. In addition to the factors such as waiting lists and thresholds for services identified by social workers, parents felt that services could have a greater impact if practitioners:

- paid greater attention to ensuring families understood what was happening and consulted them throughout the process of assessment, planning and intervention

- adopted a more honest, open and respectful approach

- provided longer-term service provision

- co-ordinated better with other service providers.

Plans, procedures and joint protocols

The extent to which agencies work together and provide a co-ordinated response to vulnerable children who live in families where there is domestic violence or parental substance misuse will depend on the priority given to inter-agency working.

A key factor in supporting collaborative working is the extent to which inter-agency and individual agency plans, procedures and protocols address the inter-relationship of these issues. To this end the research team examined key documents provided by the Area Child Protection Committee (now the Local Safeguarding Children Board, LSCB), the Domestic Violence Forum, the Drug Action Team, Community Safety, and the Children and Families Services.

The results of this scrutiny suggest ACPC and Children's Services plans were more likely to address children living with domestic violence than parental substance misuse. The greater priority given to the needs of children living with domestic violence was also found in specific service plans. For example, the Domestic Violence Forum plans generally included children living in the household, whereas children of substance misusing parents were not as frequently covered in the Drug and Alcohol Action Team plans.

The scrutiny of organisations' plans brought to light a number of innovative initiatives. For example, the Domestic Violence Forum plan in Metropolitan Borough 1 included the appointment of a children's development worker, the introduction of an awareness raising project in several secondary schools, plus the publication of articles on domestic violence in the local youth newspaper. Another example of innovative practice was found in Shire County 1 where the Domestic Violence Forum plan established a support group for children whose parent was attending a programme for perpetrators of domestic violence. In Shire County 2 the Community Safety Plan covered the funding of a full-time domestic violence co-ordinator and family support worker for families affected by drug misuse. A scrutiny of the Children's Services plans also identified innovative use of short-term funding. For example, in London Borough 2 the Children's Fund had been used to finance work with children affected by domestic violence and the Health Improvement Programme to fund work to address parental substance misuse.

A fundamental objective of the LSCB is to develop policies and procedures for safeguarding and promoting the welfare of children. These should ensure practitioners working in the statutory and voluntary sector know the action to take where there are concerns about a child's safety or welfare, including thresholds for intervention. In particular:

> agreeing inter-agency procedures for s47 enquiries, and developing local protocols on key issues of concern such as… children living with domestic violence, substance abuse, or parental mental illness… (HM Government 2006a, p.78, paragraph 3.19)

The ACPC procedures in the six participating authorities varied considerably in the attention given to children living with domestic violence and parental substance misuse. While some provided comprehensive information about the impact of both domestic violence and parental substance misuse and included a brief summary of the child protection processes, others covered the issues in a single paragraph. Moreover, the greater priority given to children living with domestic violence was evident. Prioritising domestic violence was reflected by the greater likelihood for procedures and information aimed at other agencies, to be produced by the Domestic Violence Forum.

Local services for domestic violence and substance misuse also produced helpful procedures that covered safeguarding children. For example, a local women's refuge had produced procedural documents covering what to do when there were concerns about children's welfare and safety, for their staff and residents. Similar materials had been developed by a voluntary drug services in another local authority, for use by their staff.

Information sharing between agencies with different remits (some focus on children and families and some on adults) and with different priorities is often problematic and will be supported by jointly agreed protocols. ACPC joint protocols did not routinely cover what to do when children live with domestic violence or parental substance misuse. In some local authorities joint protocols for information sharing had been developed between particular agencies, for example between the police and children's social care or between adult substance misuse services and children's social care. There was no evidence of an agreed protocol to which all the key agencies had signed up to, or of joint protocols for information sharing about children between services for domestic violence and services for alcohol or drug use.

Training

Providing plans, procedures and joint protocols will not in themselves bring about the required changes in practice. Practitioners will need training on the underlying principles and how to implement the procedures and protocols. In local authorities the ACPC was responsible for ensuring effective training for inter-agency work in safeguarding and promoting the welfare of children.

An exploration of the training plans and listening to the reports of managers showed that the higher profile given to domestic violence in the documentation was also found in relation to training. For example, ACPC inter-agency training on domestic violence tended to be more comprehensive than training on parental substance misuse. As a result managers were more likely to have attended recent training events on domestic violence. Similarly, a greater proportion of practitioners in services for domestic violence had attended training on child protection procedures than had practitioners in substance misuse services.

Providing training is one part of the equation, ensuring practitioners attend is the other. Training managers identified a number of factors that could support staff attendance. These included: planning sufficient resources to allow staff to attend and reflect on what they have learnt; targeting agencies that are more difficult to engage in inter agency training and providing single agency training; linking different training initiatives together; and auditing and monitoring training to ensure that the training has met the needs of practitioners. Training should be seen as a part of practitioners' and managers' professional development and be firmly embedded in the culture of every relevant organisation.

The extent to which managers understood the impact of domestic violence and parental substance misuse on children's development was associated with the training provided by their authority, and reflected the higher profile given to domestic violence. While two-thirds of managers (other than those working in services for domestic violence or substance misuse) reported that they had an adequate understanding of domestic violence, this fell to half when the issue in question was parental substance misuse. Similarly, practically all managers in services for domestic violence reported a clear understanding of how domestic violence impacted on children and the application of child protection procedures. Such a clear understanding related to less than two-thirds of managers in alcohol and drug services.

Implications for policy and practice
Information sharing and collaborative working
Section 11 of The Children Act (2004) places a duty on the police to make arrangements for ensuring that 'their functions are discharged having regard to the need to safeguard and promote the welfare of children'. At present after attending domestic violence incidents where there are children present the police notify children's social care. This practice tends to overwhelm children's social care and there is much variation between authorities on how notifications are dealt with – as 'contacts' or as 'referrals' (Department of Health *et al.* 2000). Patrol officers attending domestic violence incidences should be aware of the effect of such violence on children (HM Government 2006a, p.61, 2.100) and assess the situation more fully in order to be clear when they are simply informing children's social care of an incident and when they wish to make a referral. The introduction of the Common Assessment Framework (HM Government 2006b) between 2006 and 2008 could provide a tool to support the police to make more considered judgements and ensure children's social care receive better information about the cases notified to them.

Government guidance is clear that safeguarding and promoting the welfare of children and young people is everyone's responsibility and that all agencies and professionals should 'share and help to analyse information so that an assessment can be made of the child's needs and circumstances' (Government 2006a, p.34, 1.16). The findings from the study indicate that social workers rarely consult or collaborate with services for substance misuse and domestic violence in carrying out assessments or planning. Managers' reports suggest consultation depends on inter-professional trust and understanding; factors that were influenced by joint training, clear guidelines and procedures, and regular communication. Collaboration should be given greater priority because practitioners in domestic violence units, alcohol and drug services will have a better understanding of how these issues impact on adult family members and family functioning. The expertise of practitioners in these specialist services should be used to inform the social work assessments, judgements and planning. Collaborative working during these stages is likely to encourage a more proactive approach to the delivery of relevant and timely services that are co-ordinated, cost effective and appreciated by parents.

Greater priority needs to be given to engaging housing in planning for children and families. For example, the findings from the managers' questionnaires suggest contacting and working with housing organisations is not a high priority when vulnerable children live with domestic violence or parental substance misuse. This contrasts with the perceptions of families; the interviews found that practically a quarter (4/17) of parents reported that their housing circumstances were a major problem.

The findings indicate that managers and practitioners working in children's services believe colleagues in adult services do not prioritise sufficiently the needs of the children of their clients. Section 11 of The Children Act (2004) and government guidance (HM Government 2005a) make it clear that services such as the police, substance misuse, GPs and housing have a duty to take account of safeguarding and promoting the welfare of children when exercising their normal functions.

Confidentiality practices and data protection can be perceived as barriers to collaborative working and are influenced by organisational cultures. Local authorities should build on existing inter-agency protocols for information-sharing and ensure that agencies working with adults are included (HM Government 2006a). Rigid, formalised information-sharing agreements and protocols do not always match reality 'on the ground'. To ensure a better balance, agreed protocols should guide practitioners in making professional judgements about what to share, in what circumstances, and for what purposes. Finally, agreed systems that are in line with the government guidance (HM Government 2006c) on information-sharing, need to be established to resolve issues and disputes in relation to information-sharing and confidentiality should they arise.

When introducing new protocols, practices and guidance managers and those responsible for training, need to develop a clear plan for helping practitioners to become familiar with them and to understand the implications for their day-to-day practice.

Management

The research suggests that managers are not always fully aware of the services that exist locally to support children and families experiencing domestic violence or substance misuse. The timetable for 'Action on Information Sharing' laid out in *Every Child Matters* (Cm 5860, 2003) states that by 2004 local authorities should have a service directory providing comprehensive information on local providers. An easily accessible directory of all local services will make it easier for managers to be fully conversant with what is available. It is managers' responsibility to ensure that this information is effectively updated and made readily available to all relevant staff. It is also a management responsibility to ensure that practitioners use the information for the benefit of service users.

Working Together to Safeguard Children (HM Government 2006a) and the *Assessment Framework* (Department of Health *et al.* 2000) provide clear guidance on the procedures social workers should follow in assessing children when they come to the attention of children's social care. The research has highlighted that when there are concerns about the safety and welfare of children this guidance is not always adhered to. For example, there was a reluctance to carry out core assessments on complex cases. This resulted in social workers trying to gather all the required information, involve other relevant services and make considered judgements within the seven working days of an initial assessment. As a result the time-scale for carrying out initial assessments was over-run and Government targets were not met. Moreover, the high rate of re-referrals and the views of parents suggest that a desire to get assessments completed quickly (by carrying out an extended initial assessment rather than a core assessment) may mean social workers do not gain a comprehensive understanding of the child and family's circumstances: for example, relatively few cases were referred by children's social care to services for domestic violence or substance misuse following an initial assessment.

The practice of staff not following government guidance was found at all stages of the child protection process. For example, in some cases:

- referrals led directly to s47 enquiries being undertaken or to an initial child protection conference being held rather than an initial assessment and then s47 enquiries if appropriate

- core assessments were not preceded by an initial assessment
- core assessments were not carried out when enquiries were conducted under s47.

A failure to follow government guidance was related to the identity of the local authority and how fully the Assessment Framework had been implemented. The introduction of an electronic recording system, a fundamental element of the *Integrated Children's System*, should alert practitioners and line managers when agreed processes are not being followed. However, even the best intentions can be derailed when local offices experience staff shortages and have to overcome traditional local working practices and locally determined priorities. Robust senior management is required to support line managers whose responsibility it is to ensure practitioners' work is consistent with government guidance, agreed procedures and protocols. For example, local authorities should establish a system for internal auditing of social work case files and ensure that such audits are routinely carried out by managers not responsible for the cases. Senior management was also more effective when conferences for individual cases were chaired independently. Conference chairs are responsible for reviewing the process by which individual cases are managed.

Direct work with children and families

The research suggests that when statutory agencies come into contact with families with alcohol or drug problems, learning disability or poor mental health, parents may experience difficulties in understanding what is said to them or what is happening. These problems may also impact on parents' ability to remember and recall key information. Line mangers should support social workers in planning sufficient time to explain things to parents at the first encounter, and to revisit them when necessary to ensure that information has been understood and retained. Brochures and leaflets written in an easy accessible way that explain the purpose and process of assessments to children and family members can supplement the explanations provided by social workers (an example can be found in the government guidance, *Framework for the Assessment of Children in Need and their Families* (Department of Health *et al.* 2000, p.39). Parents who are unaware that an assessment is taking place will not necessarily provide all the relevant information to inform the social worker's judgements.

Parents' personal difficulties with drugs, alcohol or violence affected their working relationship with practitioners. For example, they feared that being honest about their circumstances would result in their children being taken from them. Moreover, parents found some of the issues social workers raised were challenging and they did not welcome 'hearing' what was being said. Finally, many parents felt social workers patronised them and did not treat them with respect. What parents wanted was for practitioners to be transparent, honest and open with them. Social workers should work with great sensitivity to ensure they do not alienate parents and to be particularly sensitive to parents' reactions so that they can be both supportive and robust in the messages they give.

Parents frequently felt that insufficient attention was given to assessing the difficulties they were personally experiencing. Managers need to ensure that assessments identify not only children's developmental needs, but also parents' acute and chronic difficulties. Working in partnership with parents to identify the most appropriate services and involving them in the process ensures, even when there are difficulties in accessing services, that parents feel valued. Uptake and satisfaction with service provision, and improvements in family's circumstances were shown to be linked to parents being involved in the process and the decision-making.

Plans, procedures and joint protocols

All organisations have a duty to safeguard and promote the welfare of children. To fulfil their commitment, this duty must be clearly prioritised in the organisation's strategic policy documents (HM Government 2006a, p.40, 2.8). To ensure professionals comply with government guidance, the organisation's plans, procedures and joint protocols must be readily available to all relevant staff. It is the role of managers to ensure that staff recognise their value and feel a sense of ownership of the relevant procedures and protocols. Careful thought should be given at a senior management level, to their presentation and how staff can use them in their day to day practice. Documents need to be customised for different staff with different roles in the organisation so they know how the plans, procedures and protocols apply to their particular work.

Children should be given a higher priority in all strategic local authority plans whose primary focus are adults. For example, the needs of children and young people affected by domestic violence and/or parental substance misuse should be recognised in key plans such as the:

- Domestic Violence Forum Plan.
- Community Plan.
- Crime and Disorder Reduction Strategy/Community Safety Plan.

Local authorities should ensure that their Children and Young People's Plan, a reform underpinned by The Children Act (2004) and introduced in England in 2005, adequately addresses the needs of children and young people living with domestic violence and substance misuse (HM Government 2005b).

Local Safeguarding Children's Boards (established by the Children Act 2004) need to ensure that their business plan and working procedures address the needs of children and families affected by parental issues such as domestic violence, parental substance misuse, mental illness or parental learning or physical disability.

Greater priority needs to be given to collaboration and inter-agency working between organisations providing services to meet adult needs, (such as domestic violence, substance misuse, mental illness, learning disability and housing) and those working primarily with children. To ensure collaborative working conforms to government guidance (HM Government 2006a, p.60, 2.94) joint protocols for information-sharing need to cross the divide between adult and children's services and include all relevant agencies rather than be restricted to one or two specific ones.

Training

Government guidance (HM Government 2006a) makes it clear that inter-agency training should include practitioners in voluntary, statutory and independent agencies who work regularly with children and young people, and adults who are parents or carers. The findings from this study show the importance of ensuring that practitioners providing services for domestic violence and substance misuse are included. This format can promote an understanding of the roles and responsibilities of professionals working in different organisations, their different thresholds for services, the legal frameworks within which they work, and issues surrounding confidentiality and information sharing. It will also provide opportunities to develop inter-agency networks, increase levels of trust, and provide insights into the philosophy and work of each others' organisations.

Greater priority should be given to training on domestic violence and substance misuse. Local authorities should ensure that practitioners in relevant agencies routinely attend training courses that link safeguarding and promoting children's welfare with domestic violence and parental substance misuse. Managers should regularly audit and monitor training in order to identify gaps and plan future courses.

The need for practitioners to develop this greater understanding was reflected in:

- Parents' reports – they felt social workers did not always fully understand the circumstances families like them experienced.

- Managers' reports – half the managers would appreciate more training on substance misuse and a third more training on domestic violence.

- ACPC training plans – not all local authority ACPC training plans included training on domestic violence or parental substance misuse.

Local authorities need to support training through ensuring sufficient time and resources are available, providing linked and joint training (multi-agency and joint adult and children's services training), targeting training on practitioners from agencies that are 'hard to engage', and auditing and monitoring training.

Aims and methods

Purpose of the research

This study was commissioned under the then Department of Health's Policy Research Initiative to evaluate the *Quality Protects* programme and focuses on Objective 2 *Protection from Significant Harm*. In particular the research explores how existing child protection practices and procedures respond to children who have experienced domestic violence or parental substance misuse (either alcohol or drug misuse) within their families.

Establishing an advisory group

In order to guide the research team an advisory group was established and met on two occasions during the two-year study period. The group included representatives from research, policy and practice including voluntary agencies providing services for domestic violence and substance misuse. The group also included a representative from each of the participating authorities.

Aims of the study

The study had three main aims:

- To explore how children's social care responds to families where problems require the intervention of both adult and children's services.

- To identify the factors that enable different agencies to work successfully together at the various stages of assessment, planning, service delivery and review.

- To explore children and parent's experiences of professional interventions – what factors do they find most supportive.

Research ethics

The research project was subject to Royal Holloway, University of London ethics approval process and adhered to the 2003 ethical guidelines laid down by the Social Research Association (SRA 2003) and the Department of Health Research Governance Framework. The study also gained the approval of the Research Group of the Association of Directors of Social Services who recommended the project to social services departments.

Methods of investigation

The study included three parts:

- The first part identified staff awareness of the protocols, policies, and working practices in relation to cases that involve children living with domestic violence, and/or parental substance misuse. This entailed a scrutiny of documentary evidence held within the relevant agencies and postal questionnaires completed by managers and training officers within a range of relevant agencies.

- The second part identified the factors associated with different local authority's working practices. This involved a study of social work files and particular attention was paid to identifying evidence of inter-agency working practices at all stages of the social work process.

- The third part was an in-depth study of families referred to children's social care where there was evidence of domestic violence or parental substance misuse. Interviews were carried out with parents and relevant professionals.

Selecting the authorities

The original design was to select local authorities on the basis of their inter-agency working relationships through scrutinising the policy documents of agencies represented on the Area Child Protection Committees (ACPCs) in 30 local authorities. The objective was to include local authorities with different inter-agency working practices. However, the research referees advised the research team that this would be overcomplicated and not cost-effective. As a result the selection of local authorities was carried out in partnership with the Social Services Inspectors within three of the former Social Services Inspectorate regions. The Inspectors distributed a short questionnaire to the local authorities within their region which sought information about their policies, protocols and procedures in relation to inter-agency working practices between children's social care and services for domestic violence and drugs or alcohol misuse.

Twenty-two local authorities returned a completed questionnaire to the research team. To select the six local authorities the information from the 22 questionnaires was anonymised, scored, and categorised into three contrasting groups, those with the most developed working practices, those that fell into a middle category, and those with the least developed working practices. Government statistical data were used to ensure that the selected authorities represented different types of authority. The final six authorities included two local authorities from each category and comprised two London Boroughs, two Metropolitan Boroughs and two Shire Councils.

Gaining the commitment of the local authorities

Once the six local authorities had been selected a letter seeking agreement to carry out the research was sent to the Assistant Director of Children's Social Care, with a copy to the Chair of the ACPC. This explained the purpose of the study and the relevance of the findings to policy and practice.

Whenever possible an introductory meeting was held with the Assistant Director and the Chair of the ACPC and other senior managers. This enabled the research team to explain the aims and methodology of the research and identify local agencies which provide services for domestic violence or substance misuse. The meeting was also used to establish the commitment of senior personnel to the research and to identify a lead person within the authority who would assume responsibility for liaising with the research team.

In order to inform all relevant agencies of the research and gain their co-operation, the research team presented the aims and methods of the study to a full ACPC meeting. The proposal for the research and a brief summary was circulated prior to the meeting. Once the ACPC agreed to participate in the research, arrangements were made to gain access to relevant documentation in the key agencies.

Part 1: Identifying staff awareness of the protocols, policies, procedures and working practices

Scrutinising documentation

To understand inter-agency collaboration and working, in cases where there are concerns about the safety and welfare of children living with domestic violence or parental substance misuse, each participating local authority was asked for copies of current relevant local plans, procedures and joint protocols. This resulted in a wide range and volume of documents being made available to the research team. The documents were reviewed and logged indicating their organisational source, title, date, main purpose and whether they were relevant to child protection, domestic violence or parental substance misuse.

The purpose of collecting this documentation was to:

- identify what was currently available to managers and practitioners (within relevant agencies) to guide and support inter-agency collaboration in this area of work

- compare documents across local authorities to identify good and innovative practice

- explore the relationship between the range, quantity and quality of written information and managers' awareness of the materials, their confidence in collaborative working, and their awareness of the services available to help children and families where these issues are present.

In order to review the documentation, factors known to be associated with good practice were identified and the documents assessed against these criteria. For example, the documents were examined to find out whether there was evidence of appropriate and clear ownership of the document, if it was readily accessible (was it written in a clear and concise way and well circulated), whether it was reviewed and dated, and the level of inter-agency involvement. As a result essential or primary documents, such as ACPC annual reports, Domestic Violence Forum plans, and drug and alcohol service plans, were reviewed using the following criteria:

- Dated (and up-to-date) and reviewed regularly.

- Evidence of ownership from senior management and frontline practitioners across relevant agencies.

- Evidence-based/research-based where appropriate.

- Clear, concise, accessible language for the target audience.

- Evidence of availability/access to all relevant members of staff/volunteers/carers.

- Relates to other policies, procedures, guidance and plans – and this is clearly stated.

In addition to using these criteria to establish a baseline of good practice, the submitted plans, procedures and protocols were examined for evidence of information-sharing and joint working between children's social care and domestic violence and substance misuse services. Information was recorded on a standardised pro-forma to ensure consistent information was collected.

The experience of practitioners: a postal survey

The link person in each of the six participating local authorities agreed to distribute anonymised questionnaires to the following personnel within their authority.

- *Children's social care first line managers:* managers of social work teams responsible for children and families' referrals and assessments, family centre team managers, and any other first line manager responsible for child protection services.

- *Children's social care senior managers:* senior managers within services for children and families with overall responsibility for assessment, referral, and child protection or with special responsibility for domestic violence or substance misuse.

- *Training manager:* training manager responsible for the training and development of staff within children and families service and/or multi-agency child protection.

- *Police:* officers in charge or detective inspectors within either Community Safety Units, Domestic Violence Units or Child Protection Teams or the equivalent.

- *Domestic violence personnel:* managers or senior staff in agencies providing services for domestic violence, including statutory and voluntary agencies and internal (social services) specialist staff or projects.

- *Substance misuse personnel:* managers or senior staff in agencies providing services for substance misuse (drugs and/or alcohol) including statutory and voluntary agencies and internal (social services) specialist staff or projects.

- *Health personnel:* both hospital and community-based local staff who have a specialist brief or special responsibility for child protection and/or either domestic violence or substance misuse. This included representatives from health visiting, hospital accident and emergency services, hospital neonatal/maternity units and midwives.

- *Housing personnel:* managers or senior staff in the local authority's housing directorate with responsibility for housing needs and/or homelessness, and any specialist staff with responsibility for domestic violence or substance misuse cases. This could include the housing representative on the domestic violence forum.

- *Other:* Other staff or specialists identified by the link person as having a useful contribution.

The managers' questionnaire was designed to explore four main issues:

- their awareness of relevant service providers

- their knowledge of policy and procedural guidance
- their experience of policy and procedures on practice
- their knowledge base and training.

The questionnaire sent to trainers focused specifically on training issues such as:

- The amount of training they had been responsible for during the past three years and future training plans, on issues such as:
  - The Assessment Framework
  - Domestic violence
  - Parental substance misuse
  - Child protection.
- Their experience of training on these issues on a single and multi-agency arena.

Part 2: Identifying the factors associated with different working practices: A study of social work case files

The second part of the study involved a scrutiny of social work case files. The following criteria were used to select cases for the sample:

- referred because of concerns about the child's safety
- the case progressed to an initial assessment (or other form of assessment)
- the assessment (or referral) identified concerns of either domestic violence and/or parental substance misuse.

Cases were identified retrospectively from 1 December 2002. Identifying cases retrospectively ensured that the typology of working practices used to select the local authorities remained relevant and referrals and consequent intervention, could be followed up for a period of at least 6 months.

The objective was to identify 360 cases, 60 from each participating social services department (30 where there was evidence of domestic violence and 30 where there was evidence of parental drug or alcohol misuse. In cases where both issues were present the most dominant concern was used to decide which group it should be assigned to). The plan had been to ask children's social care to identify cases from their IT database.

Two issues impacted the research team's ability to access cases: existing IT systems and assessing identified case files. These are discussed below.

Existing IT systems

Some IT systems enabled relevant cases to be identified at the point of referral – i.e. the information recorded on the system showed all the concerns at the point of referral so, for example, cases could be screened for child protection concerns *and* domestic violence. However, this was not possible in most authorities. Difficulties arose for a number of reasons including:

- The use of the then Department of Health referral codes are general categories and do not identify parental substance misuse or domestic violence.

- Cases that came to the attention of children's social care through police notifications gave a clear description of the incident but little information about the child.

- In one local authority it was difficult to decide what constituted a re-referral because their IT system included the classification of *re-referral on open cases.*

As a result, in all but one of the local authorities, children's social care staff or a member of the research team undertook the task of screening referrals to identify those that fitted the research criteria.

Accessing identified case files

Identifying the cases did not always result in accessing the case files. In one local authority only a third of the files identified as suitable from the IT database were able to be located in order for a member of the research team to carry out the initial screening. This authority was aware of their significant file storage problems and during the study period conducted an internal audit on file location.

CASES INCLUDED IN THE CASE FILE STUDY

The objective of the study was to include different types of local authority and as a result the total number of referrals made to children's social care during the study year differed markedly. It was not the intention of the researchers to link the number of research cases to the number of referrals received by the local authority. Nonetheless the difficulties in identifying and accessing case files resulted in an uneven distribution of cases across the six authorities. Table A.1 shows the distribution of the research cases and the number of referrals received by each local authority for the study year ending 31 March 2003.

Although the cases were not apportioned equally between the six authorities, one of the London Boroughs being under-represented, following discussions

Table A.1 Distribution of cases from the participating authorities

Type of local authority	Number of study cases	Number of referrals for year ending 31.03.02*
London Borough	60	5000
London Borough	37	2420
Shire County	60	7520
Shire County	65	4090
Metropolitan Borough	61	2185
Metropolitan Borough	74	2435

* Department for Education and Skills 2004b.

with the Advisory Group it was felt that this would not unduly impact on the findings, as this is a small borough. The case file study was used to explore whether the response of the children's social care to cases involving domestic violence or parental substance misuse, was associated with its inter-agency working practices. It enabled the research team to examine the relationship between the information gained at the point of referral and subsequent assessment, planning and intervention and the degree of inter-agency collaboration at each stage in the process.

Because cases follow a variety of routes within children's social care, and involve a range of different agencies and different interventions, the amount of data available can be overwhelming. To ensure that data were manageable, information was pre-coded and entered directly onto a data base using lap-top computers. This ensured the information collected from the case files was consistent across cases and authorities. In addition, contextual information relating to examples of good or innovative practice within specific departments was recorded as script.

DIFFICULTIES IN IDENTIFYING INFORMATION FROM THE CASE FILES

Gathering the information from the cases files proved an easier task when local authorities consistently used the Assessment Framework records (or similar recording formats). Where this did not happen there were difficulties locating relevant information and making sense of the case. For example, in one local authority there was little consistency in relation to the formats used to record an initial assessment. Some were recorded extremely well on a record that mirrored the then Department of Health's Initial Assessment Record, but others were recorded in a less structured way on what may have been outdated formats.

Identifying what happened following the referral was particularly problematic because information on key events and decisions was sometimes difficult to ascertain from the case record. For example, although the case record may contain notes indicating that a child protection conference had been held, locating evidence of a child protection strategy meeting/discussion, or s47 investigations having been undertaken was sometimes extremely difficult. In many cases a scrutiny of the social worker's running record was necessary.

A further factor that affected the research team's ability to get the full picture of what happened once children came in contact with children's social care was the custom in two local authorities of not routinely recording a core assessment when cases progressed to a child protection conference. Information about the child's developmental needs and circumstances was incorporated into the child protection conference notes.

Part 3: Understanding the experiences of families: A qualitative study

The aim of the third part of the research was to carry out case studies of 42 families identified from the case file study (seven from each of the six participating local authorities). The initial objective had been to interview the child's parent or carer, the young person when 10 years and over and when appropriate, and the relevant professionals such as the child's social worker or health worker.

Interviewing parents and practitioners enables individual accounts of events to be balanced by the views of others. For example, the stress parents are undergoing at the time of the initial assessment, or the effects of their problem drug taking, may mean parents have difficulty in recalling important information.

To talk to parents about the difficulties their families are experiencing and what they think of the services they have received, requires establishing quickly a relationship of trust. The members of the research team were either qualified social workers or child psychologists and had considerable experience in carrying out research-focused interviews. Police checks were carried out prior to any interviews taking place. Members of the research team carried an identity card issued by the University of London.

Gaining access to families

All cases selected for the qualitative study had to have a social worker currently assigned to the family. Safety issues with regard to approaching the family were discussed with the social worker prior to any approach being made. Moreover, any efforts to locate and interview the non-resident parent were only done having taken guidance from the social worker, and with the consent of the parent living with the child.

When seeking the participation of families in research it is essential that their dignity, rights, safety and well-being is an integral part of the design (Department of Health Research Governance Framework 2001). The research took a staged approach to gaining access to families which has been found to empower potential participants to make informed decisions and offers a number of opportunities to withdraw from the study with dignity (Cleaver and Freeman 1995; Cleaver 2000).

STAGE 1

The aim of the qualitative study was to include seven cases from each of the six participating local authorities. Previous experience in carrying out research on emotive areas of people's lives suggests that approximately half of the families approached will not wish to be involved (Cleaver and Freeman 1995). In the light of this, 20 cases (that fitted the research criteria) were identified by the research team from the survey of case files in each authority (a total of 120). The group was equally divided between those with evidence of domestic violence and those with evidence of parental substance misuse. The list was discussed with the relevant social work manager and practitioner to decide the most sensitive strategy to use to seek access to the family.

Once suitable cases were identified the social worker responsible for working with the family, or a practitioner from another agency such as the health visitor, made the first contact. Their purpose was to discover whether parents and young people were interested in becoming involved in the study and agree to a member of the research team contacting them.

To enable the social workers and other practitioners to cover all the relevant issues when introducing the study to parents, and to facilitate a consistent approach, a brief summary of the issues to be discussed (a crib sheet) was provided by the research team.

Following the initial approach social workers passed to the research team the names and addresses of families who wanted to be involved in the study. They also informed the researchers when letters needed to be translated into the parents' language of choice.

STAGE 2

In cases where parents were willing to be involved, an introductory letter was sent seeking their co-operation. This explained how the research team had gained their name and address, who we were, the purpose of the study, the topics that were to be covered during the interview, how long it was likely to take, and issues of confidentiality. When the family included a young person over the age of 10 years, a similar letter to the young person was enclosed. A suggested date for the interviews was given. An enclosed reply slip (translated when appropriate) gave parents and young people (a) the opportunity to re-negotiate the timing of the interview and (b) an opportunity to decide not to be involved in the research.

STAGE 3

Families who did not withdraw were telephoned (when possible), the proposed date confirmed and the family visited. In cases where there was evidence to suggest one or both parents had a history of violence, two members of the research team visited.

When both parents were living with the child at the time of the referral but by the time of the interview were not, having consulted the social worker and with the consent of the resident parent, efforts were made to locate and interview the absent parent.

When both parents continued to live with the child the first part of the interview involved both parents. It sought their informed consent, agreement to interview their child (when aged 10 years or more), to interview their current social worker and other relevant professionals, and to read their case file. Throughout parents were encouraged to ask questions and were assured that they were under no obligation to participate. The second stage of the interview explored the parent's experiences and was, wherever possible, conducted in private.

Difficulties in gaining access to families

Gaining access to families proved particularly difficult. Families were lost to the research at all stages in the accessing process. For example, discussions with the social workers revealed practically half (42.5%) the selected cases had been closed in the months following our case file survey. Cases were also lost because the social worker felt an approach was not appropriate, either because the case was at a very sensitive stage ($n = 14$, 11.7%), or the family was violent ($n = 10$, 8.3%). When the social worker did try to contact the families, five could not be found and 10 (8.3%) declined the invitation to participate in the study. As a result 32 families agreed in principle to take part in the research. Unfortunately agreement in principle did not always translate into practice. In 14 cases the research team failed to gain access to the family. Some families had moved house, others simply did not answer our calls, others agreed to be interviewed but were not in or found the time inconvenient on the day, rearranging the interview resulted in further excuses. This continual erosion of the sample group resulted in only 18 families agreeing to take part in the in-depth study.

The sample shrank once more at the point of interview when one mother reported that, although in the past there had been incidents of domestic violence which resulted in the study child being looked after, the current referral had not resulted in any services being provided. Indeed, the mother reported that the family was experiencing no problems at the time of the referral.

> I wasn't having any problems at the time. Social services contacted me saying they'd had an anonymous call saying that I was not feeding my children and that I was letting them run around naked. They came round, saw there were no problems and closed the case... I said I didn't need any help.

Finally, the plan to include the experiences of young people had to be abandoned. The 17 families included only three young people aged 10 years and over, only one of whom it was appropriate to interview.

Designing and piloting the interviews

Interviews were designed in a semi-structured way in order, as far as possible, to mirror ordinary social interactions (Burgess 1988; Hammersley and Atkinson 1983). To ensure the interviews covered the issues parents felt were important, a group of parents who were receiving services from an agency working with substance misusers were consulted and commented on the draft interview schedule. The interview schedule was altered in the light of their comments and then, along with the social worker interview, was piloted with four families and final adjustments made.

Interviews with parents

Parents were, whenever possible, interviewed in their own homes. Considerable effect was made to engage with fathers as well as mothers. This resulted in nine cases where the mother was the sole parent interviewed, three cases where the father was the sole parent interviewed, and six cases where both parents (or the parent and his or her partner) were interviewed.

The interview covered the following issues:

- the difficulties facing the family at the time of referral and what help they wanted
- their experiences of professional assessment and planning processes
- aspects of professional interventions which they found helpful
- their views on how to improve professional responses and service provision.

Interviews with practitioners

To give a more all-round picture of the services provided to the family and how well agencies worked together on individual cases, the aim had been to interview both the current social worker and any other relevant practitioner working with the family. Interviews with a social worker were carried out in 14 cases. In the other three cases either the social worker was not available for interview because of sickness or a new social worker was in place who did not know the history of the case. In only two cases had it been possible to interview a practitioner from another agency; in both cases this was a health professional. Interviews with practitioners were conducted at their convenience and held in their own offices or conducted over the phone if this suited them better.

The interviews with practitioners covered issues such as:

- the difficulties facing the family at the time of referral

- their experience of inter-agency co-operation

- their perception of the value of the intervention.

Managing the data

The study used four main methods of information gathering:

- A scrutiny of documentary evidence including plans, procedures and joint protocols.

- A questionnaire survey involving managers in relevant agencies.

- A study of social work case files.

- A qualitative interview study involving parents and practitioners.

Information from a single source such as the managers' questionnaires provided, for example, information about the agencies they would contact and involve in cases where children were living with domestic violence or parental substance misuse. However, data from a number of sources were used to provide a more comprehensive understanding of an issue. For example, issues affecting inter-agency working relationships were informed by information gathered by scrutinising (a) protocols, procedures and training plans; (b) the manager questionnaires; and (c) social work case files. Finally, the interviews with parents provided insights into their experiences of how well different agencies worked together.

The data gathered from the various methods of investigation were subjected to both quantitative and qualitative methods of analysis.

The information gathered from examining the documentation (annual reports, business plans, procedures and joint protocols) was recorded on a standardised pro-forma to ensure consistency. Qualitative methods were used to identify commonalities and differences between the same documents, for example between the ACPC business plans developed by the six authorities, and the implications for practice identified.

The questionnaires for social work managers included both closed and open questions. The replies to the closed questions were analysed using SPSS (Statistical Package for Social Sciences) and answers to open questions provided illustrative material. The sample size meant that many of the cell sizes were too small for tests of significance and the data was presented in terms of frequency counts.

The information gathered from the case file study was subjected to quantitative methods of analysis using SPSS. Finally, the size of the interview sample ($n =$ 17) meant the data could not be subjected to any sophisticated statistical analysis. Qualitative methods were used to identify themes and the findings were used in a descriptive manner to aid the understanding and interpretation of the findings from the case file study and provide insights into the experiences of families.

Summary points

- The study explores how existing child protection practices and procedures respond to children who have experienced domestic violence or parental substance misuse within their families.

- The research encompassed three parts.

  ○ The first identifies practitioners' awareness of existing policies, protocols and working procedures in relation to cases where there were child protection concerns and evidence of domestic violence and/or parental substance misuse.

  ○ The second explores how such cases were dealt with by children's social care.

  ○ The third explores the experiences of families.

- Six local authorities participated in the research. The authorities represented different working practices and different types of local authority.

- A range of research methods was used to collect information.

  ○ A proforma to record information from the documentary material.

  ○ Postal questionnaires to explore the experiences of managers and trainers.

  ○ Interviews to explore the experiences and views of parents and relevant practitioners.

- The research team encountered a number of difficulties in gathering the data.

- ○ Social services' IT data bases were not able to always identify cases that met the research criteria and staff in children's social care or members of the research team had to screen referrals.
- ○ Cases for inclusion in the in-depth interview study failed to materialise. Half the identified cases had been closed in the months following the case file survey, other cases were lost to the study because social workers thought an approach was not appropriate, and a few families simply could not be contacted. As a result only 17 families were included in the in-depth study.

- The data were subjected to both quantitative and qualitative methods of analysis. Qualitative methods were used to analyse both the information gathered from the documentary material and the findings from the interviews with parents and practitioners. The questionnaires for managers and trainers included both closed and open questions; the replies to the closed questions were analysed using the computer statistical package SPSS, and answers to open questions provided illustrative material. The information gathered from the case file study was analysed using SPSS.

Appendix II

Family Stories

Story 1: Thomas family from Shire County 2

Ms Thomas is a single parent with one child, a 2-year-old boy called Nicky. She comes from a fairground family who constantly moved around England. Domestic violence was an accepted part of family life. Ms Thomas's mother admitted that she had been subjected to extreme violence from her husband for some 18 years, much of which had been witnessed by her children. Mrs Thomas senior had not sought help from the police during these years because she was convinced no action would have been taken. Eventually the violence resulted in serious injury and she found the strength to tell her husband to leave. He is still working in a circus and she hears from him every now and then.

Ms Thomas's experience of domestic violence mirrors her mother's; intervention was not sought until the violence resulted in serious injury. Ms Thomas explains what happened.

> There was a lot of violence that Nicky was seeing. Andrew was drinking. He was verbally aggressive. It was after an England football match that he had been drinking and he lashed out at me and broke my arm. He is Nicky's dad and I did not want Nicky to be without a dad. He was then arrested by police and bailed to a hostel. He was threatening to set fire to my mum's house and was threatening me in the street. He got involved in car offences and he broke my fingers in the street. He then disappeared and there is an arrest warrant out for him now. He comes round to the house sometimes and I have told the police but they do nothing. He is not supposed to come to the house and they are supposed to arrest him.

The injury led Ms Thomas's mother to contact the police and children's social care. If her mother had not acted Ms Thomas indicated she would not have gone to the authorities and felt angry towards her mother and what happened as a result of her initiative. The authorities took the case seriously, as the social worker explained:

The mother had presented in hospital with a broken arm and the explanation given by mother was not accepted by the hospital staff who alerted the police. The police domestic violence officer interviewed Mum who said initially that she had fallen through a window, but they were certain she was lying. It transpired that there had been an argument in the home and Andrew, the partner, had assaulted Mum and as a result her arm was broken. As Nicky was in the household the police referred to the social services.

As a consequence of the police and children's social care involvement Nicky was placed temporarily with his grandmother. A social work assessment and child protection proceedings followed which resulted in Nicky's name being placed on the child protection register. Ms Thomas found the process bewildering, and her social worker difficult to talk to, she was uncertain whether an assessment had been carried out, and felt important issues had not been discussed.

Ms Thomas wanted both practical help and emotional support. She wanted someone to listen to her, to provide her with advice and information, but felt no one gave her the help she needed. She also wanted financial and practical help; her partner having broken a door, smashed the windows, sold the TV and destroyed the furniture and inside fabric of the house. It took £4500 to repair all the damage and Ms Thomas is still in debt having had to borrow the money. She felt bitter that no financial assistance had been forthcoming.

Nicky has returned to live with his mother and his grandmother supports the family. Ms Thomas continues to fear her ex partner who is still threatening her; she has little faith in the police's ability to protect her.

Story 2: Penhurst family from Shire County 2

Mr Penhurst is a father of five children, four from a previous relationship who live with their mother, and baby Peter who is the child of Mr Penhurst and his then partner Michelle. The parents are now separated. Mr Penhurst and Michelle had a history of mutual violence and drug misuse; using amphetamines, ecstasy and heroin and alcohol.

Around the time of referral Mr Penhurst was arrested for motoring offences, including driving while under the influence of drugs and alcohol. He explained that he would frequently drive his motor cycle at excessive speeds while under the influence, a practice which had resulted in a serious accident; Mr Penhurst received a six-month prison sentence. On release he found Michelle had sold everything from their home to pay for drugs. A number of men were living in the house and Michelle was prostituting herself to fund her drug habit.

Further domestic violence between Mr Penhurst and Michelle followed, and within a few days of being released from prison he was rearrested for assaulting

Michelle; allegations made by Michelle that he assaulted Peter were dropped. Mr Penhurst was remanded to a bail hostel. While in the hostel he received telephone calls and letters from a man who graphically described the nature of his sexual activities with Michelle. Mr Penhurst cut his wrists in a suicide attempt.

Mr Penhurst received a further prison sentence for the assault on Michelle. While in prison he became determined to come off drugs and attended a number of courses including: anger management, alcohol and drug awareness, offending behaviour and communication skills. As a result of the courses Mr Penhurst stopped misusing drugs and learnt new skills.

On release from prison Mr Penhurst found another man was with Michelle and baby Peter. Michelle was continuing with her drug and alcohol lifestyle. She made further allegations to the police about Mr Penhurst being violent. Although the police investigation resulted in no charges, Mr Penhurst left to live in a hostel for the homeless. Baby Peter continued to live with his mother until her arrest for burglary. Child protection proceedings followed and Peter has placed with foster carers because of neglect, the serious nature of the drug and alcohol misuse and the level of violence within the home.

Since his last prison sentence Mr Penhurst successfully stayed off drugs. He has found employment as a fork lift truck driver, returned to live with his mother and her partner, and in his own words has 'sorted my life out'. At this time children's social care looked into whether he would be a suitable carer for Peter; as a result Peter returned to live with his father, subject to a supervision order.

Mr Penhurst acknowledges the assistance given him by children's social care. He recognises the serious mistakes he made and does not attempt to avoid responsibility for his behaviour. He thinks that to some extent his driving offences, which were very serious both to him and to others, were motivated by a desire to kill himself. Within two years he has turned his life round and now appears to be a responsible father, holding down a job and has successfully applied for the tenancy of a house. He has been off drugs now for about 12 months, and hopefully has a chance of continuing a drug-free life. At the time of the interview Michelle had no contact with either Mr Penhurst or Peter. It would appear that she continues to misuse drugs and alcohol.

Story 3: Pine family from Shire County 1

Mr Pine is the father of 10-year-old Ian. Ian's mother left the home when he was about three years old to live in Australia and there has been no contact since. There are no other children. Mr Pine is a problem drinker, admitting to consuming about two bottles of vodka every day. Since Ian's mother left them Mr Pine and Ian have experienced a number of moves, most recently having been accommodated temporarily in a hotel before leaving to move between a network of friends who all drank heavily. Mr Pine has a learning-disabled partner who lives with him and Ian on what he calls a part-time basis. The couple are frequently violent towards each other, usually following a long period of drinking.

It was while living with one set of drinking friends that a neighbour, concerned about the violence and Ian's welfare, contacted children's social care. At this time Mr Pine was subject to a Community Rehabilitation Order because of drink-driving. The probation service also referred Ian to children's social care concerned that Mr Pine's alcohol consumption was adversely affecting his parenting. The referrals to children's social care led to the involvement of the police and the health service.

The social worker's perception of the circumstances at the time of referral provides a clear picture of the concerns.

> Ian is a resilient young boy, but he was having to behave like a much older child: he had to look after himself, take responsibility for getting to school and to generally care for himself because of his dad's serious drinking. Dad was unable to offer reasonable parenting. Ian was also witnessing domestic violence which was of concern to us. The son and father had in effect changes roles – Ian had become the carer, with Dad the dependent person. This was not good for Ian.

Following the referral an assessment was undertaken, but Mr Pine thought that the process had not been explained to him, that he was told rather than consulted, and was not involved in decisions. The assessment led to Ian's name being placed on the child protection register. Copies of conference reports were sent to Mr Pine, but he felt that his comments about the reports, especially when he identified mistakes in them, were not always addressed by social workers.

Mr Pine was also upset at how he was made to feel at core group meetings and became angry and frustrated at the way he was spoken to and made to look. Mr Pine used words such as 'patronised', 'unfriendly' and 'poor attitude', when referring to the social worker.

As a result of the assessment and child protection plan Ian and his father received a range of services. These included Mr Pine being referred to a voluntary alcohol service, support from a counsellor and from a social worker, some financial assistance for practical household items, and financial help for Ian to attend days out with school and a voluntary organisation. Some of the work with Ian focused on his feelings about his absent mother. Mr Pine also referred himself for detoxification to the National Health Service, and received ten days' in-patient treatment.

While feeling that he and Ian had benefited considerably from these services, Mr Pine also believes that he had no choice in the selection of services, or whether he accepted them or not, apart from the detoxification service to which he had referred himself:

> We have all benefited, Ian is more secure and has a stable lifestyle. I am receiving support and have managed to control my drinking. My partner and myself no longer fight as we used to and there is no domestic violence present.

Mr Pine believes that he and Ian now have a much better life. He feels he has done everything asked of him by children's social care, has recognised his problems and is making every effort to deal with them. However, he is frustrated that children's social care did not appear to share his view and would prefer them to 'back off a little' and show in some way that they recognise the steps he has taken to improve his situation.

However, the social worker does not share Mr Pine's positive perception of the family's future:

> We were very concerned about the impact of chronic and very serious alcoholism on Ian's [aged 10 years] life. Dad is very ill, the alcohol has effected both his physical condition and his mental condition. He has problems walking with a very unsteady gait, and his short-term memory is seriously affected. He will probably be dead within a short period. His condition is deteriorating and yet he is unable to stop drinking.

Story 4: Sheridon family from Metropolitan Borough 1

Mr and Mrs Sheridon live with their three children, Mike 13 years, Daniel 11 years and Susie 7 years. Both parents are learning-disabled. There is a background of alcohol misuse, domestic violence, inadequate parenting, constant house moves and periods of homelessness.

There has been social services involvement with the family since shortly after the birth of their first child, when a health visitor expressed concern about the baby's safety. A health visitor was also responsible for making the current referral, worried about Mrs Sheridon's very heavy drinking, the children being left at home alone when the parents were out drinking, and the two older children's very aggressive and violent behaviour directed at both their parents and each other. The situation was exacerbated by the death of Mr Sheridon's mother who had supported the family.

The referral resulted in an assessment. Although Mr Sheridon had not been aware of the assessment he felt the subsequent services had been helpful. The child in need plan included family support from the family centre, support workers visiting the family home to provide intensive practical support three hours a day, five days a week. Behaviour management was discussed and the parents were helped with parenting skills.

> The children started to eat properly, they went to bed at a decent time and did not fight as much. They were good in the house and stopped swearing at us. They went for days out and it was much better.

Both parents referred to these as 'happy' times when they had some control over their children's behaviour and the quality of their family life improved. Mrs Sheridon said she was not drinking as much because she felt a lot better.

Although both parents had asked children's social care for help and advice about Mrs Sheridon's alcohol problem, this had not been forthcoming. Mrs Sheridon eventually got support from the family doctor at her own request, and was admitted to a detoxification ward for in-patient treatment. The parents believed that children's social care objected to Mrs Sheridon being away from her children and as a result she discharged herself before the detoxification course had been completed.

The situation deteriorated once again; Mrs Sheridon resumed her excessive alcohol consumption, the children's behaviour returned to their earlier violent pattern and the parents were once again resorting to aggression and violence in their interactions with each other. Mr Sheridon also became aggressive in his dealings with social workers and support workers, blaming children's social care for his behaviour.

> If social services had been honest with me and treated me with respect, even if I'm not going to like what they say, then it would be a lot better, I would not get so angry with them. I know I get upset and angry and I shouldn't, I try not to but when they don't tell me anything until they have to it gets me angry.

A further referral led to child protection procedures and the children becoming looked after. Susie, the youngest child was placed with foster parents who communicate regularly with Mr and Mrs Sheridon. They in turn are happy with the situation because they feel involved in what is happening to their daughter, are able to talk with her regularly, and have supervised contact. In contrast, Daniel and Mike are with foster parents with whom they have little contact. Mr and Mrs Sheridon feel frustrated at the lack of information they receive about their sons' welfare. Attempts to gain information from children's social care have met with little success and Mr Sheridon is angry believing this has made things more difficult for himself and his wife.

Story 5: Caine family from Shire County 1

Mrs Caine is the mother of three children, brothers Tom aged 8 years and Charles aged 7 years and their half sister 3-year-old Jackie. The family was known to social services in one local authority because there were concerns of emotional abuse and neglect as a result of maternal alcohol abuse and domestic violence. When they moved to another authority they soon came to their attention. Mrs Caine describes the family's circumstances and what led to the current referral.

> I was drinking and there had been a lot of violence from my husband – he beat me up and he caused me a miscarriage by sticking his fist up me. He also forced me in to prostitution. It was then I became pregnant again with Jackie. [Jackie is of dual heritage, either Indian or Chinese]. It all started in London then we moved here to start again, but nothing changed, he [husband] still beat me. Tom was beaten by his dad, and there was an occasion when his dad attempted to strangle him. Then we split up, but I got into a fight with Bill [husband] in the street and the social services got to know – they came around at night and took all of them [the children] away. They put them with my mum and dad.

Mrs Caine lives with a new partner in his house and is in the process of divorcing her husband, the father of Tom and Charlie. She feels the intervention of children's social care has not been helpful. All contact with her children must be supervised, and as they are with her parents this means she can only see her parents by special arrangement. Contact is currently twice a month and she understands that this is being reduced.

Mrs Caine thought that during the assessment she had been completely honest with her social worker, openly discussing the violence and heavy drinking. However, on reflection she thinks her honesty worked against her and she now distrusts social workers.

> They say they are helping you but they are not. They use it [what you tell them] against you.

When speaking about her social workers Mrs Caine descends into foul language, quite different to the language she uses normally. When talking with her social worker Mrs Caine frequently swears and her temper is demonstrated through violent acts such as kicking doors. This has not promoted a good relationship with her social worker or forwarded her cause for greater contact with her children.

When interviewed in the morning (for the research) it was obvious that Mrs Caine had already been drinking, a partly drunk litre bottle of white wine was beside her and she continued to drink from it throughout the interview. She readily admitted that she was still drinking very heavily.Children's social care is supporting the grandparents in seeking a residence order in respect of all three children.

Story 6: Murch family from London Borough 1

Mr and Mrs Murch have three children, Daniel aged 11 years, Jenny aged 8 years, and Joshua aged 4 years. Mrs Murch is physically disabled because of a progressive illness. To get around she uses a wheelchair most of the time but can walk slowly. Mr Murch is the main carer and gave up his job to assume this role. He has a long history of violence both domestically and more generally. Mrs Murch herself grew up in a violent household.

Children's social care became involved initially following a referral by the health visitor because of Mrs Murch's disability and the difficulties the family were experiencing in managing the behaviour of the older two children. A second referral was made by the school, concerned that the children were being physically abused by their father.

Mrs Murch explains the family's difficulties:

> Jenny was aggressive towards her father. He has an aggressive temper and used to smash up the home... We didn't notice Jenny's difficulties at first. I've had a violent upbringing – it was like living through that again! It was stressful. We noticed with Daniel – he was aggressive with Jenny, copying his dad.

The family were not aware that their children had been referred to children's social care until the social worker called on them. Once social workers became involved Mr and Mrs Murch felt that they had been kept informed about what was being done. As a result of an assessment the names of all three children were placed on the child protection register.

Mr and Mrs Murch's experienced a number of different social workers and their opinion varied with the worker.

> The first two social workers were like friends, the next one wasn't so good, the one we've got now is brilliant.

Moreover, Mr and Mrs Murch felt that the frequent changes in social worker created problems for their family, particularly the children.

> They should stop giving you so many social workers, the children won't talk to them and then the social workers wonder why. We should be able to choose the social worker.

As a result of the assessment the family received a package of services. They were moved from a two to a three-bedroom property, Mrs Murch received counselling from Surestart, after school club activities were provided for Jenny and Daniel, both parents attended parenting sessions, Mr Murch attended anger management sessions and a new wheelchair was provided for Mrs Murch. To some extent this sudden input from a number of different agencies was overwhelming, but ultimately both parents felt that things had improved considerably, the children were happier, and their names were removed from the child protection register.

Overall the parents felt that their experience with the children's social care was a positive one that helped the family considerably. Of greatest benefit was the anger management course Mr Murch had attended.

Story 7: Hendy family from Metropolitan Borough 2

At the time of the referral Mrs Hendy was living with her husband, their own child Dick aged 3 years and two children by her previous relationship, James aged 9 years and his sister Bethany aged 6 years.

Mrs Hendy and her present husband have a long history of domestic violence. The police have been called to the home on at least 15 occasions prior to the current referral. Her previous partner also made allegations that Mrs Hendy was using illicit drugs, but this was never proven. Mrs Hendy explains her circumstances:

> Me and my husband were constantly fighting, I was calling the police every week or every other week, he was hitting me where the marks wouldn't show and pulling big chunks of hair out, he used to smash the house up as well.

Mrs Hendy believed that they had been able to shield the children from the violence; the older two children tended to be with their father when fights occurred and Dick was always in bed. However, she did acknowledge that James was very quiet, seemed to be hiding his feelings, and was very protective towards her. The social worker's view suggests a rather different picture.

> All of the children are aware of the domestic violence which is affecting them emotionally, and they are possibly at risk physically.

At an early stage in the intervention it was made clear that the children would be removed from home if Mr Hendy did not move out. At the time Mrs Hendy's previous partner was applying for a residence order in respect of his two children.

As a result of the assessment, in which Mrs Hendy felt fully involved, the names of all three children were placed on the child protection register. A comprehensive plan was drawn up. Mr Hendy agreed to attend an anger management course, Mrs Hendy accepted counselling from a voluntary domestic violence service, and attended parenting sessions provided by children's social care. Both parties agreed to end their marriage.

Mrs Hendy found some services more helpful than others. For example, the counselling provided by the voluntary service was not particularly useful and Mrs Hendy discontinued her attendance. However, she found the parenting sessions provided by children's social care, beneficial.

> It was good to share some experiences with others.

Since the end of the involvement of children's social care Mr Hendy continues to harass his estranged wife. He presents himself at the home and occasionally assaults her. She is very reluctant to phone the police fearing renewed children's social care involvement with her family. Moreover, she feels the police were unhelpful in the past.

> If the police had done their job in the first place it wouldn't have happened.

Divorce proceeding are going ahead.

Although Mrs Hendy acknowledges the help she received from children's social care, nonetheless she found the process very stressful. She feels she 'lost her life', which seemed to revolve around meetings with the social worker, core meetings or court appearances.

Story 8: Linden family from Metropolitan Borough 2

Ms Linden lives with her partner, their son Morgan aged 4 years and her daughter Jackie aged 8 years from a previous partner. Ms Linden grew up in local authority care and has been intermittently involved with children's social care ever since. The social worker explained the family history.

> She has been heavily into drugs and there have been serious child care problems. At one point she left her child at our office door. She was also not keeping the child's medical appointments and these were very important. The child was born an hermaphrodite. They decided it was more appropriate for her to be a girl but she needed constant medical attention and drug therapy and this she was not getting. Mum had difficulty relating to Jackie.

The current referral came from the health visitor because of a number of concerns about Jackie's health and welfare.

> Jackie had a very serious medical condition that needed long-term management and close follow up – it was a major life-threatening condition, a congenital condition, and without proper medical oversight puberty could onset very early. The child was also witnessing drug misuse, and there was a lack of a role model. She had no friends, they would not come to the home, were not allowed to come to the home because of the known drug users that were frequently there. Jackie was being ostracised. Men were frequenting the home to use drugs and Jackie was unsupervised and this presented as a threat to her. There was also

the lack of extended family support as they had, in effect, given up on Mum. They had become isolated from all normal areas of society. There was no routine, no regular meal times and no food in the cupboards. Also Jackie was losing weight – with her condition weight can fluctuate, but she was losing too much weight. The whole picture was very concerning.

Ms Linden explained that she was using heroin and cocaine to block out feelings of depression. She was concerned about her daughter, worried about her diet, her schooling, her fear of her partner, and the emotional impact of seeing adults taking drugs regularly.

Jackie had to do a lot of her own care, her schooling was affected as Jackie had to get herself up and ready for school which made her late a lot, Jackie's diet wasn't good; although she ate she didn't have a good diet, Jackie was intimidated by my boyfriend and all the others that were always in the house taking drugs, it wasn't good for her emotionally at the time; Because I was using drugs I didn't see the effect it was having on her. Morgan was younger, so I don't think he was as affected at the time, Jackie looked after him.

Following the referral, children's social care carried out an assessment. Ms Linden felt able to participate fully in the assessment process and believed she was consulted over decisions. However, she continually feared that it would result in her children being taken away. The assessment showed that Ms Linden's parenting was satisfactory when she was not under the influence of drugs.

As a result of the assessment a package of services was provided including: parenting classes for Ms Linden, Jackie to attend a young carers' scheme, Ms Linden to work with the drug team who would provide some 'listening support' and a heroin substitute. More intensive counselling for Ms Linden was planned but was not forthcoming. Ms Linden felt that the services that had been provided had helped, although she felt she needed additional counselling and specialist help to resolve her own emotional and mental health problems. Adult mental health services were not involved.

The support provided to Ms Linden had positive results and her lifestyle improved. Her partner left and she moved to a new house which, when seen at the time of the research interview, was well-maintained and clean.

As a result of the overall improvement in the family's circumstances, children's social care closed the case. Ms Linden, however, feels children's social care withdrew their support prematurely and she feels very vulnerable. At the time she was still on the heroin substitute.

Story 9: Reed family from Shire County 1

Mr Reed is the lone father of daughter Alice, who is three years old. He has a moderate learning disability and is unable to read or write. Mr Reed has never used illegal drugs. Alice's mother has another child by a previous relationship who is in local authority care. She has been known to social services since she was a child and has a history of violence and drug and alcohol abuse. The social worker gives a brief description of the family history.

> Alice's mother had been out of control since she was only about 13. She became pregnant at 15 (with Alice's older half-brother) and was involved in drugs and alcohol from a very early age. Dad was mentally ill and on drugs; the child's name was placed on the Child Protection Register at birth. Dylan, Alice's half-brother, was disabled and spent a lot of time in hospital. There was a lot of domestic violence between the parents... Mum went into prison. She then left Dad and got a new partner, the dad of Alice. She continued to use drugs and was stealing – she went to prison and Alice's dad got residence of the child. A long-term ongoing case known to the service for a long time.

Mr Reed recalls that when he met Alice's mother he was unaware of her background and for a time she was not taking drugs. When off drugs there were no issues over her parenting. Her drug-taking resumed and the need to consume a cocktail of cannabis, speed and ecstasy led to a lifestyle of stealing. The relationship became violent; 'she stabbed me in the foot with a knife, in the head with a fork while Dylan and Alice were there'. She was sent to prison for street robbery and drug offences.

Shortly after Alice was born the relationship ended and Mr Reed had no contact with his daughter until children's social care contacted him to ask if he would look after his child as her mother was not in a fit condition to do so. He went to her house to find her 'out of her head with drugs. I phoned emergency social services as I found two men also on drugs looking after Alice. I got custody the following Monday.'

The social work assessment resulted in both children being placed for a brief period in care. Mr Reed soon took over the care of his daughter, but Dylan's father was unable to look after him because of his own chronic substance misuse and poor mental health, and he remained in local authority care. Alice's mother was referred to an agency to undertake a drug rehabilitation course, but this did not work out and she continues to misuse drugs. Contact was arranged and she currently sees Alice every other week at her own mother's house.

Mr Reed received practical help and support from the children's social care, including help with child care, and financial help to purchase appliances such as a fridge and oven. He also received 'home help' support. Overall, he felt the services were well co-ordinated and helpful. 'It was a good plan, it helped me; I did not know how to be a father.'

Mr Reed gained a residence order in respect of Alice and although the case is closed to children's social care he is aware that he can always ask for help.

> They help if you ask for help. Pick up the phone and ask for help. Social services are good at their job but they're not mind readers.

He has a new relationship and his girlfriend stays with him three or four nights a week. Both the Mr Reed and children's social care consider things have worked out well.

> The case in now officially closed but Steve [father] still comes in every now and then for supportive visits. He is doing really well and giving Alice good care [social worker].

Story 10: Peel family from Shire County 2

Mrs Peel is a single mother with three children, John who is 11, George aged 15, and their 17-year-old sister Sandy. Mrs Peel is divorced from the father of her three children.

Mrs Peel's background is in stark contrast to her present circumstances. She is an educated woman, a qualified nurse and when married lived in a five-bedroomed house. They had a middle-class lifestyle and kept horses. After the divorce she moved away and lived with a new partner. She explained that things started to go wrong when she became pregnant.

> I lost the baby and he seemed to blame me. He was hitting me, it had been going on a long time and he was taking my money. He then told me to leave home and go and live with my parents in XXX. He took me there in a car and dumped me. I stayed with my parents for a while but it was overcrowded and I got a place with the council on a really rough estate.

Life on the estate was not easy for the family. They were burgled three times, but Mrs Peel was too frightened of the suspected culprits to report them to the police. She was not accepted by the community, neighbours verbally abused her because of her accent and background and started reporting her to children's social care for being drunk and not looking after the children. Things at home were little better. John aged 11 years was bullied at school and refused to go, and bullied at home by his brother George. George who had been violent, difficult and rebellious for some time was hitting his mother, stealing from her and telling neighbours that 'mum has not given me anything to eat. She is always drunk.' The difficulties led to him leaving home to live with neighbours against his mother's wishes.

> I complained about this as he was only 15 and they were heavy drinkers and so was he, but they [children's social care] allowed him to stay there. He is still there.

Mrs Peel formed a new relationship with Ian. This man, she discovered, had a conviction for burglary and continued his criminal behaviour using stolen credit cards to raise funds. Mrs Peel explained that his relationship with her sons was complex.

> Ian then took John and said I could not have him back. I am not sure what happened then but he [Ian] phoned social services to say I had abandoned John.

Following this referral to social service an assessment of the children was carried out. Mrs Peel felt she had been involved in the process and had been honest about the difficulties facing her family. However, she felt the focus of the assessment had been exclusively on the children and no one looked at her needs. She had wanted someone to listen to her story, wanted advice and information, and to feel that someone was on her side. She felt that she got none of these things. She admits that although she had been invited to a number of meetings she had been too intimidated to attend. The social worker tells a rather different story, explaining that Mrs Peel disappeared for some months during the period of assessment, planning and service delivery which had hampered their ability to involve her.

The assessment resulted in George remaining privately fostered with neighbours, and John being placed with foster carers 40 miles from the family home. The distance made contact difficult. Her 17-year-old daughter remained living at home. Mrs Peel was referred to the local drug and alcohol team and a voluntary project, but did not attend. At this time Mrs Peel says she became very depressed and started drinking heavily, not able to see a positive future for her family.

> I don't know if I will ever get John back. I am not yet strong enough to ask that question. I am frightened of the answer. However, I am not drinking as much and things are better in some ways. I am getting my life together again.

Story 11: Fox family from London Borough 1

This family consists of Ms Fox, a young white mother with mild learning disabilities, her partner who was either an asylum seeker or possibly an illegal immigrant and their young daughter Sasha. Ms Fox's partner did not live within the household but visited regularly. The housing and domestic facilities were good and there were no concerns over Ms Fox's parenting. Ms Fox described the difficulties facing her family at the time of the referral.

> I had a problem with my partner [Sasha's father]. He accused me of cheating and he pushed me and that. I was new to having a baby, but he was throwing her in the air; I explained he wasn't supposed to do that.

The family were referred to children's social care by the police who had been called to the home because of an incident of domestic violence. Children's social care then carried out an assessment in which they were able to fully involve Ms Fox, although involving Sasha's father proved more difficult.

> In some meetings he would come in glaze-eyed – as if he was on drugs. He could also be threatening and aggressive.

Ms Fox felt the key issues had been explored during the assessment but because she feared her daughter might be taken away she worried about how honest and open she could be with the social workers. The assessment found that Ms Fox was being subjected to violence from her partner which had resulted in a non-accidental injury to Sasha. It was felt that Ms Fox needed support and help in protecting her daughter.

As a result of the plan the following services were provided: a childminder twice a week; the domestic violence unit provided support to Ms Fox; a health visitor also supported the mother; and contact with Sasha's father had to be supervised.

Ms Fox feels that things have improved since the involvement of children's social care and other agencies. She hopes that she will be able to re-establish her relationship with her partner and she thinks that the agencies are helping her achieve this.

Story 12: Harding family from Metropolitan Borough 1

Ms Harding and her partner had a violent relationship which deteriorated further when she became pregnant.

> I was in a bad relationship, my partner was battering me black and blue; it started when I was pregnant.

They had a son Jimmy who was 10 months when she called the police because of her partner's violence. She separated from her partner. The police made a referral to children's social care.

The first Ms Harding knew of the referral was when she received a letter from the children's social care saying they wanted to talk to her about concerns over the safety and welfare of her son. The referral resulted in an assessment. However, Ms Harding had not realised that this was taking place and complains that this had not been explained to her and no one had asked her what she needed.

As a result of the assessment children's social care decided that Jimmy should go and stay with his maternal grandmother, and that his mother's visits must be supervised. This decision left Ms Harding angry and bewildered.

> I was no longer living with my partner and thought I could be left alone, all I wanted was to have Jimmy back to live with me and to get on with my life. If I knew all this was going to happen because I called the police for help I wouldn't have bothered.

During the assessment period Ms Harding's partner was given a prison sentence, and because she gave this information to the children's social care department she was able to have unsupervised contact with her son. However, she felt it needed a prison sentence for children's social care to believe that she was not having contact with her ex-partner. She thought she had been punished for his violent behaviour.

In retrospect Ms Harding believed that if she had been advised to separate from her partner and move away from the area with her son, she would have done this and life would have been different. She felt that she had never been asked what help she wanted. She felt very strongly that mothers who are the victims of domestic violence should not be punished, but given appropriate help and support. At the time of the research interview Ms Harding was in the process of taking social services to court because of the way they handled her case.

Story 13: Booth family from London Borough 2

Mr and Mrs Booth live together with their 5-year-old daughter Hannah. Mr Booth has a mild learning disability. Mrs Booth explained the family circumstances at the time of the referral.

> Silly verbal threatening – at the time I put up with it, I was so frightened I would cower away from him [husband]. We were in a lot of debt at the time. It was years of violence, he was being verbally abusive to Hannah and me. It escalated – we were shouting and swearing – I wouldn't back down anymore... She [Hannah] was behaving bad, her insecurities about Mummy and Daddy fighting. Us shouting and yelling, she would say 'stop it' and cover her little ears.

The referral was triggered by Hannah telling her mother that her father had 'tickled her privates'. Mrs Booth went to see her solicitor who referred her to a voluntary organisation concerned with domestic violence. This organisation then referred the family to the children's social care and the police.

From this time on it appears that things were not handled as sensitively as they could have been. Mrs Booth recalls that a social worker and a member of the police child protection team arrived one night on her doorstep to demand her husband left immediately. Mrs Booth said she felt very bullied and threatened by them and feared that if she didn't co-operate Hannah would be taken away. Because she was not clear of their or her own legal position she phoned her solicitor who agreed to come to the house immediately. Mrs Booth recalls that once it became known that a solicitor was on his way the social worker told Mrs Booth that they would leave and return at another time. Her husband left the family home as a result of the visit despite Mrs Booth being convinced that he no longer posed any threat to either Hannah or herself.

Some months later Mrs Booth telephoned children's social care to ask if her husband could return. The social worker's response, as Mrs Booth recalls, was to tell her that 'the case is closed, don't come back to me'. Mrs Booth says she wrote lots of letters of complaint to the social worker and her manager but never really knew who to address them to. After a few months her husband returned to live with them and Mrs Booth wrote and told children's social care about the change in the family's living arrangements. This led to the involvement of children's social care; a different social worker was assigned to the case and an assessment was carried out. Mr and Mrs Booth were aware that an assessment was being undertaken and the family's difficulties were discussed. However, Mrs Booth could not recall being asked what help she wanted or needed.

As a result of the assessment Hannah's name was placed on the child protection register and a number of services were offered to support the family. Hannah's father enrolled in an anger management course, and both parents attended a parenting programme. Mrs Booth had also expected a referral to a family therapist, but was still awaiting an appointment at the time of the research interview. The intervention led to improvements within the family, much of which were attributed to the parenting programme and the support given by the current social workers. Mrs Booth contrasts her current workers very favourably with previous workers, believing they had gathered a full picture of her family's circumstances, were honest, and that things were run better.

At the time of the research interview the family were living together, the allegation of sexual abuse had been withdrawn, and the domestic violence apparently had come to an end. Mrs Booth's confidence in her parenting capacity had improved considerably. However, there remain concerns about how well the family would cope once support and monitoring is totally withdrawn.

Reflecting on the intervention of children's social care Mrs Booth felt things could have been much less traumatising if the professionals had been more honest and 'up front with us'. She was adamant that families like hers should not be pre-judged or assumed to be lying.

Story 14: Evans family from Shire County 1

Ms Evans is a single mother with two children, Steven aged 13 and his sister Shannon aged 6. The family had a history of social services involvement. Six years ago Ms Evans's partner was physically assaulting both herself and her son Steven; there were also allegations that Steven had been sexually abused by this man. These allegations led to the involvement of the police and children's social care and resulted in Steven being looked after for approximately four months. Ms Evans separated from her partner.

An anonymous referral brought the family once again to the attention of children's social care. The allegation was that Ms Evans was not feeding her children and that they were allowed to run around naked. On this occasion the children's social care called around unexpectedly, were satisfied that there were no problems and closed the case.

Because of her previous contact with children's social care the current referral frightened and shocked Ms Evans who was extremely concerned that they would again take action to remove the children.

> When social services contacted me I just flipped, I wanted to know who had reported me but they would not tell me.

As a result of the referral an assessment was carried out, although at the time Ms Evans had not been aware that this was happening. However, she does remember the social worker asking about her family and feeling sufficiently confident to answer all the questions honestly. Following the assessment there were no plans to provide any services because the social worker thought the allegations were unfounded and the case was closed.

Story 15: Krausse family from Shire County 1

Mrs Krausse lives with her partner and her 8-year-old son Mike. Her partner drinks heavily and there is evidence of domestic violence. Mike has two half-brothers, Peter who is 27 and lives locally and Aliceo aged 17 who lives in South Africa. Mrs Krausse has a background of domestic violence, poor mental health and problem drinking. Her eldest son has a history of offending and Mike experiences learning difficulties; he suffers dyspraxia and functions some two years below his chronological age. Mike is the subject of a statement of special educational need. Mr Krausse was South African and died in suspicious circumstances, as the social worker explains.

> He had died under peculiar circumstances. Mum at one stage said she had been involved in his death and Interpol had been involved. No action against Mum. It is apparent that Dad died a violent death. Dad query schizophrenia. It would also

appear that when in South Africa she had been involved in prostitution. Child Protection procedures initiated.

Mrs Krausse returned to England when she was 6 months pregnant with Mike. Her recollections of why she came back and what subsequently happened provide a picture of the family's circumstances prior to the referral.

> I had returned from South Africa when I was 6 months pregnant with Mike due to domestic violence. When I returned home my eldest son Peter, who had always lived in England, was in a young offenders' institute. When he was released he wanted to live with me, but I didn't think it was suitable as I was living in a 'rough area'. Peter found this hard to accept. Over the next few years there was a lot of trouble due to this and I was suffering from depression. I didn't drink every day but once I had a drink I couldn't stop, I was binge drinking.

The referral to children's social care was made by the education service because of growing concerns about Mike's welfare.

> Mike was missing school and was soiling himself. His speech was deteriorating and he was constantly tired. Mike got to the point where he would not talk.

The referral was triggered when the transport services, responsible for taking Mike home, could not get Mrs Krausse to answer the door. She explained that distressed after a violent argument with her son Peter she had taken a large number of sleeping tablets and had not heard the knocking. The transport services called the police. Mike was taken to a place of safety until Mrs Krausse's partner came back from work, at which point Mike returned home.

Children's social care remained in contact with the family. Mrs Krausse's depression deepened resulting in a hospital admission for a drug overdose. She had a history of self-harming and at one point when thinking she might be pregnant, stabbed herself in the stomach.

Children's social care carried out an assessment which resulted in a number of interventions.

Mrs Krausse was admitted to hospital for rehabilitation and detoxification and Mike became looked after by foster carers. His mother was given supervised contact. It was agreed that Mrs Krausse needed psychiatric help, but children's social care experienced difficulty in accessing this. Mrs Krausse moved house but financial difficulties may result in her losing her home. Mrs Krausse's depression is ongoing, domestic violence continues, and both parties remain problem drinkers. However, Mike has benefited from his placement, as the social worker explains.

> Since Mike has been in foster care his behaviour and speech have really improved, and he is a contented boy now. It would be totally wrong to return

him to his mum with all of the problems still there. He wants to stay with the foster carers but he also wants to see Mum.

The social worker is far less positive about Mrs Krausse's future.

I think that the prospects for Mum are very bleak. In the child's interest we are going for a full care order with a view to very long-term care for him in the foster home, with only limited supervised contact for Mum, perhaps about six times a year. When she fully realises what is happening I think there is a real danger of her committing suicide. She really needs a separate adult worker to work supporting her.

Story 16: Davis family from London Borough 2

Mrs Davis is a lone mother living with her two children; Rachel aged 5 years and her 8-year-old brother Billie. There is a long history of domestic violence and alcohol misuse by her husband, the father of the two children. A particular violent episode resulted in Mr Davis being given a prison sentence.

While her husband was in prison, Mrs Davis asked her health visitor for help with the children who, with her agreement, referred the case to children's social care. Mrs Davis explained how affected the children were by the family's circumstances.

It was unbearable; we were all living on the edge. We couldn't be normal. Billy was very insecure and he still is – won't sleep on his own and at one time he couldn't go upstairs to the loo without all of us going up. He didn't want to leave me to go to school he was scared we would bump into Ian [father] whenever we went out. Rachel was younger – she acted more aggressive and her behaviour got worse.

On his release from prison Mr and Mrs Davis separated, although Mr Davis continued to see his children at the family home. However, there were difficulties over contact as the social worker explains.

The issues of domestic violence were affecting both of the children and Mum's ability to protect the children around the times of contact. She didn't have much control at all over when Dad saw them – he still had keys etc. At the time there was no agreed contact order or residence order; they were going through the divorce at the time.

The social work assessment resulted in a range of services. The family centre provided help which included individual work with both children, and Mrs Davis was provided with training to better manage her children's behaviour. In addition, a plan was made to ensure contact, between Mr Davis and his children, was safe. Mr Davis was re-housed.

Mrs Davis and her social worker agree that the referral and consequent services have improved the family's situation. The social worker reports that supported contact is working well and the children are no longer exposed to violence. Mr Davis has greater control over his drinking and co-operates with the contact arrangements. Mrs Davis is able to manage her circumstances better and feels the children are happier. The mother's description shows her perspective on how the services helped her family.

> Things have improved for me – more confident, the children are a lot better and more relaxed around the house.

Story 17: Cossins family from London Borough 2

Ms Cossins is 20 years old with a baby daughter, Katie. She has a long history of drug abuse and became pregnant while still a teenager. She continued drug-taking throughout her pregnancy. While in prison her pregnancy and drug use was recognised and a referral made to children's social care. The social work assessment started while Ms Cossins was still incarcerated. When Ms Cossins left prison she returned to live with her mother. The three-bedroom accommodation was overcrowded as it housed Ms Cossins and her daughter, her own mother and her partner, and Ms Cossins' 22-year-old sister.

The social work assessment revealed Ms Cossins' deep-seated drug problems, her lack of parenting skills and the overcrowding and tension within the household. As a result a support package was provided. This included on-going support from a social worker, child day care 4 days a week, support for Ms Cossins from the community drug team and from a support group for parents with drug and alcohol problems. The social worker explained the aim of the services.

> The overall aim was for Tia [Ms Cossins] to remain at home with Katie and the grandma. She worked with the community drug team well initially and was assessed quickly – they were good when she engaged.

The expectation was that Ms Cossins should be helped to get her own accommodation, but while she remained a drug abuser to live with her mother thus ensuring baby Katie was safe and her welfare promoted.

Some services were more successful than others. For example, Ms Cossins appreciated the child day care support but derided the drug withdrawal programme provided by the local drug clinic.

> The clinic were a waste of time, they were supposed to help with a withdrawal programme but they have got a bad attitude.

Both children's social care and the family were disappointed at the housing department's lack of action; at the time of the interview Ms Cossins and Katie continue to live in overcrowded accommodation with her mother. Ms Cossins thinks the intervention of children's social care has not improved her situation.

> Nothing's really changed or moved on. Still taking drugs, still living here which isn't working for any of us.

Story 18: Hammond family from London Borough 2

Mr and Mrs Hammond are separated. Mrs Hammond has two children by a previous partner who live with their father. Mr Hammond has five children by a previous partner, four of whom live with their mother and one with his paternal aunt. Mr and Mrs Hammond have a daughter Annie aged 3 years.

Both parents have a long history of drug and alcohol misuse and domestic violence. Mrs Hammond has a history of mental illness. Mrs Hammond explained her circumstances and what led to Annie becoming looked after.

> XXX, where I live, were already involved with the family because of my mental health and drug problems, and I had postnatal depression and psychosis with my second child. I just could not cope any more when I had Annie. I did not have any support with her. I was taking crack, alcohol, dope, medicating myself to survive. It was the best thing at the time to give up the kids... I neglected the children, I couldn't protect them – I wasn't protecting myself so I just couldn't protect them.

At this time Mr and Mrs Hammond separated and Mrs Hammond moved to another local authority. As a result of the social work assessment Annie was placed with her paternal aunt who was already looking after her 8-year-old half-sister. A number of services were provided to the family. Mrs Hammond received services from the drug and alcohol team, attended a drug rehabilitation course, the social worker visited to provide support once every two weeks, and a mental health worker also provided a service.

As a result of this package of services Mrs Hammond has stopped taking drugs reporting that she is now *clean*. She found the services helpful in that they enabled her to gain insight into her situation and improve her relationship with her husband. However, she is distressed that Annie continues to live with what she describes as *that family* and thinks she should return to live with her.

References

Abel, E.L. (1997) 'Maternal alcohol consumption and spontaneous abortion.' *Alcohol and Alcoholism 32*, 3, 211–219.

Bancroft, A., Wilson, S., Cunningham-Burley, S., Backett-Milburn, K. and Masters, H. (2004) *Parental Drug and Alcohol Misuse: Resilience and Transition Among Young People.* York: Joseph Rowntree Foundation.

Barnard, M. (2007) *Drug Addiction and Families.* London: Jessica Kingsley Publishers.

Birchall, E. and Hallett, C. (1995) *Working Together in Child Protection.* London: HMSO.

Brisby, T., Baker, S. and Hedderwick, T. (1997) *Under the Influence: Coping with Parents who Drink too Much.* London: Alcohol Concern.

Burgess, R.G. (ed) (1988) *Studies in Qualitative Methodology, Volume 1.* London: JAI Press.

Butler, S., Atkinson, L., Magnatta, M. and Hood, E. (1995) 'Child maltreatment: the collaboration of child welfare, mental health and judicial systems.' *Child Abuse and Neglect 19*, 3, 355–362.

Butt, J. and Box, L. (1998) *Family Centred: A Study of the Use of Family Centres by Black Families.* London: Race Equality Foundation.

Cabinet Office and Home Office (1999) *Living without Fear – An Integrated Approach to Tackling Violence against Women.* London: Women's Unit. Website: www.womens-unit.gov.uk

Cawson, P. (2002) *Child Maltreatment in the Family: The Experience of a National Sample of Young People.* London: NSPCC.

Chief Inspector of Social Services, Director for Health Improvement, Commission for Health Improvement, Her Majesty's Chief Inspector of Constabulary, Her Majesty's Chief Inspector of the Crown Prosecution Service, Her Majesty's Chief Inspector of the Magistrates' Courts Service, Her Majesty's Chief Inspector of Schools, Her Majesty's Chief Inspector of Prisons, Her Majesty's Chief Inspector of Probation (2002) *Safeguarding Children: A Joint Chief Inspectors' Report on Arrangements to Safeguard Children.* London: Department of Health. Website: www.dh.gov.uk/assetRoot/04/06/ 08/33/04060833.pdf

Chief Inspector – Commission for Social Care Inspection, Her Majesty's Chief Inspector for Schools, Her Majesty's Chief Inspector of Court Administration, Her Majesty's Chief Inspector of Probation, Her Majesty's Chief Inspector of Constabulary, Her Majesty's Chief Inspector of Prisons, Chief Executive – Healthcare Commission, Her Majesty's Chief Inspector of the Crown Prosecution Service (2005) *Safeguarding Children: The Second Joint Chief Inspectors' Report on Arrangements to Safeguard Children.* London: Department of Health. Website: www.safeguardingchildren.org.uk

Cleaver, H. (2000) *Fostering Family Contact.* London: The Stationery Office.

Cleaver, H. and Freeman, P. (1995) *Parental Perspectives in Cases of Suspected Child Abuse.* London: HMSO.

Cleaver, H., Wattam, C. and Cawson, P. (1998) *Children Living at Home: The Initial Child Protection Enquiry, Ten Pitfalls and How to Avoid Them: What Research Tells Us.* London: NSPCC.

Cleaver, H., Unell, I, and Aldgate, J. (1999) *Children's Needs–Parenting Capacity: The Impact of Parental Mental Illness, Problem Alcohol and Drug Use, and Domestic Violence on Children's Behaviour.* London: The Stationery Office.

Cleaver, H. and Walker, S. with Meadows, P. (2004a) *Assessing Children's Needs and Circumstances: The Impact of the Assessment Framework.* London: Jessica Kingsley Publishers.

Cleaver, H., Barnes, J., Bliss, D. and Cleaver, D. (2004b) *Developing Information Sharing and Assessment Systems.* Research Report 597. Website: www.dfes.gov.uk/research.

Cleaver, H., Cleaver D. and Cleaver, D. (2004c) *Information Sharing and Assessment: The Progress of Non-trailblazer Local Authorities.* Website: www.dfes.gov.uk/research

Cleaver, H. and Nicholson, D. (2005) *The Development and Use of a Local Prototype Common Referral, Information and Assessment Record in Cumbria.* Cumbria: Cumbria Children's Fund.

Cm 5730 (2003) *The Victoria Climbié Inquiry. Report of an Inquiry by Lord Laming.* London: The Stationery Office.

Cm 5847 (2003) *Safety and Justice: The Government's Proposals on Domestic Violence.* London: The Stationery Office.

Cm 5860 (2003) *Every Child Matters.* London: The Stationery Office. Website: www.dfes.gov.uk/everychildmatters/pdfs/EveryChildMatters.pdf

Cm 5861 (2003) *Keeping Children Safe: The Government's Response to the Victoria Climbié Inquiry Report and Joint Chief Inspectors' Report Safeguarding Children.* Norwich: The Stationery Office.

Children Act (1989). London: HMSO.

Children Act (2004). London: The Stationery Office.

Coleman, R. and Cassell, D. (1995) 'Parents Who Misuse Drugs and Alcohol.' In P. Reder and C. Lucey (eds) *Assessment of Parenting: Psychiatric and Psychological Contributions.* London: Routledge.

Commission for Social Care Inspection (2005) *Safeguarding Children: The Second Joint Chief Inspectors' Report on Arrangements to Safeguard Children.* Newcastle: Commission for Social Care Inspection.

Crime and Disorder Act (1998). London: The Stationery Office.

Darlington, Y., Feeney, J.A. and Rixon, K. (2005) 'Interagency collaboration between child protection and mental health services: Practices, attitudes and barriers.' *Child Abuse and Neglect 20,* 1085–1098.

Debbonaire, T. (1999) 'Domestic violence and inter-agency child protection work: An overview of recent developments.' In N. Harwin, G. Hague and E. Malos (eds) *The Multi-agency Approach to Domestic Violence: New Opportunities, Old Challenges?* London: Whiting and Birch.

Department for Education and Skills (2004a) *Safeguarding Children in Education.* London: Department for Education and Skills.

Department for Education and Skills (2004b) *National Statistics, Statistics of Education: Referrals, Assessments and Children and Young People on Child Protection Registers: Year Ending 31 March 2003.* Norwich: The Stationery Office.

Department for Education and Skills (2005) *Government Response to Hidden Harm: The Report of an Inquiry by the Advisory Council on the Misuse of Drugs.* Nottingham: DfES publications. Available at www.everychildmatters.gov.uk

Department for Education and Skills (2006a) *About the Integrated Children's System.* Available at www.everychildmatters.gov.uk/ICS/about/

Department for Education and Skills (2006b) *The Common Assessment Framework for Children and Young People: Practioners' Guide.* London: DFES. Available at www.everychildmatters.gov.uk.

Department of Health (1991) *The Care of Children: Principles and Practice Guidance and Regulations.* London: HMSO.

Department of Health (1995) *Child Protection: Messages from Research.* London: HMSO.

Department of Health (1998) *Making an Impact: Children and Domestic Violence. Training Resource.* London: NSPCC.

Department of Health (1999) *The Government's Objectives for Children's Social Services.* London: Department of Health.

Department of Health (2000a) *Framework for the Assessment of Children in Need and their Families. Guidance Notes and Glossary for: Referral and Initial Information Record, Initial Assessment Record and Core Assessment Record.* London: The Stationery Office.

Department of Health (2000b) *Assessing Children in Need and their Families: Practice Guide.* London: The Stationery Office.

Department of Health (2002) *Integrated Children's System.* Website www.everychildmatters.gov.uk/ics

Department of Health (2003) *Guidelines for the Appointment of General Practitioners with Special Interests in the Delivery of Clinical Services. Child Protection.* London: Department of Health Publications

Department of Health, Home Office and Department for Education and Employment (1999) *Working Together to Safeguard Children: A Guide to Inter-agency Working to Safeguard and Promote the Welfare of Children.* London: The Stationery Office.

Department of Health, Department for Education and Employment, and Home Office (2000) *Framework for the Assessment of Children in Need and their Families.* London: The Stationery Office.

Department of Health, Cox, A. and Bentovim, A. (2000) *Framework for the Assessment of Children in Need and their Families: The Family Pack of Questionnaires and Scales.* London: The Stationery Office.

Department of Health, Home Office and Department for Education and Skills (2001) *Safeguarding Children in whom Illness is Induced or Fabricated by Carers with Parenting Responsibilities: Supplementary Guidance to Working Together to Safeguard Children.* London: Department of Health.

Department of Health and Department for Education and Skills (2004) *Core Standards: National Service Framework for Children, Young People and Maternity Services.* London: Department of Health Publications.

Department of Health and National Treatment Agency for Substance Misuse (2006) *Models of Care for Alcohol Misusers.* Website: www.dh.gov.uk/publications

Domestic Violence, Crime and Victims Act (2004) The Stationery Office.

Drugs Strategy Directorate (1998) *Tackling Drugs to Build a Better Britain.* Website: www.drugs.gov.uk/drug-strategy/overview/

Dutt, R. and Phillips, M. (2000) 'Assessing black children in need and their families.' In Department of Health, *Assessing Children in Need and their Families: Practice Guidance.* Norwich: The Stationery Office.

Education Act (2002) The Stationery Office.

Ehrle, J., Scarella, C.A. and Geen, R. (2004). 'Teaming up: collaboration between welfare and child welfare agencies since welfare reform.' *Children and Youth Services Review 26*, pp.265–285.

Family Law Act (1996) HMSO.

Farmer, E. and Owen, M. (1995) *Child Protection Practice: Private Risks and Public Remedies – Decision-making, Intervention and Outcome in Child Protection Work.* London: HMSO.

Freeman, P. and Hendy, J. (1998) *Parental Perspectives on Care Proceedings.* London: The Stationery Office.

Forrester, D. and Harwin, J. (2003) *Parents Who Misuse Drugs and Alcohol: Effective Assessments and Interventions in Social Work and Child Protection.* Chichester: Wiley.

Göpfert, M., Webster, J. and Seman, M.V. (eds) (1996) *Parental Psychiatric Disorder.* Cambridge: Cambridge University Press.

Hallett, C. (1995) *Interagency Coordination in Child Protection.* London: HMSO.

Hague, G. and Malos, E. (1998) *Domestic Violence: Action for Change.* London: New Clarion Press.

Hammersley, M. and Atkinson, P. (1983) *Ethnography: Principles in Practice.* London: Tavistock Publications.

Harbin, F. and Murphy, M. (2000) *Substance Misuse and Child Care.* Dorset: Russell House Publishing.

Harwin, N., Hague, G. and Malos, E. (eds) (1999) *The Multi-Agency Approach to Domestic Violence: New Opportunities, Old Challenges?* London: Whiting and Birch.

Hart, D. and Powell, J. (2006) *Adult Drug Problems – Children's Needs: Assessing the Impact of Parental Drug Use – A Toolkit for Practitioners.* London: National Children's Bureau.

Hendry, E. (2000) 'Setting the scene.' In C. Marian and E. Hendry (eds) *Training Together to Safeguard Children: Guidance on Inter-agency Training.* London: NSPCC.

HM Government (2005a) *Statutory Guidance on Making Arrangements to Safeguard and Promote the Welfare of Children under Section 11 of the Children Act 2004.* London: Department for Education and Skills.

HM Government (2005b) *Guidance on the Children and Young People's Plan.* London: Department for Education and Skills. Website: www.everychildmatters.gov.uk/resources-and-practice/search/ ?cat+29978

HM Government (2006a) *Working Together to Safeguard Children: A Guide to Inter-agency Working to Safeguard and Promote the Welfare of Children.* Norwich: The Stationery Office. Website: www.everchildmatters.gov.uk

HM Government (2006b) *The Common Assessment Framework for Children and Young People: Practitioners' Guide.* London: Department for Education and Skills. Website: www.everychildmatters.gov.uk/caf

HM Government (2006c) *Information Sharing: Practitioners' Guide.* London: Department for Education and skills. Website: www.everchildmatters.gov.uk

HM Government (2006d) *What to Do if You're Worried a Child is Being Abused.* London: Department of Health Publications.

Home Office (2000) *Domestic Violence: Breaking the Chain: Multi-agency Guidance for Addressing Domestic Violence.* London: Home Office Publications. Website: www.homeoffice.gov.uk/ violenceagainstwomen

Home Office (2003) *Hidden Harm. Responding to the Needs of Children of Problem Drug Users. The Report of an Inquiry by the Advisory Council on the Misuse of Drugs.* Website: www.drugs.gov.uk.

Home Office (2004) *Domestic Violence, Crime and Victims Act 2004.* Website: www.homeoffice.gov.uk

Home Office, HM Customs and Excise, Office of the Deputy Prime Minister, DfES, DoH, DWP and Foreign and Commonwealth Office (2002) *Updated Drug Strategy.* London: Home Office.

Hudson, B. (2000) 'Inter-agency collaboration – a sceptical view.' In A. Brechin, H. Booth and M.A. Elby (eds) *Critical Practice in Health and Social Care.* London: Sage Publications.

Humphreys, C. and Stanley, N. (eds) (2006) *Domestic Violence and Child Protection: Directions for Good Practice.* London: Jessica Kingsley Publishers.

Itzin, C. (2006) *Tackling the Health and Mental Health Effects of Domestic and Sexual Violence and Abuse.* London: Department of Health.

James, G. (1994) *Department of Health Discussion Report for ACPC Conference: Study of Worker Together 'Part 8' Reports.* London: Department of Health.

Joint Chief Inspectors (2002) *Safeguarding Children. A Joint Chief Inspectors' Report on Arrangements to Safeguard Children.* London: Department of Health.

Jones, D.P.H. (2003) *Communicating with Vulnerable Children: A Guide for Practitioners.* London: Gaskell.

Jones, D.P.H. and Ramchandani, P. (1999) *Child Sexual Abuse: Informing Practice from Research.* Abingdon, Oxon: Radcliffe Medical Press.

Klee, H., Jackson, M. and Lewis, S. (2002) *Drug Misuse and Motherhood.* London: Routledge.

Kroll, B. and Taylor, A. (2003) *Parental Substance Misuse and Child Welfare.* London: Jessica Kingsley Publishers.

Lindstein, T. (1996) *Working with Children of Alcoholics.* Stockholm: Stockholm University.

Littlechild, B. and Bourke, C. (2006) 'Men's use of violence and intimidation against family members and child protection workers.' In C. Humphreys and N. Stanley (eds) *Domestic Violence and Child Protection: Directions for Good Practice.* London: Jessica Kingsley Publishers.

Malos, E. and Hague, G. (1997) 'Women, housing, homelessness and domestic viollence.' *Women's Studies International Forum 20,* 3.

Mullender, A. and Morley, R. (eds) (1994) *Children Living with Domestic Violence.* London: Whiting and Birch.

Murphy, M. and Oulds, G. (2000) 'Establishing and developing co-operative links between substance misuse and child protection systems.' In F. Harbin and M. Murphy (eds) *Substance Misuse and Child Care.* Dorset: Russell House Publishing.

National Family and Parenting Institute and Alcohol Concern (2001) *Putting the Children First: Helping Families to Deal with the Effects of Parent's Heavy Drinking on Family Life.* London: A National Family and Parenting Institute and Alcohol Concern publication.

Protection From Harassment (Act 1997) HMSO.

Reder, P. and Duncan, S. (1999) *Lost Innocents? A Follow-up Study of Fatal Child Abuse.* London: Routledge.

Sanders, R. (1999) *The Management of Child Protection Services.* Aldershot: Ashgate.

SCODA/Standing Conference on Drug Abuse (1997) *Drug Using Parents: Policy Guidelines for Inter-agency Working.* London: Local Government Association Publications.

SRA (2003) *Ethical Guidelines.* London: Social Research Association. Accessed on 21 June 2007 at www.the-sra.org.uk/ethical.htm.

Stevenson, O. (ed) (1998) *Child Welfare in the UK.* Oxford: Blackwell Science.

Strategy Unit (2004) *Alcohol Harm Reduction Strategy for England.* London: Strategy Unit.

Thoburn J., Lewis, A. and Shemmings, D. (1995) *Paternatism or Partnership? Family Involvement in the Child Protection Process.* London: HMSO.

Thoburn J., Wilding, J. and Watson, J. (2000) *Family Support in Cases of Emotional Maltreatment and Neglect.* London: The Stationery Office.

Tunnard, J. (2002) *Parental Drug Misuse – A Review of Impact and Intervention Studies.* Dartington: Research into Practice.

Turning Point (2006) *Bottling it Up: The Effects of Alcohol Misuse on Children, Parents and Families.* www.turning-point.co.uk

Velleman, R. (1993) *Alcohol and the Family.* London: Institute of Alcohol Studies.

Velleman, R. (1996) 'Alcohol and drug problems in parents: an overview of the impact on children and the implications for practice.' In M. Gopfert, J. Webster and M.V. Seeman (eds) *Parental Psychiatric Disorder: Distressed Parents and their Families.* Cambridge: Cambridge University Press.

Velleman, R. and Orford, J. (2001) *Risk and Resilience: Adults who were the Children of Problem Drinkers.* Amsterdam: Harwood Academic Publishers.

Webster, A., Coombe, A. and Stacey, L. (2002) *Bitter Legacy. The Emotional Effects of Domestic Violence on Children.* London: Barnardos.

Subject Index

age, of children in study 33, 37, 45, 47, 50
agencies *see* service providers; specialist agencies
Alcohol Harm Reduction Strategy 19–20
alcohol misuse *see* substance misuse
Area Child Protection Committees 67, 68, 73, 75–6, 132–4, 142–4
  training *see* training
  see also Local Safeguarding Children Boards
assessment 51–2, 54, 93–6, 98, 102–4, 181
  see also Common Assessment Framework; core assessments; initial assessments

business plans
  ACPC 132–4
  assessment criteria 132
  Children and Young People's Plans 141–2, 184
  Crime and Disorder Reduction Strategies 139–40, 184
  domestic violence forums 134–7, 184
  drug and alcohol teams 137–9
  police 15–16
  recommendations 184–5

case study families
  access to records 100–102
  assessment issues 93–6, 102–4
  characteristics 84–6
  details of
    domestic violence 202–4, 206–211, 213–22
    parental substance misuse 203–9, 211–14, 219–23
  outcomes 114–20
    factors in 120–24
  parent–social worker relations 96–100, 123–4, 125–7, 183–4
  referral issues 86–92
  services
    length of provision 128

needed 110–112, 120–21, 127–8
received 106–8
views on 108–112, 115–16, 117–20, 122, 123–8
social work contacts 85–6, 91–2
views on joint working 112–14, 128
child development
  knowledge after training 156–60
  needs of children 38–9, 40, 41–2
Child in Need Plans 48–9, 95, 181
child protection
  in DAAT procedures 145–6
  in domestic violence forum plans 135–7
  in domestic violence procedures 145
  and initial assessments 36
  knowledge after training 160–62
  legal context 13–15
  police role 15–16, 72, 180
  prioritisation of 72
  process, effects on 23–4
  and referrals 30, 31
  training opportunities 153, 154–5
child protection conferences 48–50, 54, 182
children
  at child protection conferences 50
  characteristics of 33–4, 37, 40, 45, 47, 84, 85–6
  effects on 21–4, 89–90
  see also case study families; parents
Children Act (1989) 14, 25, 71
  see also s47 enquiries
Children Act (2004) 14, 15, 16, 25, 180, 181, 184
Children and Young People's Plans 138–9, 141–2, 184
children's social care
  contact with case study families 85–6, 91–2
  involvement of 60–61
  involvement of police 63

managers' knowledge of 59, 60
quality of inter-agency relations 65, 66–7
reports to child protection conferences 50
responses to referrals 29, 30, 32–3
see also assessment; managers; referrals; services; social workers
co-morbidity 23, 30, 37–8, 40–42, 43, 120
collaborative working *see* joint working
Common Assessment Framework 24–5, 29, 78, 156, 171, 180, 182, 183, 194
communication
  and inter-agency relations 67, 70–71, 73
  parents' views on 125
  see also confidentiality; information sharing; records
Community Plans 138, 184
Community Safety Plans 139–40, 184
confidentiality 24, 72, 75–9, 113–14, 181–2
core assessments 43, 45, 46–9, 54–5, 182, 183
  see also Child in Need Plans; s47 enquiries
Crime and Disorder Act (1998) 16
Crime and Disorder Reduction Strategies 139–40, 184

data protection *see* confidentiality; information sharing
domestic violence
  addressed in business plans 15–16, 134–8, 140, 142
  and assessment 36, 37–8, 39, 40, 46, 47, 51–2, 94–6
  case studies
    access to records 101
    assessment issues 94–6
    characteristics of parents 84–5
    outcomes 115, 116–19, 122, 123–4

parent–social worker relations 97–8, 99, 100, 123–4, 125–7
parents' views on services 108–9, 111–12, 115, 117–19, 124–5, 126–8
referral issues 87, 88, 89–90
services received 106–8
and child development 39, 40, 41, 157, 158–9
effects 21–4, 89–90
family and environmental factors 41–2
legal context 16–18
and parenting capacity 21, 41
procedures 68, 73, 142–5
and referrals 29, 30, 31
statistics 16, 20, 23, 38
training opportunities 153–5, 156, 163, 167, 185–6
training plans 151–2, 157, 158–9
see also child protection; co-morbidity
Domestic Violence, Crime and Victims Act (2004) 17–18, 135
domestic violence forums 134–7, 144–5, 152, 184
domestic violence services
information sharing protocols 75–9, 146–7
involvement of 51, 52, 53, 54, 60, 61–2, 102–4, 181
involvement of police 63
quality of inter-agency relations 66, 67–8, 70
referrals by 78
referrals to 42, 43, 52, 53
shortage of 104, 107
drug abuse see parental substance misuse; substance misuse
drug and alcohol teams 43, 51, 52, 54, 137–9, 145–6

Education Act (2002) 16
education services
involvement of 51, 52, 53, 54, 64, 102
referrals by 28, 29, 31, 32
environmental factors see family and environmental factors
ethnicity, of children in study 33–4

family and environmental factors 36, 39–40, 41–2
see also relationships
Framework for the Assessment of Children in Need and their Families 25, 183

friendships see relationships
funding, for training 163–4

gender, of children in study 33, 45, 47

health services
involvement of 51, 52, 53, 54, 63, 102
involvement of police 63
quality of inter-agency relations 65, 66
referrals by 28, 29, 31, 32
Hidden Harm 18–19, 157–8, 159–60
housing services
collaboration with 51, 62, 64, 102, 181
need for 127
quality of inter-agency relations 65, 66, 69

information sharing 75–9, 134, 146–7, 180–82, 185
see also communication; confidentiality; records
initial assessments
children seen 37
delays in 35–6, 182
findings 37–42
joint working in 51–2
not done 44–5, 46, 49, 182–3
outcomes 42–4, 52–3, 182
reasons 36
Integrated Children's System 25, 183
inter-agency relations
and communication 67, 70–71, 73
quality of 64–8, 69, 70

joint working
addressed in business plans 134, 136, 137, 139–40
in assessment 51–2, 54, 102–4, 181
and confidentiality 24, 72, 75–9, 113–14, 181–2
guidance 16–17, 51, 69, 73–4
importance of 24–5
involvement of different agencies 60–64
negative factors 24, 71–2, 74–81, 103–4, 113–14, 120–21
parents' views 112–14, 128
positive factors 68–74, 158
problems in 14, 24, 103
recommendations 181, 185
at referral 51, 92
at strategy discussions 53

training 24, 72–3, 151, 152, 153–4, 165, 167, 185
see also information sharing; inter-agency relations

Local Authorities
service directories 60, 73, 182
variations
in business plans 134, 135–7, 138–9, 140
in core assessments 46, 47
in knowledge of services 59, 61, 62–3
in procedures 143–6
in training 151–2, 157, 158, 161
see also children's social care; social services
Local Safeguarding Children Boards 15, 16, 20, 133, 143, 185
see also Area Child Protection Committees
managers
involvement of different agencies 60–64
knowledge
of child development 156–60
of child protection 160–62
of service providers 59–60, 73
multi-agency working see joint working
multiple-problem cases 40–41, 43
see also co-morbidity

National Policing Plan 15–16

parent–child relationships 22
parental substance misuse
and assessment 36, 37–8, 39, 40, 46, 47, 51–2
business plans, references in 134, 137–8, 140, 142
case studies
access to records 101
assessment issues 93, 94–6
outcomes 114–15, 118–20, 121–3, 124
parent–social worker relations 97–8, 99, 100, 124, 125–7
parental characteristics 84–6
referral issues 86–92
satisfaction with services 108, 109, 111–12, 115, 118–20, 124
service improvement needs 125–7, 128
services received 106–8

parental substance misuse *cont.*
  and child development 39, 40,
    41–2, 157
  effects 21–4, 89, 90
  and family and environmental
    factors 41, 42
  government strategy 19
  information sharing protocols
    147
  legal context 18–20
  and parenting capacity 21, 41,
    42
  procedures 73, 142–4
  and referrals 30, 31, 43, 52, 53
  statistics 19, 20, 37, 38
  training opportunities 153–5,
    156, 163, 167, 185–6
  training plans 73, 151–2,
    157–8, 159–60
  see also child protection;
    co-morbidity; substance
    misuse services
parenting capacity 21, 39, 40, 41,
    42
parents
  awareness of referrals 31, 32,
    90–91, 96–7
  case studies *see* case study
    families
  characteristics 37–8, 84–6
  at child protection conferences
    50
  consultation with 94–6, 98,
    101–2, 112, 126–7
  information for 43–4, 94–6,
    100–102, 183–4
  initial social work contacts 91–2
  relationships with social workers
    96–100, 123–4, 125–7,
    183–4
  support for 14, 184
  views
    on communication 125
    of joint working 112–14,
      128
    on services 108–112,
      115–16, 117–20, 122,
      123–8
partnership working *see* joint
  working
plans *see* business plans; Child in
  Need plans; strategy
  discussions
police
  involvement of 51, 52, 53, 54,
    63, 102
  procedures 145
  quality of inter-agency relations
    66
  referrals by 28, 29, 31, 32

role in safeguarding children
    15–16, 72, 180
practitioners
  training needs 23–4, 81
  see also managers; social workers;
    staff retention
priorities, divergence of 71–2
procedures 67, 68, 73–4, 142–6
protocols 75–9, 134, 146–7,
    181–2, 185

racism, and service take-up 34
rating scales 47–8
records
  parents' access to 100–102
  problems with 27–8, 33, 38, 45,
    51
  see also information sharing;
    Integrated Children's System
recruitment, of social workers 26,
    62, 79–80
referrals
  case study issues 86–92
  characteristics of children 33–4,
    40, 84, 85–6
  children's social care responses
    29, 30, 32–3
  see also assessment; Child in
    Need Plans; strategy
    discussions
  joint working in 51, 92
  methods 29–30
  outcomes 182–3
  parental awareness of 31, 32,
    90–91, 96–7
  practice guidance 29–30, 32
  re-referrals 30, 182
  reasons 30, 31, 86–90
  sources of 28–9, 30, 31, 32, 33,
    78, 80, 90–91
  to specialist agencies 42–3, 45,
    52–3, 182
relationships
  effects on 23
  parent–child 22
  parent–social workers 96–100,
    123–4, 125–7, 183–4
research
  advisory group 187
  aims 187
  context 25–6
  data analysis 199–200
  ethics 188, 195–6
  methods 48–9, 150–51, 188–99
  sample 188–9, 191, 192,
    193–4, 196, 197–8
resources
  lack of
    and joint working 79–80,
      103–4

and service provision 104,
    107, 111–12, 120–21,
    127–8
  for training 163–4, 167
  see also staff retention

s47 enquiries 44, 45–6, 47, 49, 54,
    182
  see also core assessments
safeguarding *see* child protection
scales and questionnaires, in core
  assessment 47–8
schools *see* education services
self-referrals 28
service providers
  culture, and inter-agency
    relations 24, 71–2
  directories of 60, 73, 182
  managers' knowledge of 59–60,
    73
  see also children's social care; drug
    and alcohol teams; education
    services; health services;
    housing services; police; social
    services; specialist agencies
services
  factors in take-up 23, 34, 96
  parents' views 108–112,
    115–16, 117–20, 122,
    123–8
  provision of, lack of resources
    104, 107, 111–12, 120–21,
    127–8
  see also case study families,
    services
social relationships *see* relationships
social services departments
  information sharing protocols 77
  referrals by 28, 29, 31, 32, 80
  see also children's social care
social workers
  changes, effects 99–100
  initial contacts with parents
    91–2
  perspectives on case study
    parents 88
  preconceptions 80–81, 86
  recruitment and retention 26, 62,
    63, 74, 79–80
  relationships with parents
    96–100, 123–4, 125–7,
    183–4
  see also practitioners
specialist agencies
  commissioning assessments from
    43, 48
  referrals to 42–3, 52–3, 182
  see also domestic violence
    services; substance misuse
    services

staff retention 26, 62, 63, 74,
    79–80
    see also recruitment
strategy discussions 43, 44–5, 49,
    53
substance misuse
    Government strategy 18
    procedures 145–6
    see also parental substance misuse
substance misuse services
    information sharing protocols
        75–9
    involvement of 51, 52, 54, 60,
        61, 62, 102, 181
    involvement of police 63
    quality of inter-agency relations
        66–7
    referrals by 78
    referrals to 52, 53
    services for children 159–60
    see also drug and alcohol teams

training
    amount of 155
    auditing 166–7
    guidance 150, 151, 167
    inter-agency 72–3, 151, 152,
        153–4, 165, 167, 185
    for new initiatives 156, 164
    opportunities for 153–5, 156,
        163, 164, 167, 185–6
    outcomes 156–62
    plans 73, 151–3, 157–60, 186
    practitioners' needs 23–4, 81
    purpose 153
    quality of 155–6
    recommendations 185–6
    resources for 163–4, 167
    support for 164–7
    targeting 165–6
    time for 162–3, 164, 167
trust 80, 97–8

voluntary agencies, referrals by 28,
    29, 31, 32

waiting lists 109
Working Together to Safeguard Children
    14–15, 20, 166–7, 182

Young People's Plans 138–9

Author Index

Abel, E.L. 21
Advisory Council on the Misuse of Drugs 18–19
Alcohol Concern 19
Aldgate, J. 13
Atkinson, P. 198

Baker, S. 20
Bancroft, A. 22
Barnard, M. 21, 22, 23, 66, 67
Bentovim, A. 48
Birchall, E. 68, 75
Bourke, C. 23
Box, L. 34
Brisby, T. 20, 80
Burgess, R.G. 198
Butt, J. 34

Cabinet Office 16–17
Cassell, D. 23
Cawson, P. 21, 30
Chief Inspector of Social Services 15, 24
Cleaver, H. 13, 20, 21, 22, 23, 24, 26, 30, 32, 33, 35, 38, 39, 40, 42, 48, 49, 74, 80, 81, 84, 86, 88, 90, 92, 94, 96, 97, 98, 99, 120, 128, 196
Coleman, R. 23
Commission for Social Care Inspection 24, 69, 72, 74
Coombe, A. 89
Cox, A. 48

Darlington, Y. 64, 75, 121
Debbonaire, T. 23
Department for Education and Skills 15, 19, 24, 25, 26, 29, 30, 33, 35, 58, 194
Department of Health 11, 14, 15, 16, 19, 20, 24, 25, 26, 29, 30, 32, 35, 37, 39–40, 44, 46, 48, 49, 51, 58, 92, 94, 95, 98, 101, 132–3, 141, 150, 151, 171, 180, 182, 183, 196
Drugs Strategy Directorate 18
Dutt, R. 34

Farmer, E. 20, 23, 96
Feeney, J.A. 75
Forrester, D. 24
Freeman, P. 24, 86, 88, 92, 97, 98, 99, 128, 196

Göpfert, M. 121

Hague, G. 23, 24
Hallett, C. 68, 75
Hammersley, M. 198
Harbin, F. 21, 23
Hart, D. 21
Harwin, J. 24
Hedderwick, T. 20
Hendry, E. 80
Hendy, J. 128
Home Office 16–17, 18–19, 24, 81, 134, 135, 137, 157–8, 159–60, 162
Hudson, B. 75
Humphreys, C. 21, 22

Itzin, C. 21

James, G. 23, 121
Jones, D.P.H. 50, 96

Klee, H. 21
Kroll, B. 21, 22, 68, 80, 81

Lewis, S. 20
Lindstein, T. 21
Littlechild, B. 23

Malos, E. 23, 24
Meadows, P. 20
Morley, R. 21
Mullender, A. 21
Murphy, M. 21, 23, 24

National Family and Parenting Institute 19
National Treatment Agency for Substance Misuse 19
Nicholson, D. 32

Orford, J. 21
Oulds, G. 24
Owen, M. 20, 23, 96

Phillips, M. 34
Powell, J. 21

Ramchandani, P. 96
Rixon, K. 75

SCODA 18
Seman, M.V. 121
Shemmings, D. 20
SRA 188
Stacey, L. 89
Stanley, N. 21, 22
Strategy Unit 19

Taylor, A. 21, 22, 68, 80, 81
Thoburn, J. 20, 100, 128
Tunnard, J. 21
Turning Point 23, 24

Unell, I. 13

Velleman, R. 21, 22, 23

Walker, S. 20
Watson, J. 128
Wattam, C. 30
Webster, A. 89
Webster, J. 121
Wilding, J. 128